Business Resources

BUSINESS RESOURCES

An Economic and Social Perspective

DAVID FAIRHURST

Cert Ed, BA (Hons) Econ, MA
Senior Lecturer in Management and Professional Studies
Blackburn College

HEINEMANN: LONDON

William Heinemann Ltd
10 Upper Grosvenor Street, London WIX 9PA
LONDON MELBOURNE TORONTO
JOHANNESBURG AUCKLAND

First published 1986
© D. W. Fairhurst, 1986

British Library Cataloguing in Publication Data
Fairhurst, D. W.
    Business resources: an economic and social perspective
    1.   Industrial management – Great Britain
    I.   Title
    658'.00941   HD70.G7

ISBN 0 434 90601 8

Printed in Great Britain by
Redwood Burn Ltd, Trowbridge, Wiltshire and
bound by Pegasus Bookbinding, Melksham, Wiltshire

For MYRA, LISA, and AMANDA

Contents

Preface

Business Resources aims to provide the modern business or management student with one of the essential foundations of a sound business education and to help to prepare him or her for a variety of careers in business or public administration. The book has been designed specifically to meet the needs of students of the core learning modules, 'Resources for Business' and 'The Organization in its Environment' on Business and Technician Education Council Higher Diploma and Certificate courses, but will also be invaluable to students on professional and degree courses in business studies or management.

Using a multi-discipline approach, the author provides a clear and comprehensive analysis of the acquisition and utilization of human, financial, capital, energy, and material resources by organizations in both the private and public sectors of Britain's mixed economy.

Business Resources promotes the personal and professional development of the student in two ways:

1. Through the presentation of detailed 'business knowledge' designed to provide insights into the resource implications of organizational aims and policies.
2. Through the many 'real world' case studies and student assignments included in the book in order to encourage students to become independent, self-directed learners and to develop their problem-solving, decision-making, and communication skills.

At a time of high levels of unemployment, rapid technological change, rising concern about present and future resource scarcities, and environmental protection, the author is especially concerned to examine the wider implications of resource policies both for business organizations themselves and for the society with which they interact. Consequently, *Business Resources* touches on some important social, political, and ecological constraints upon business activity.

D. W. Fairhurst
1985

PART I

THE CONTEXT

1

The Basic Economics of Resource Allocation

1.1 What Economics is About

Economics is the scientific study of how human societies allocate their productively versatile but limited resources to provide for their needs and wants. Economic analyses figure importantly in several BTEC Higher National learning modules other than Resources for Business, most notably perhaps in Business in its Environment. For this reason, only those bare elements of economic theory relating directly to resource allocation decisions in different economic systems are presented here. By introducing some of the basic analytic tools and ideas that economists have developed to help explain the complex processes of resource allocation in the modern economy, this opening chapter offers the reader a background context against which the more detailed analyses of business resource activities of later chapters can be viewed.

Resources are *scarce* relative to the wants they can satisfy: no society's capacity to produce goods and services has yet been sufficient to satisfy all the needs and wants of its people. Because virtually infinite human wants are constrained by finite resources choices about the use of resources in production inevitably arise. In a world of abundant resources there would be no need to decide

- what goods to produce and in what quantities;
- which amongst many technically possible methods of production should be used;
- how the resulting products should be shared out between different groups and individuals in the population.

1.2 Choice and Opportunity Cost

Because resources are scarce every choice about their use carries with it a sacrifice in terms of the foregone opportunity to use those same resources in other ways. In wartime, for example, the real cost of the increased allocation of resources to the production of armaments is the loss of those consumer goods – cars, perhaps, or household goods – which could have been produced using the same resources.

At the family level a decision to buy a new car may involves the loss of a family holiday which cannot now be afforded and which is the real cost of the new car.

The real cost of a government decision to increase hospital building may be the schools which will now not be built. Having A always means going without B in a world of finite resources. Thus the real or *opportunity cost* of any good is the most desirable alternative foregone. In reality, of course, choices may not be starkly 'all or nothing' ones. More commonly decisions are about producing more of A and less of B rather than relinquishing B absolutely.

1.3 Economic Resources

All output requires a combination of scarce resource inputs. Traditionally, economic theory views production as a process in which inputs of the separate 'factors of production' as the resources are called, are combined by business firms to produce a variety of goods and services. The many and varied factor inputs that constitute an economy's productive base are grouped into four broad categories – land, labour, capital, and enterprise.

LAND

The term 'land' is used to denote the vast array of natural resources used in production. Land, therefore, incorporates the total surface area of the planet including lakes, rivers, oceans and ocean beds; sunshine, rain and climate; soil fertility; and mineral and fossil fuel deposits in the crust of the earth. Most of these inherited 'free gifts of nature' are of no use in economic production until (a) they have been 'discovered' and (b) technical knowledge and capital have been applied in order to convert them into natural resources. Although research is under way as part of the space programmes of the Super-Powers the potential for 'harvesting' resources for the economy from outer space has yet to be assessed. However, the enormous energy requirements for exploring and transporting resources from outer space would seem to preclude significant developments in this direction.

LABOUR

All human activity involved in the production of economic goods or services is included under this heading. The size of the labour force available to an economy will depend primarily on population size which in turn will depend on birth rate, death rate, and net international migration flows. The flow of labour inputs (i.e. the number of man hours per year) from any given population will depend upon the age and sex structure of the population; legislation on the school leaving age and retirement age; and social convention e.g. attitudes to married women working. Merely to add numbers, however, indicates neither the extent or nature of people as resources. The extent to which people effectively participate in the production and distribution of goods and services depends upon many factors including expenditure on education, skill training, and health care, as well as on social class, social attitudes, mobility, working arrangements, and so on. In return for labour services people are rewarded by the payment of wages or salaries.

CAPITAL

Capital refers to all man-made resources which are useful in production. 'Fixed' capital consists of the inherited stock of buildings, plant, machinery, tools, transportation systems and so on. 'Floating' capital consists of stocks of raw materials, components, finished, or semi-finished goods. Social capital as distinguished from industrial capital comprises roads, schools and colleges, hospitals and clinics – these assets are usually but not exclusively in public ownership.

As capital is used up or wears out in the course of production, a proportion of newly produced capital is required to replace it. The remaining proportion adds to the nation's capital stock, which is an important determinant of its productive capacity.

ENTERPRISE

Entrepreneurs (who supply enterprise) decide what goods and services will be produced, and organize the other factors of production into productive relationships. Entrepreneurs also bear the (uninsurable) financial risks that arise because production takes place in advance of sales and because the future is always uncertain. These risks are borne in the anticipation of profits which is the reward to enterprise.

In the eighteenth and much of the nineteenth century the two functions of enterprise i.e. organization and risk-taking tended to be carried out by the same persons. One-man businesses or partnerships were the usual form of business organization in which the owner managers invested their own money. In the late twentieth century it is more difficult to identify the 'entrepreneur'. The job of organizing the factors is undertaken largely by salaried teams of managers often working for massively scaled corporations whose ordinary shareholders bear the risks.

In the UK's mixed economy government also plays an important role in risk-taking through its financial support for investment both nationwide and in the assisted areas (see Chapter 7). The broad aims of such support are to improve industrial competitiveness and to encourage the growth of employment and investment. Government involvement in this way is especially important for new technological innovation. For example in March 1985 government grants of up to 20 per cent were available for selected capital projects involving the production and design of advanced micro-electronics, fibre optics, optic electronic components and related activities. 20 per cent grants (up to a maximum of £40,000) were also available for the acquisition of computer-aided design for the design of integrated circuits.

The rewards to capital, enterprise and land – respectively, interest profits and rent – are distinguishable in principle but rarely in practice.

In reality it is often impossible to separate resource inputs into production in the way suggested by the above categorization. Land (in its literal sense), for example, is improved by the application of capital in the form of irrigation or drainage schemes, or fertilisers. The extraction of ores or fossil fuels is impossible without the use of huge amounts of capital equipment and labour.

In the case of labour, much of the acquired abilities or skills of a worker will be the result of past 'investment' in education and training. To imply that entrepreneurs exclusively bear the risks of production is also unrealistic. Workers face not only the financial risks of unemployment, but health hazards at work of an almost infinite variety.

1.4 Economic Goods

The link between human wants and economic resources are goods. Goods (used here to denote services as well as physical goods) are produced from resource inputs and are necessary to satisfy needs and wants. More fundamentally, since resources are both scarce and may in varying degrees be employed in alternative productive uses, and since wants are infinite, it is *choice* that links resources to wants through the selection of which goods will be produced. We may distinguish between private and collective goods.

Private goods are privately owned and privately consumed. Typically these are the goods involved in transactions where money exchanges for goods, and goods exchange for money. Most consumer goods are private goods. Such goods may be used by only one person at a time. Their use is *competitive* i.e. either you use them *or* I use them. Pure private goods are, however, exceptional, because most goods give rise to 'spillover' effects or externalities' (see p. 24 below).

Collective goods are *not* competitive in use. More than one person, in some cases large numbers of people, can use them simultaneously, without diminishing supply. The reception of television or radio signals is a collective good since any number of people can tune in without forcing any other to tune out. National defence, law enforcement, and national parks are among many publicly provided goods which, within limits, confer benefits on large numbers of people without diminishing the benefits derived by others.

Many but not all collective goods are provided by the State. In Britain education, health care, and transport are provided privately and by the State and there is ongoing debate about the merits of private vs public provision of these services.

1.5 The Allocation of Resources

Let us now return to the fundamental economic problem – that of reconciling scarce resources capable of alternative uses with infinite consumer wants. The purpose of economics is to analyse ways of allocating our limited resources in such a manner as to maximize our economic wellbeing. How can the wants of people best be provided for from available resources?

Broadly there are two alternative systems for linking consumers with resources. In the **planned economy** what, how, and for whom to produce, are decided by a central planning authority and its agencies. The alternative is the **market economy** where outcomes are determined by the operation of impersonal market forces, with relative *prices* signalling what the pattern of production and distribution should be.

1.6 The Planned Economy

In the planned economy *political* choices determine priorities in the allocation of resources. In such economies resources tend to be in public ownership, with government claiming to represent the public.

In the Soviet Union the responsibility for planning lies with Gosplan, the state planning organization and its subordinate organs representing each of the Soviet Republics and eighteen larger economic regions. Gosplan works closely with other government ministries and is account- able to the USSR Council of Ministers.

The development of the Soviet economy proceeds through a series of plans. Within the framework of the 10 to 15-year long-term reference plan more detailed five-year and one-year plans operate. Five-year plans have tended to emphasize the allocation of resources to capital goods and heavy industry based on the belief that this is the best way to improve the rate of economic growth. In the period of Stalin's control planning was highly centralized. Stalin and a small number of party elite around him decided on the direction of the economy and a small group of planners in Moscow developed a detailed plan to carry out his decisions. The plan governed all Soviet enterprises in detail and was law.

A recent (1976–80) five-year plan aimed to increase national income by 24–28 per cent with investment concentrated on railways, energy and fuel, chemicals, metallurgy, and industry. In 1980 priority in the allocation of funds, materials, and plant and machinery was given to a number of projects including nuclear power stations, large-scale cellulose and asbestos producing plants, thousands of kilometres of oil and gas pipelines, extensions to the railway network, and road construction and improvement. Investment in high technology industries, especially computers, was also emphasized.

The Soviet system works as follows. On the basis of goals set by the Council of Ministers and information transmitted upwards from enterprise level a plan for the whole economy is drafted, although production and allocation details are provided for only about 2,000 commodities. The draft plan is then shown to all agencies down the ladder to the level of the enterprise. After each agency and enterprise have added their comment and suggestion, Gosplan produces the final draft. The plan will aim for sufficient investment to achieve targeted rates of growth of output and to produce the particular desired assortment of goods decided by political criteria.

After the plan is enacted into law it is passed down the committee structure of the economy with detailed commands, expanded at each stage. At the end of the chain the enterprise managements receive a very detailed document telling precisely what each is expected to produce in what time periods, what techniques are to be used, what prices are to be charged and so on. Since 1965 managers have been allowed wider discretion, for example, over the retention and utilization of profits for various purposes such as employee welfare schemes, bonuses, and decentralized investment.

Economic planning confronts the authorities with formidable problems. One of the most difficult issues is the question of how the planners are to decide what goods society should produce. In the market economy where production is for profits it is relatively a simpler matter to decide which goods will be produced from given resources than when the objective is to maximize social wellbeing, or something even more nebulous in the minds of the planners. If relative market prices guide the allocation of resources in the market economy how should relative prices be set in the planned economy where political choice determines the product mix?

The diversion of resources – highly skilled manpower and computers, for example – which is necessary to find answers to these and other fundamental questions of planning will be considerable. The use of many officials in implementing the plan is likely to lead to a proliferating bureaucracy, red tape, excessive form filling and delayed decision making. Large-scale bureaucracy may also tend to spawn corruption and bribery. The planned economy is characterized by formidable problems of co-ordination, of ensuring for each particular industry that inputs match targeted outputs, that supply matches demand, that the best technologies are used in each enterprise, and that the myriad decisions carried out by each committee and enterprise are consistent.

The consequences of failing to solve these various problems may all too often be shortages of key materials, components, machinery, or man-power; queues and 'black markets' for some consumer goods and over production of others as enterprises strive to meet targets unrelated to demand and irrespective of whether they can be sold; disruptions to production, and so on.

1.7 The Free-market Economy

The alternative to planning is the free-market economy in which resource allocation decisions are decentralized to millions of consumers and hundreds of thousands of business firms whose voluntary transactions are co-ordinated by an 'invisible hand' of free competition and self-interest. What, how, and for whom to produce are all determined by market forces.

The distinguishing feature of the modern private enterprise or capitalist economy is the private ownership of the means of production, i.e. of land, factories, machines, tools, and stocks. The most important social institution in these economies is the market, defined here in intangible terms as 'the negotiation of exchange transactions and the determination of the terms on which such transactions shall take place'. The main decision-making units in the market economy are **households** which sell or hire out resources – labour power, land, finance – to business **firms** which in the course of production transform these factor inputs into goods and services for sale on the market. In return for factor services firms make payments of wages, rents, interest, and dividends thus providing income to house-holds. Households in turn spend their income in buying goods and services from firms, and this expenditure constitutes the firm's income. Figure 1.1 depicts a highly simplified model of these flows of income and expenditure.

In the real economy there are hundreds of thousands of markets for the different goods and factor services, with market prices providing the crucial link between households and firms, between supplies and demands in both goods and factor markets. Market prices move in response to

Figure 1.1.   Simplified model of income and expenditure flows in the market economy.

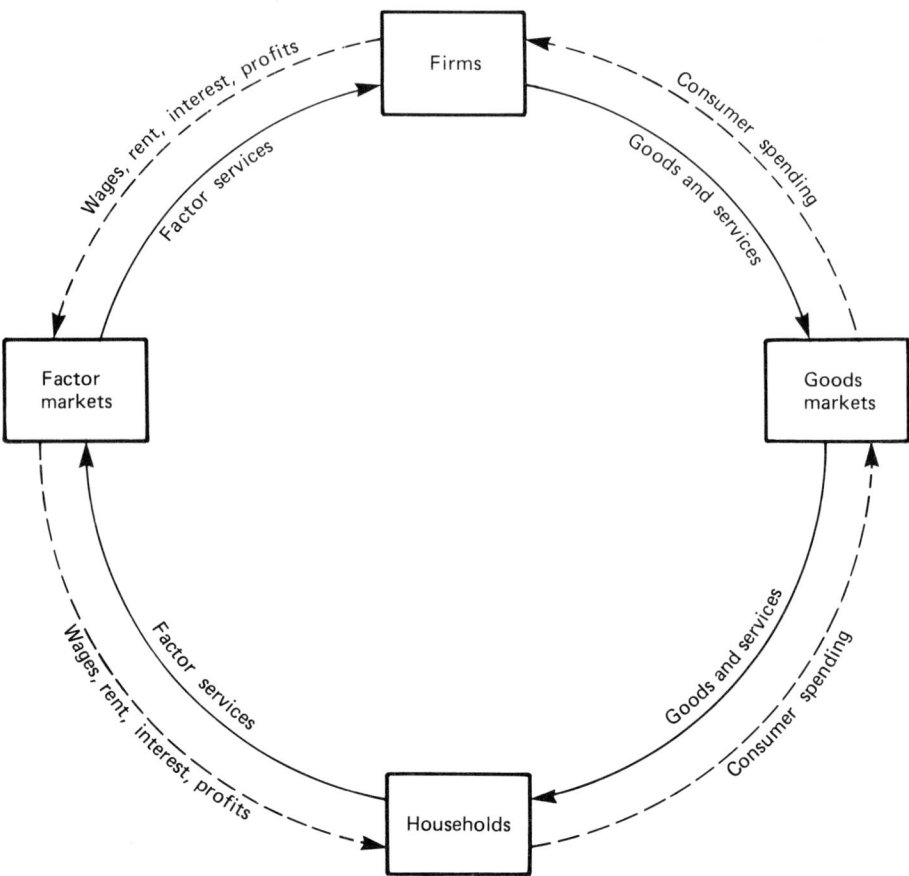

changes in the conditions under which demand and supply take place. If demand rises relative to supply, price will tend to rise; if demand falls relative to supply, price will tend to fall. Such price changes act as signals and provide incentives to the decision-making households and firms who adjust their behaviour accordingly, by altering the way in which they allocate their limited resources – income in the case of households, productive resources in the case of firms.

1.8 The Operation of the Price Mechanism

Let us examine this more closely. A market is essentially two-sided; buyers wish to exchange money for goods and sellers wish to exchange goods for money. The amount of a good that buyers wish and, are able, to buy during a given period and at a given price is referred to as **demand**. It is important to emphasize that demand here does not refer to realized expenditure or purchases but to intentions, desires, or plans to purchase.

For demand to be *effective* potential buyers require purchasing power, i.e. income. Thus demand is not necessarily related to need. A homeless person who desperately seeks a place to live but lacks income adds nothing to the market demand for accommodation.

Supply is defined similarly as the quantity of a good that sellers would wish to sell during a given period and at a given price.

Thus both supply and demand are held to depend on price.

1.9 Demand

A demand schedule relates various prices of a good to the amounts of that good that people would like to buy at each of these prices. If we imagine, for example, that a large television manufacturer polled the British people in order to establish the number of a particular model that people would want to buy at different market prices, the results might be something like those shown in Table 1.1

The graphical representation of this schedule in Figure 1.2 provides us

Figure 1.2. Demand curve for standard television sets.

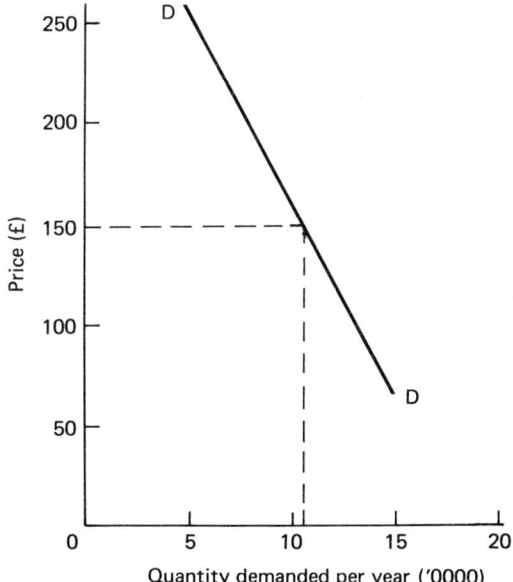

Table 1.1. Demand schedule for standard television set.

Price (£)	Quantity demanded per year (tens of thousands)
100	15
150	12
200	9
250	6

with the normal downward sloping *demand curve* so prominent in the literature of economics showing that the lower the price the higher will be the quantity demanded and vice versa.

Any demand curve is relevant only for a *given* level and distribution of income, a *given* set of prices for other goods, *given* consumer tastes and preferences, and *given* time periods. If any of these so-called 'conditions of demand' change, the views of consumers towards the good in question will also change, and consequently a new demand curve will have to be constructed.

Suppose for example, consumers' preferences shift away from the standard model towards a television set with facilities for video recording.

Figure 1.3. Increase and decrease in demand.

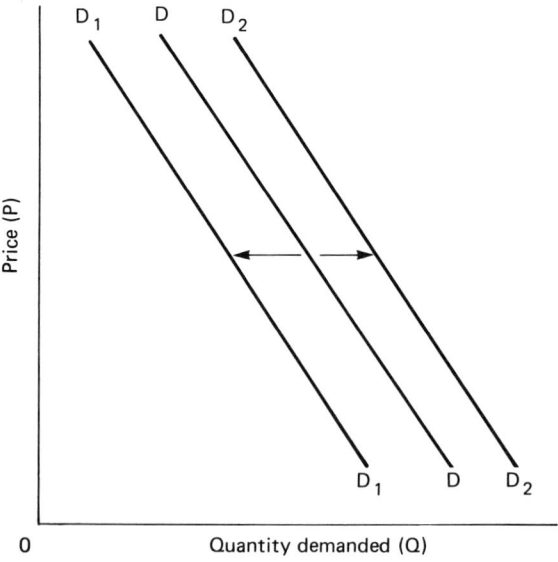

The effect is that the public is now willing to buy *fewer* of the original sets than formerly at *every* possible market price. The result is a shift in the position of the demand curve downwards and to the left to D_1 in Figure 1.3.

A general rise in income levels, other things remaining unchanged, would tend to generate a greater willingness to buy *more* of the original type of television receiver than formerly at *every* market price causing the demand curve to shift upwards to the right to D_2 in Figure 1.3 reflecting the increase in demand.

1.10 Supply

Economic theory assumes that entrepreneurs aim solely to maximize profits. We have already defined supply as the amount of a commodity which firms are willing and able to offer for sale during a given period at a given price. Given the profit-maximizing assumption it is obvious that firms would like to offer more for sale when the price is high and less when it is low. Reverting to our original television market, the supply schedule may look something like Table 1.2.

Table 1.2.   Supply schedule for television sets.

Price (£)	Quantity supplied (hundreds of thousands)
100	3
150	6
200	9
250	12

From the schedule we may derive the typical upward sloping supply curve. (Figure 1.4.)

The supply curve is relevant only for a *given* set of prices of other goods, *given* costs of production, and *given* technology. Should any of these 'conditions of supply' change, firms will tend to adjust their production and marketing plans accordingly.

If, for example, the cost of materials used in the manufacture of television sets falls then, other things being equal, we would expect manufacturers to be willing to offer more sets for sale at every market price than formerly in order to take advantage of the higher profit margin now available. Consequently the supply curve would shift to the right (S_1 in Figure 1.5). Conversely an increase in labour costs would shift the supply curve to the left (S_2 in Figure 1.5).

Figure 1.4.   Supply curve for television sets.

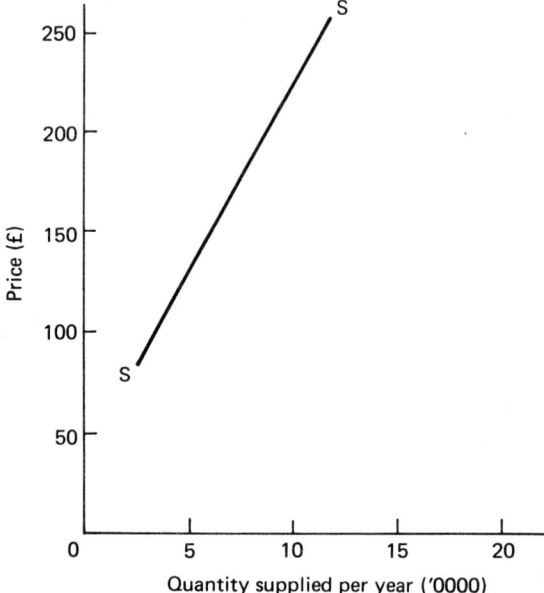

Figure 1.5.   Increase and decrease in supply.

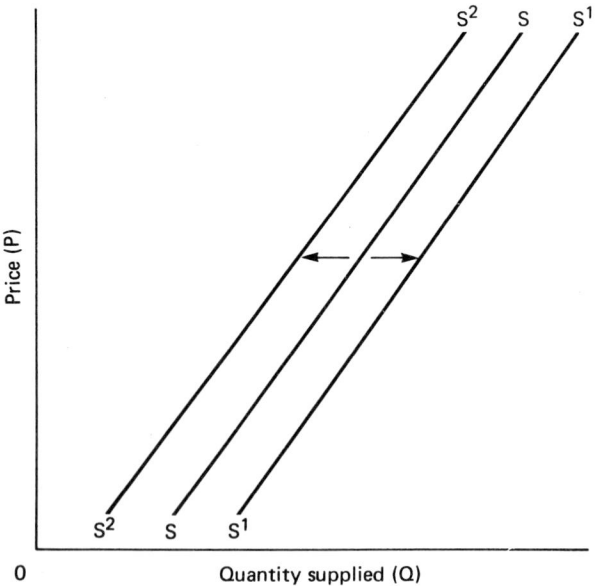

1.11 Demand, Supply, and Price

In every market there will be one, and only one price at which demand is exactly matched by supply. Bringing together our original demand and supply schedules for television receivers gives us the following:

Table 1.3. Demand and supply for television sets.

Price	Demand	Supply
100	15	3
150	12	6
200	9	9
250	6	12

At a price of £200 the amount which firms are willing to offer for sale is the same as the amount which consumers are willing to purchase. At this price the desires of buyers and sellers are consistent and both are able to conduct their desired exchanges.

In this situation when the desires of buyers and sellers are mutually consistent the market is said to be in *equilibrium*. The equilibrium price is that price at which all parties are satisfied and there are no forces likely to work to cause change. In Figure 1.6 the equilibrium price (*OP*) and

Figure 1.6. Demand, supply and equilibrium price.

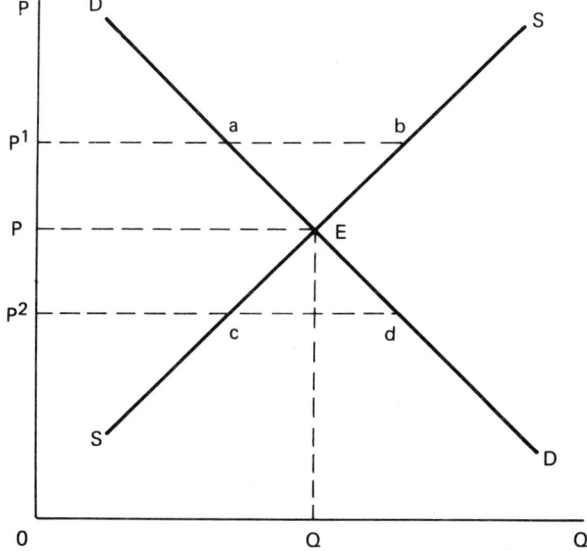

equilibrium quantity traded (*OQ*) are shown graphically at the point at which the market demand and supply curves intersect. The rectangle *POQE* represents the total revenue (price × quantity demanded) from TV sales.

If market price happens temporarily to exceed equilibrium price, then supply will exceed demand. At *OP*₁, for example, excess supply equal to *ab* exists. The excess supply will tend to cause television manufacturers and stockists to bring down the price in order to induce consumers to buy the unsold stocks. At any price below the equilibrium, at *OP*₂ for example, demand will exceed supply. Queues and waiting lists will indicate to dealers and manufacturers that they can sell their product at a higher price. Their search for higher profits will lead them to increase price.

Thus if there is a disequilibrium in the market manifested either by surplus or shortage, market forces will automatically produce price alterations in the direction of the equilibrium where supply matches demand. Thus the market can be seen as a self-equilibriating mechanism which eliminates surpluses and shortages alike.

We now have the necessary theoretical tools to explore the process of resource allocation in the free-market economy. In an ideal market system consumers ultimately decide what will be produced by expressing their preferences for particular goods and services by paying for them in the market. If, for whatever reasons, consumers' preferences change in favour

Figure 1.7.   Changes in demand and equilibrium price.

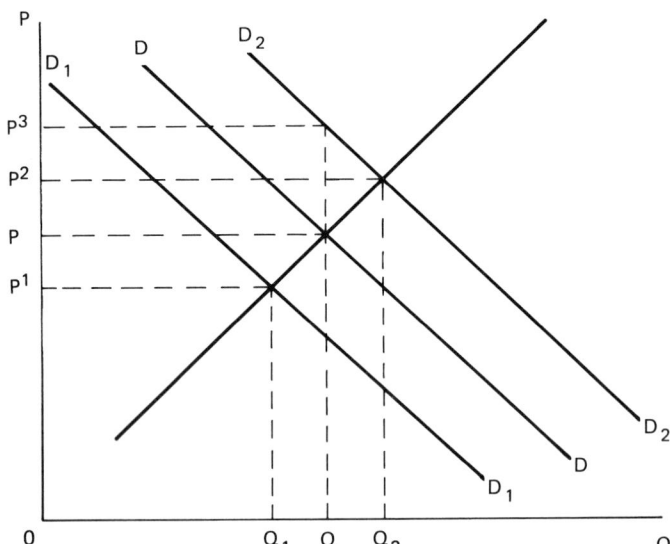

of a good there will be an increase in demand for this good. This is shown
in Figure 1.7. Given the supply curve, this increase will be represented by
a shift to the right in the position of the demand curve (to D_2) leading to an
immediate rise in the price from OP to OP_3. This higher price will act as a
signal to profit-seeking firms to allocate more resources to the production
of this good to meet the increased demand. The market will eventually
settle at a new equilibrium price of OP_2.

A decrease in demand (to D_1) will have the opposite effect. Equilibrium
price will fall to OP_1, signalling firms to produce less (OQ_1) of the
commodity. Consequently fewer resources are used.

If we now assume the demand curve to be given, changes in the
conditions of supply will also change market equilibrium. An increase in
supply, perhaps due to falling production costs, is represented in Figure
1.8 by a shift to the right of the supply curve to S_1. The consequent fall in
price to OP_1 signals consumers to adjust their expenditure and at the new
price the quantity traded increases to OQ_1. A shift in the supply curve to
the left (to S_2) representing a decrease in supply, leads to an increase in
price to OP_2 and a decrease in the quantity exchanged to OQ_2.

In summary, in the ideal market economy the price mechanism
produces a series of automatic signals to which very large numbers of
decision-making firms and consumers can react. The market responds to
the collective reactions of either producers or consumers. Without anyone

Figure 1.8.   Changes in supply and equilibrium price.

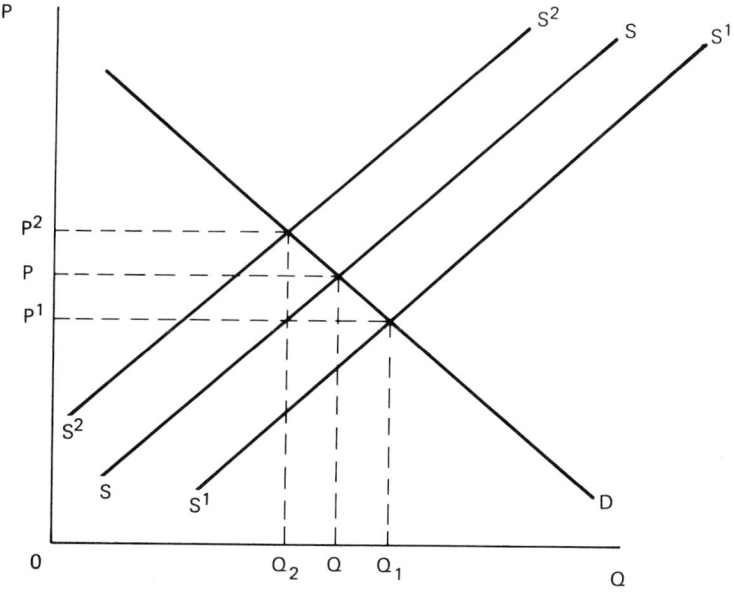

consciously co-ordinating decisions, systematic changes in demand and supply take place. In most markets an increase in demand leads to an increase in price which 'calls forth' an increase in the amount supplied. In turn this implies an increased allocation of resources to the production of this commodity. Conversely, a fall in demand leads to a fall in price and through this to a reduction in the amount supplied and thus in the resources used in producing this commodity. In these ways changes in relative market prices both in goods and resource markets change profit opportunities and provide the mechanism by which changes in resources use are effected.

STUDENT ASSIGNMENT 1.1

Visual Delights

Visual Delights PLC manufactures video recorders. On the diagram D and S represent the original demand and supply curves respectively for Visual Delights' video recorders.

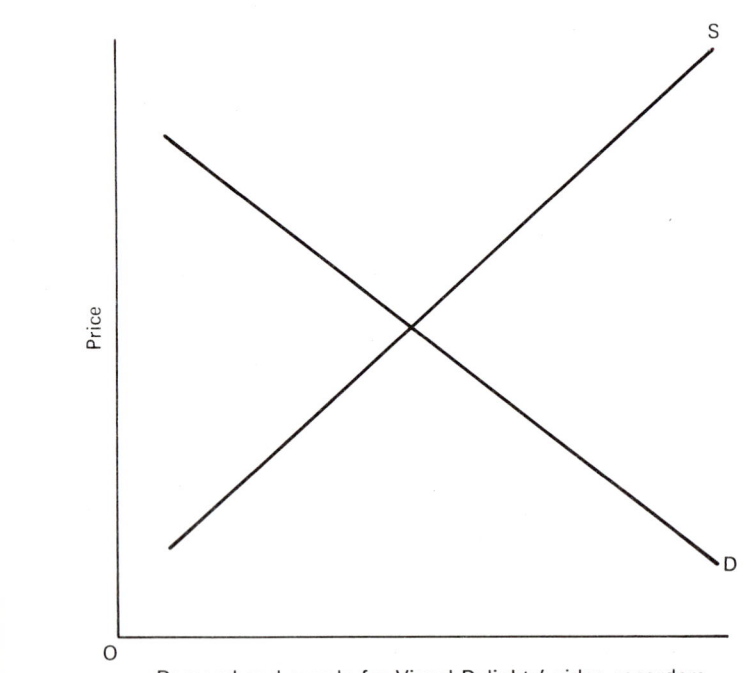

Demand and supply for Visual Delights' video recorders

Reproduce the diagram and show on it the effects of each of the following changes on Visual Delights' video market:

(a) a general rise in incomes associated with an upturn in the national economy;
(b) a large increase in earnings of Visual Delights' employees;
(c) an intensive TV and press advertising and promotion campaign for Visual Delights' video machines;
(d) an investment in advanced technology for the manufacture of Visual Delights' machines;
(e) a large surcharge on the licence for televisions having video recording facilities.

In each case note the change in the allocation of resources to the production of video recorders. How would other markets be affected by these changes?

STUDENT ASSIGNMENT 1.2

The British 'Pinta'

In February 1983 the EEC Court of Justice ruled that Britain was acting illegally by insisting that imports of UHT (ultra-heat-treated) milk be re-treated on arrival in Britain. The British practice, ostensibly to protect health, had long been suspected as a measure to protect the British dairy industry from EEC competition.

In November 1983, Agriculture Minister Michael Jopling announced that all restrictions on imports of not only UHT milk but also of 'sterilized' milk were to be ended.

Traditionally, British taste has favoured fresh pasteurized milk not popular in the EEC and impossible to import because of 'souring' en route. The British dairy industry grudgingly recognized that 'free' imports of UHT milk were inevitable, but protested strongly about the Minister's decision to allow imports of sterilized milk which lasts as long as UHT but tastes much more like the traditional doorstep 'pinta'.

The dairy industry argues that the new imports will spell doom for the milkman and his pinta. Britain's price fixed by Government at 21p a pint compares unfavourably with prices in Europe which average around 17p per pint but which can be as low as 12p. Since both UHT and sterilized milk are long life, milkmen will be unable to benefit from the lower prices. Daily delivery is pointless for milk that keeps for several weeks. Consequently customers will be lured to the shops for their milk. A swing of only 5–10 per cent could make milk rounds uneconomic.

This trend has in fact been apparent for some time. Over the past decade the proportion of milk bought in shops rose from 9 per cent to 14 per cent. Most supermarkets can undercut the maximum price because transport costs are less.

Assuming that in the new situation of unrestricted milk imports the total demand for milk (i.e. both delivered and long-life milk purchased in shops) remains constant, use suitable diagrams to analyse:

1. the likely effects on the separate markets for (a) fresh daily delivered milk and (b) long-life shop milk;
2. the likely effects on the bottle-making industry's market.

We have seen that in the free-market economy the price mechanism functions as a marvellously simple allocative device. Scarce resources are allocated with a minimum of inconvenience and, if people are left free to pursue their own self interest, in such a way as to reflect expressed preferences of consumers for particular goods and services. Goods in the right quantities and of the right quality are made available at prices that consumers are willing to pay. All this is achieved without the need for expensive bureaucracy, red tape, and all the other shortcomings associated with non-market allocative mechanisms.

1.12 The Distribution of Income

The process of resource allocation through the price mechanism in the market economy has often been described as one of economic democracy. Consumers 'vote' in favour of various 'candidates' – goods and services offered and promoted by firms – by choosing to spend their limited incomes on these goods. In this way, as we have seen, firms are signalled (via movements in relative prices) to deploy their resources in ways that reflect consumer preferences.

Just how democratic the market system will prove to be in practice will depend largely on the way in which voting power – i.e. income – is distributed between consumers. Obviously the many votes of the rich man will carry more weight in the market than the few of the poor, even though the purchasing decision of the latter may be more crucially important to his family's well-being than an equivalent expenditure by a wealthier man. In most market capitalist economies income (and wealth) is very unevenly distributed. Table 1.4 shows the income distribution picture in the United Kingdom and how this changed between 1961 and 1976–7. The reader is reminded that for most of this period the country was governed by a Labour administration with egalitarian and welfare ideals at the centre of its political philosophy.

Table 1.4. Percentage shares of original and final (i.e. after taxes and benefits) income by decile groups.

Group	Original Income			Final Income		
	1961–63	*1971–73*	*1976–77*	*1961–63*	*1971–73*	*1976–77*
	%	%	%	%	%	%
Top 10%	27.4	26.9	26.0	23.5	23.4	23.2
Top 30%	56.1	57.6	55.7	51.5	51.8	52.5
Bottom 30%	8.0	6.7	10.8	11.9	12.3	12.6
Bottom 10%	0.2	0.1	N/A	1.8	2.6	2.3

Source: Royal Commission on Distribution of Income and Wealth, Initial and Fourth Reports of the Standing Reference.

Given this sort of distribution of purchasing power, the allocation of resources and goods may fall a long way short of maximizing social well-being, as the rich are able to bid away scarce resources from essential uses into the production of their luxuries. For example, as two economists from the University of California point out, the medical care industry in the United States places more importance on the psychiatric care of the neurotic pets of the wealthy than on minimal health services for the children of the poor.*

CASE STUDY 1.1

The Distribution of Income and Market Resource Allocation

However we might wish it otherwise, it simply is not possible to use prices to transmit information and provide an incentive to act on that information without using prices also to affect, even if not completely determine, the distribution of income. If what a person gets does not depend on the price he receives for the services of his resources, what incentive does he have to seek out information on prices or to act on the basis of that information? If Red Adair's income would be the same whether or not he performs the dangerous task of capping a runaway oil well, why should he undertake the dangerous task? He might do so once, for the excitement. But would he make it his major activity? If your

* Hunt, E. K. and Sherman, H. J., *Economics: an Introduction to Traditional and Radical Views*, 3rd Ed., Harper and Row, 1978, p. 171

income will be the same whether you work hard or not, why should you work hard? Why should you make the effort to search out the buyer who values most highly what you have to sell if you will not get any benefit from doing so? If there is no reward for accumulating capital, why should anyone postpone to a later date what he could enjoy now? Why save? How would the existing physical capital ever have been built up by the voluntary restraint of individuals? If there is no reward for maintaining capital, why should people not dissipate any capital which they have either accumulated or inherited? If prices are prevented from affecting the distribution of income, they cannot be used for other purposes. The only alternative is command. Some authority would have to decide who should produce what and how much. Some authority would have to decide who should sweep the streets and who manage the factory, who should be the policeman and who the physician.

(*Source:* M. Friedman, *Free to Choose*, Penguin Books, 1980)

It is a question of great social significance as to why, in the midst of such historically unprecedented wealth in Western societies, poverty still persists. One explanation asserts that the poor constitute an indispensable component of the market economies of such societies offering 'the sole moral justification for the necessary dynamic to growth and expansion'.*
For two centuries or longer the wealthy have argued that it is only by further wealth-creation that poverty can be alleviated, but for the same length of time the poor have obdurately remained.

Few would argue that it is the West's incapacity to produce that ensures the survival of poverty. 'Once the basic cause of poverty (a natural dearth of resources) is removed, this must be replaced by an elaborate and artificially created sense of insufficiency...nothing could be more damaging to industrial society than that the people should declare themselves satisfied'.**

1.13 The Mobility of Resources

In practice, resources are far from being perfectly mobile between alternative uses in production, as the theory assumes them to be. Structural and regional unemployment in Britain and other industrialized countries provides abundant evidence that as old industries decline labour and capital are neither occupationally nor geographically mobile. Even when workers move it is often not from choice but because they are forced to by lack of work in a given locality. And economists do not often refer to

* Seabrook, Jeremy, *Landscapes of Poverty*, Blackwell, 1985
** *ibid*

the social *disharmony* that may be produced by labour mobility in terms of the breakdown of the extended family, of elderly parents isolated from their children and grandchildren, of the breakdown of the community and the destruction of roots.

1.14 Market Imperfections

The structure of the modern capitalist economy is vastly different from the universe of small firms existing in highly competitive markets implied by the traditional model of market allocation. In the industrialized world of today very large corporations control a significant proportion of economic activity and resource allocation. In such economies, competition between a few typically very large enterprises, or *oligopoly* as it is called, is the dominant form of market behaviour. The essence of oligopoly is that each 'giant' will have to consider the reactions from its rivals to any policy changes it might introduce. For example, before raising its product prices, firm A must consider how firms B and C will react to this. Because oligopolistic firms are consequently interdependent, economic theory can only be constructed on the basis of assumptions about the reactions of rivals to specific policy changes by one oligopolistic corporation. Many sophisticated models have been developed to explain the behaviour of oligopolistic firms, but have tended to yield little in terms of predicting the real world behaviour of the corporate giants, many transnational in character, who dominate both the industrialized and the developing world.

The prevalence of oligopoly and of other imperfectly competitive conditions severely limits the effectiveness of the market economy as an efficient resource allocator. In a perfectly competitive world, competition between the many would force price down to the level at which firms make only 'normal' profits. In today's circumstances profits have ceased to be a reliable indicator both of efficiency and of what consumers want produced. Rather they arise from the market power of firms to charge consumers prices higher than those necessary to make 'normal' profits and hence to exploit rather than serve the consumer by redistributing income in favour of producers. In such cases prices no longer indicate consumer preferences but rather producer power, and supply is no longer responsive to price changes in the manner suggested by simple market theory.

Galbraith* has highlighted an important feature of the behaviour of the modern giants which appears to destroy much of the traditional theory of market resource allocation. In a world of highly technological processes, products may take many years, even decades, to develop. Such develop-

* Galbraith, J. K., *The New Industrial State*, Hamish Hamilton, 1967

ment will usually require massive commitments of capital and manpower. Given these long lead times corporations will do all they can to ensure by sophisticated management of consumer behaviour that the market will want what they have to offer. Wherever possible they will secure advance contracts to make doubly sure that what they produce will be bought. National governments, of course, are the best markets for long-term contracts and they want, in particular, all those goods required for the arms race. As the supply of arms is increased to one country, the demand for armaments rises in their rival countries. Supply creates its own demand, profits for the corporations, jobs for the workers. So long as wars continue to be confined to the Third World our awareness of the barbarity of the arms trade is obscured and our moral judgement fudged by self interest.

Market manipulation of this kind and magnitude is a long way from the benign and efficient resource allocation of traditional market theory.

1.15 Social Costs

Yet another reason why the market will fail to allocate resources optimally arises from the fact that the true costs of producing goods are often not measured in the money costs met by firms. Most productive activities involve spillover effects or 'externalities' as they are called. When producers cause detrimental effects on others by polluting air, land, or water, or by uglifying or despoiling the countryside, or by creating excessive noise, they impose costs on the community which are not paid for by the firm. This important point is developed more completely in later chapters.

1.16 Collective Goods

Market allocation of resources suffers from the further limitation that some essential services calling upon the use of resources, but not 'profitable' in a narrow accounting sense, would not be produced, or not produced in adequate amount, if left to private enterprise. Collective goods like defence, law and order, and the judiciary, could not be provided adequately by the market. To some extent the same is true of basic 'merit' services like education, medical care, universal old-age pensions, and other forms of social security.

1.17 Unemployment

It is quite obvious that if the market economy fails to make full use of available resources it fails to allocate them optimally. Experience before the Second World War was of periodic and often large fluctuations in the level of economic activity and employment associated with the booms and slumps of the so-called trade cycle, culminating in the Great Depression and mass unemployment of the 1920s and 1930s.

STUDENT ASSIGNMENT 1.3

Economic Systems

Compare and contrast market and command economic systems by answering the following questions:

1. Who own the basic productive resources?
2. Who decides the national economic goals of the economy?
3. How are the activities of individual consumers and enterprises co-ordinated to achieve these goals?
4. On what criteria are the decisions about *what* is to be produced from the nation's scarce resources made?
5. State what you consider to be the two most important strengths and weaknesses of each system and why.

Background Reading

P. Dalton, *Economic Systems and Society*, Penguin Books, 1974.
P. Donaldson, *Economics of the Real World*, BBC/Penguin Books, 1980.
M. Friedman, *Free to Choose*, Penguin Books, 1980.
Lloyds Bank Economic Bulletin, August 1980.

1.18 Summary

1. Economics is the study of the allocation of scarce resources between alternative uses.
2. Scarcity gives rise to unavoidable choices about what, how, and for whom to produce.
3. Every choice about the use of resources in production involves a sacrifice or opportunity cost in terms of the most desirable alternative production foregone.
4. A traditional classification divides resources into the four factors of production – land, labour, capital, and enterprise.
5. Private goods tend to be competitive in use. Large numbers of people can use collective goods without diminishing the benefits derived by others.
6. In the planned economy political choice determines priorities in the

allocation of resources which tend to be in public ownership.

7. The planning apparatus is complex and involves a significant diversion of scarce resources into the planning process.

8. Among the formidable problems of economic planning are those concerning the co-ordination of resource inputs for targeted outputs, matching supply with demand, and ensuring that decisions are mutually consistent. Failure to resolve these may result in shortages, black markets, 'bottlenecks' in production or overproduction.

9. In the free-market economy decision-making is de-centralized to millions of households and firms who jointly influence the allocation of resources.

10. Changes in the conditions of demand or supply produce signals in the form of altered market prices and profit opportunities to which households and firms respond and alter the way in which resources are allocated.

11. The price mechanism allocates resources with minimum inconvenience and avoids the shortcomings of the planned economy.

12. A highly unequal distribution of income in the market economy is incompatible with socially optimal resource allocations.

13. Resource immobilities, the divergence of private and social costs, the inability to provide collective goods, and the persistence of unemployment all call into question the efficacy of market resource allocation.

14. Powerful oligopolistic national and multinational corporations dominate resource allocation in many sectors of the market economy.

Exercises

1. Review your understanding of the following:

economic resources	demand
opportunity costs	supply
resource allocation	market equilibrium
planned economy	price mechanism
free market economy	

2. Using Alan Morrice's book (*The Fundamentals of Economics*, Heinemann, 1983) or other introductory textbook on economics revise or read and make brief notes on

   price elasticities of demand and supply
   the law of diminishing returns.

2

The Management of the UK Mixed Economy

2.1 Introduction

The extent to which, and the manner in which, UK governments have attempted to manage the economy in the post-war period has had significant effects on:

- the allocation of resources and the composition of national output;
- the distribution of resources (i) between the regions of the UK and (ii) between the private and public sectors of the economy;
- the extent to which resources have been employed or unemployed;
- the rate at which new (capital) resources have been developed.

Economic policy is also an important determinant of the economic environment within which organizations operate and policy changes significantly affect the constraints and opportunities for organizations in both private and public sectors of the economy.

The broad purpose of the complex and essentially political task of managing the economy is to alter the course of the economy in order to achieve certain social objectives. Put another way the object of economic management is to achieve a set of outcomes different from that which would result from leaving it all to the interplay of market forces. There is an implicit belief, therefore, that government intervention can produce socially superior results than those which would result from the free play of unregulated market forces operating through the price mechanism.

Economic management comprises several components important amongst which are:

- the formulation of objectives;
- an analysis of how the economic system works (i.e. a set of theories or models);

- the determination and implementation of policy;
- an accurate and detailed knowledge of where the economy is now and of how it is likely to develop.

2.2 The Objectives of Economic Management

Throughout the post-war period economic policy has been chiefly concerned with one or more of four objectives – full employment, economic growth, an adequate balance of payments with the rest of the world, and stable prices. In addition to these, post-war governments have attempted to improve the balance between the various regions of the kingdom; to liberalize international trade; to maintain a stable exchange rate; and to redistribute income and wealth.

The emphasis laid on the various macroeconomic objectives has varied considerably over the period. This has been partially due to the differing political and social priorities of Labour and Conservative governments. For example, the extent to which government intervention in the economy is either desirable or necessary is strongly disputed by the political parties. Priorities are also partially influenced by the fact that objectives often conflict.

CASE STUDY 2.1

Policy Objectives

Governments in the UK have, since the War, pursued the broad economic policy objectives of growth, a high level of employment, control of inflation and balance of payments equilibrium.

The long-term objectives of the present Government were and are no different. It has, however, put greater emphasis than in the past on control of inflation as a pre-requisite for long-term growth and a high level of employment.

The main instrument chosen to control inflation has been the monetary mechanism; this has been accompanied by a shift away from short-term demand management as the central element of economic policy, a trend evident since 1976.

The cornerstone of the Government's strategy is the Medium-term Financial Strategy. It is within this framework that a progressive reduction in monetary growth, inflation and interest rates is to be achieved.

Control of the overall level of nominal expenditure can result in lower output and employment initially. However, the policy is based on the view that as expectations about inflation are revised downwards, so growth of output and employment will re-emerge within the overall monetary constraints set by the Government.

Complementary to this strategy, current policy also reflects a determination to alter the behaviour of the UK economy by letting or making markets forces work more freely and actively, through increasing incentives and flexibility, enhancing competition and shifting the balance of economic activity more towards the private sector. This form of supply-side approach emphasizes more limited intervention in order, in the long-term, to create an economic climate more conducive to entrepreneurship, risk-taking and wealth creation.

(*Source:* Extract from a Memorandum by the Director-General of the
National Economic Development Council on
The Progress of Economic Policy, July 1981)

STUDENT ASSIGNMENT 2.1

Managing the UK Economy

Refer to Case Study 2.1 and carry out the following investigations:

1. Using some of the sources listed below* discover what has happened in relation to the major economic policy objectives over the past decade.
2. Comment on your findings and evaluate the present government's achievements since it took office. In your opinion, is it fair to pass judgement on the present government's handling of the economy at the time you carry out your investigations?
3. Present your findings in the form of a short report.

* Economic Trends
  National Income Blue Book
  British Business
  Employment Gazette
  Monthly Digest of Statistics

2.3 Keynesian Theory and Post-War Economic Policy

For most of the post-war period the basis of British economic policy has been the Keynesian analysis, and for most of the period the emphasis on Keynesian demand management has brought considerable success in preventing unemployment from returning to the high levels of the inter-war years.

In the *General Theory of Employment, Interest and Money* (1936), which was to revolutionize our understanding of how the economy worked, Keynes traced the origins of mass unemployment to a deficiency of overall spending in the economy. The demand for labour is derived from the demand for goods and services. If the overall or aggregate demand for goods and services fell short of that needed for full employment the result would be unemployment. In an unregulated market economy the expenditure plans of millions of diverse economic agents considered together were most unlikely to be sufficient to produce the level of output that would employ the whole of the available labour force. If by some means, those agents could be induced to spend more, the level of output would rise and the level of employment with it.

This is not the place to explore the full rigour and subtleties of Keynesian theory; the following highly simplified treatment based on a two-sector economy (government and foreign trade are excluded) will suffice to illuminate the practical implications which have guided post-war policy-makers. Essential to an understanding of Keynes is the notion of *macro-economic equilibrium*. The volume of national output will accommodate itself to the current level of aggregate demand for goods and services. The economy is in equilibrium when national output has expanded or contracted to be just equal to the amount that economic agents spend on that output. In Figure 2.1, the 45° line gives all the points at which national output can be in equilibrium, i.e. at which the amount that

Figure 2.1. Equilibrium income, full employment income and the deflationary gap.

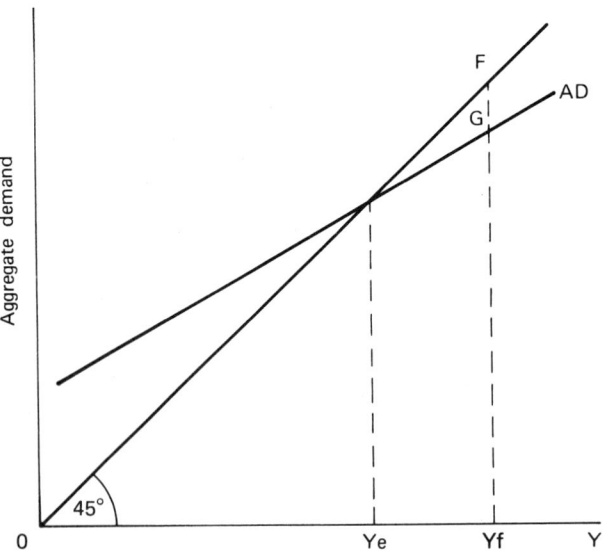

economic agents are willing to spend on the output of the economy (AD) is equal to the output that firms are willing to produce (Y). Given the expenditure function in Figure 2.1, national output will be stabilized at Ye. Thus the equilibrium level of output is determined by the position of the total spending (AD) function which will depend on the numerous spending decisions of consumers and firms. It is apparent that an almost infinite number of equilibria are possible, each associated with a different level of employment, and only one unique level associated with full employment.

Given the level of technology, the theoretical upper limit on what the economy can produce is **full employment output**, i.e. that level of output which would result if all available economic resources were fully employed, designated Yf on Figure 2.1. The problem of unemployment emerges wherever the demand function gives an equilibrium income (Ye) which is lower than Yf as in Figure 2.1.

The position of the aggregate demand function indicates that output will stabilize at a level well below Yf where a considerable proportion of the labour force will remain unemployed. This unemployment can only be eliminated if policies are introduced to expand demand, i.e. to raise the demand function to a position where it intersects with the 45° line at point F. The shortfall in demand at full employment output or the **deflationary gap** (FG) will then be eliminated and income will be stabilized at the full employment level, Yf. The question then is how can spending be raised to close the deflationary gap? Keynes' answer was demand management through the manipulation of taxation and public expenditure, i.e. through the use of **fiscal policy**.

In particular Keynes advocated government spending on 'public works' for example Council house building, road construction and so on financed by a **budget deficit** as the way to close the deflationary gap and thereby to gain full employment. A budget deficit results when government spends more than it raises in taxation. This implies government borrowing to finance the deficit spending. Thus there is an increase in non-tax financed public spending injected into the economy which will raise national output by some multiple of itself.

This **multiplier process** takes place as a result of the fact that the initial increase in government spending creates income and gives rise to a number of further spending rounds. Assume an increase in government spending on hospital building of £100 million. This sum is paid out to the suppliers and workers and others in the construction industry who jointly receive £100 million income, some of which they will spend, creating income for another group of people and so on. Let us assume that people spend a constant proportion, say 80 per cent, of any additional income on domestically produced goods, i.e. in Keynesian jargon the **marginal**

propensity to consume (MPC) = 0.8 and the **marginal propensity to save** (MPS) = 0.2. In this case successive spending rounds will be as follows:

Increase in Government spending	generating increase in income of
£100m	£100m + £80m + £64m + £51.2m . . .

The sum of this geometric series is found using the formula

$$\frac{1}{1 - \text{common ratio.}}$$

The common ratio in this example is 0.8, i.e. the MPC. Thus the value of the multiplier (i.e. the ratio of the final increase in national income to the initial injection of expenditure) is found by applying the formula

$$\frac{1}{1 - \text{MPC}} \text{ or } \frac{1}{\text{MPS}}$$

In our example

$$\frac{1}{0.2} = 5 \times \text{£100m} = \text{£500m} = \text{final rise in income.}$$

We are now in a position to see the way in which fiscal policy has been used to generate additional employment through an expansion in demand.

In Figure 2.2, AD_1 shows the demand function that appears likely in the absence of intervention. Since full employment output is estimated as

Figure 2.2.   Closing the deflationary gap.

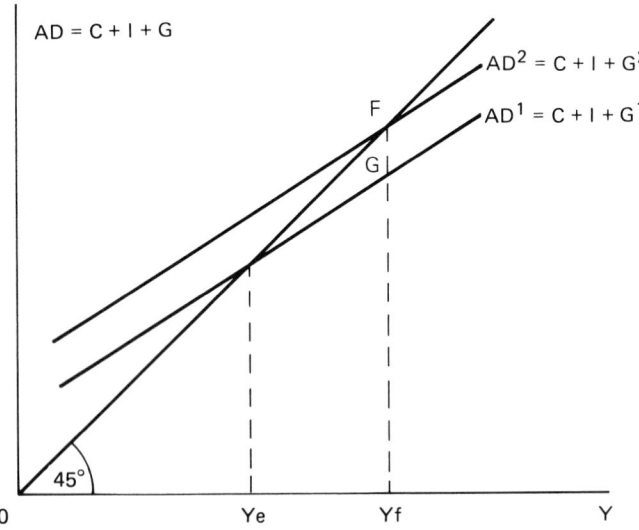

Yf, demand is insufficient as evidenced by a deflationary gap *(FG)*. The government budgets for a deficit to close the deflationary gap. Through the multiplier process this injection of demand causes national output to rise from *Ye*, to *Yf*. As a result firms will have raised their demand for labour to produce the additional output necessary to meet the higher level of demand.

Keynes explained the causes of inflation using similar analyses in terms of excessive demand. When the various economic agents attempted to purchase more than the economy was capable of producing (i.e. when *AD* exceeded *Yf*) the result would be shortages, production bottlenecks, and an **inflationary gap**. The Keynesian remedy for inflation was a **budget surplus** of taxes over public spending, in order to reduce the excess demand, and, as the multiplier process worked in reverse, to close the inflationary gap.

STUDENT ASSIGNMENT 2.2

The Multiplier Process

In the imaginary economy of Keynesland, a recent public investment into motorway construction cost £100 million, which was not financed from taxation. Of this £40 million created income in the form of corporate profits and £60 million in the form of wages and salaries.

The companies earning the £40 million profits paid corporation tax of £8 million retained (i.e. saved) £5 million and paid out £27 million as dividends. The shareholders, all of whom were private individuals paid dividends tax of £2 million leaving them with disposable income of £25 million. Of this £25 million, they (*i*) spent £12 million on domestic consumption (of which £3 million was VAT and other expenditure tax); (*ii*) spent £6 million on imports; and (*iii*) saved £7 million.

The recipients of the £60 million wages and salaries paid income tax amounting to £12 million leaving them a disposable income of £48 million. Of this £48 million they (*i*) spent £35 million on domestic consumption (of which £5 million was VAT and other expenditure tax); (*ii*) spent £8 million on imports; (*iii*) saved £5 million.

Calculate:

1. The marginal propensity to consume.
2. The value of the multiplier.
3. The total increase in income resulting from the public investment.
4. Assuming that each £10 million increase in income generates 1000 extra jobs, the resulting increase in numbers in employment.

2.4 Inflation and the Balance of Payments

Increasingly during the 1960s and 1970s governments were concluding that demand management was not enough to solve all the problems. Boosting domestic demand, to prevent unemployment invariably led to balance of payments problems and rising inflation. When domestic demand rises a greater volume of imports are sucked in and exports are diverted to the home market. Though imports are positively related to income, exports are determined by many other factors and will not necessarily rise concurrently. The result is a trade deficit, which as we shall see below constrains the government's efforts to tackle unemployment.

2.5 The Rise of Monetarism

By 1976, Keynesian orthodoxy was being increasingly questioned. Increasingly, too, governments were being seduced by an economic doctrine which was almost its complete antithesis. Whereas the Keynesian analysis is rooted in a profound disbelief in the efficiency of market forces, Friedmanite monetarism is underpinned by faith that, though the market economy may have its problems, it is superior to any other system if left to itself. Friedman argues that it is above all else government intervention that interferes with market efficiency.

At its simplest, the monetarist explanation of inflation is based on an observed relationship between movements in a nation's money supply and subsequent movements in the price level. There is impressive historical evidence to show that every increase in money supply has been followed by inflation and a rising level of prices. The cure for inflation therefore is in the hands of government who control movements in money supply. In the monetarist scheme of things governments should concentrate on managing the money supply, allowing it to grow at a steady rate roughly in line with the increase in productive capacity, i.e. with economic growth. Increases in money supply above this will result in inflation.

Monetarists are highly sceptical of governments' ability to reduce the rate of unemployment below what Friedman calls 'the natural rate of unemployment', i.e. the structural unemployment (caused by changes in the pattern of demand or technological innovation, for example) which exists when the overall supply and demand for labour has been brought into balance by movements in the real wage rate. Government demand management may succeed in *temporarily* reducing unemployment below its natural rate by running a budget deficit financed by borrowing. However, the budget deficit will invariably lead to an expansion in the money supply which will subsequently accelerate the rate of inflation. As the rate of inflation accelerates, people's expectations of future inflation will be continually revised in an upwards direction. The changed expectations will be incorporated into all monetary contracts including wage bargains, ensuring that the expectations are self-fulfilling. Thus the change in expectations about the future course of inflation is built into the system and becomes an important determinant of the actual rate of inflation. With inflation rising and the balance of payments deteriorating, the government 'applies the brakes' to contract demand, but the rate of inflation relative to the level of employment remains permanently higher than before.

The escalation of inflation during the latter part of the post-war period is the product of various government attempts to spend their way out of unemployment by running budget deficits. These have inevitably resulted in over-expansions of the money supply and *accelerated* the rate of inflation. The monetarist solution is to be found in a much less interventionist government, whose economic policies should be largely confined to controlling the money stock.

The displacement of Keynesianism by Friedman's monetarism (at the end of the 1970s in Britain) has set in train a series of political shock waves. The post-war consensus that government spending could be used to guarantee full employment was shattered. By early 1982 unemployment had risen to an unprecedented post-war figure in excess of three million as the Conservative Government, accepting the Friedmanite doctrine, desperately tried to arrest the rate of growth in money supply.

By January 1985 and on the basis of a revised count which excluded unemployed men over sixty (who were no longer required to register) the unemployment figure stood at 3,341,000, almost 14 per cent of the workforce. In addition an estimated 465,000 people were in jobs, training, or early retirement as a result of government special employment and training measures including 330,000 on the YTS Scheme and 131,000 on the Community Programme.

By May 1985 after four years of continuous economic growth, but with unemployment still rising, inflation had edged up again, having risen from an annual rate of 4.6 per cent in December 1984 to 7 per cent less than six months later. At the same time government ministers and the Prime Minister herself continued to insist that the government would not ease up in the fight against inflation and that there would be no return to 'the bad old days of the 1970s'. In the government's view 'nothing would do more to destroy the prospect for jobs'.

2.6 Conclusion

Economic management has been described as 'an attempt to pick one's way forward from a present which is highly constrained to a future which is highly uncertain'. In the necessarily selective and simplified account of economic management little has been said about the many *constraints* which governments face. As an open economy, the UK is part of the world economy and this means that no British government can ever be fully in control of the economic situation. Membership of international organizations – e.g. the EEC, the General Agreement on Trade and Tariffs (GATT), the IMF – may further limit a government's freedom of action. Unpredictable events at home or abroad – strikes, wars, the discovery of a new source of raw materials, for example – may constitute further constraints or opportunities. Case Study 2.2 illustrates some of the problems that can arise. The magnitude, timing, and even sometimes the direction of economic-policy effects on employment, growth, and prices, for example, are highly uncertain.

CASE STUDY 2.2

Managing the Economy – Problems with the £ Sterling

One of the effects of Britain's North Sea oil production is that in the foreign exchange markets the £ sterling is seen as a petro-currency. Consequently its exchange value tends to fluctuate with actual or anticipated changes in the price of oil on the world market. Thus, in the early months of 1985 market fears that OPEC was about to cut oil prices caused currency speculators to sell their £s in order to invest their money in other safer currencies. This together with other factors (notably the strength of the US dollar) triggered sharp increases in nominal and real interest rates to record levels in order to prevent the exchange rate falling to the politically unacceptable parity level (i.e. £1 = $1). Protecting the £ in this way, however, had many adverse effects on the domestic economy; as well as deterring industrial investment and removing purchasing power from the economy, the hikes in interest rates pushed up the cost of mortgages and, via the increased cost of imports, added to the rate of inflation. All-in-all, these effects made it much more difficult for government to achieve its macro-economic objectives of growth, employment, and price stability.

Perversely even the good news that the miners' strike had ended hit the £ even further as the resumption of coal supplies removed the need for Britain to import the £2 billion extra oil – a phenomenon which had underpinned the price of oil on the world market.

STUDENT ASSIGNMENT 2.3

Indicators of Economic Recovery

1. Using *British Business, Employment Gazette, Economic Trends* and/or other sources investigate the statistical trends since 1979 in

   the volume of (non-oil) exports
   investment
   the share of profits in total income
   company profitability
   new company formation
   company liquidation

2. From your findings to No. 1 (above) what appear to have been the effects of government economic policies on either

   (i) business organisations in general
   (ii) a particular industry or sector of the economy
   (iii) a particular company or other organisation.

3. Write a short report on your findings.

2.7 Summary

1. Management of the economy has important effects on the allocation, distribution and employment of the nation's resources.
2. The major policy objectives of economic management in the post-war period have been
   - full employment
   - growth
   - balance of payments equilibrium
   - price stability.
3. Labour and Conservative governments disagree about (*a*) the emphasis which should be given to each objective and (*b*) the extent to which governments should intervene in the market economy.
4. The history of post-war economic management reveals conflicts between objectives and changing priorities in their pursuit.
5. Keynesian theory explaining unemployment in terms of demand deficiency has formed the basis of economic policy for most of the post-war period.
6. The Keynesian analysis implies the use of fiscal policy to manage the level of aggregate demand in order to achieve policy objectives.

7. From the late 1970s Keynesian ideas were increasingly questioned as problems of inflation, payments deficits and slow growth persisted.
8. In the period since 1979 government has intervened less in the economy, and monetary measures have been used to manage the economy.

Exercise

1. Review your understanding of the following:

   aggregate demand
   propensity to consume
   multiplier process
   equilibrium level of income
   full employment output
   deflationary gap
   inflationary gap
   budget deficit
   budget surplus
   quantity theory of money

2. Using Alan Morrice's book (*The Fundamentals of Economics*, Heinemann, 1983) or other introductory economics textbook, revise or read and make notes on

   national income accounts
   quantity theory of money

Further Reading

Donaldson, Peter, *10 X Economics* (Penguin Books, 1982).
Maunder, Peter (ed.) *The British Economy in the 1970s*, (Heinemann).
National Institute of Economic and Social Research, *The United Kingdom Economy* (5th ed.) (Heinemann, 1982).

3

Resource Allocation in the Public Sector

3.1 Public Expenditure and the Public Sector

The public sector is defined here as that part of the economy over which government has direct control. It includes

- central government;
- local government;
- nationalized industries and other public enterprise.

The most important single indicator of the *relative* size of the public sector is public expenditure expressed as a ratio of the total economy. However, statistical problems arise in defining public expenditure and in selecting the most appropriate measure of national output with which to compare it.

Brown and Jackson* have compared U.K. public expenditure ratios for 1980 using different national income aggregates. Their results range from 50 per cent when public expenditure is compared with GDP at market prices to 62.3 per cent when it is compared with national income at factor cost. Which ratio is 'correct'? Is the 'true' size of the public sector nearer 60 or 50 per cent? The authors conclude that no single ratio is the true one; all are arbitrary.

Significant differences in public expenditure/GDP ratios yielded by using different recent official definitions of public expenditure have been highlighted by Heald.** If, for example, a broadly based pre-1977 definition and the narrower definitions of the 1982 public expenditure

* Brown, C. V. and Jackson, P. M., *Public Sector Economics*, Martin Robertson, 1982, p. 131
** Heald, D., *Public Expenditure*, Martin Robertson, Oxford, 1983

White Paper are applied to 1980 the resulting ratios are 55 per cent in the former case, and 43 per cent in the latter.

The distinction between **exhaustive** public expenditure on goods and services (e.g. government spending on health or defence) and **transfer payments** (e.g. pensions, social security payments) raises further questions. Whereas in the case of exhaustive expenditure, governments directly allocate a proportion of the nation's resources to the production of final goods and services, transfer payments merely redistribute income from taxpayers to beneficiaries with government acting as an intermediary. Thus whilst the public expenditure/GDP ratio may be an appropriate measure of what needs to be financed from taxation and public borrowing, the public sector's claim on national resources is better indicated by expressing *exhaustive* public expenditure as a ratio of GDP. This latter ratio has remained relatively constant at about 25 per cent over the past decade, but is expected to fall to an estimated 22.5 per cent in 1985–86.

The decision to measure public expenditure at **current prices** (i.e. in cash terms) or at **constant prices** (i.e in volume terms) as later sections show, has important implications for planning and control.

Given the many problems, interpretation of public expenditure/GDP ratios is very tricky and 'the potential for confusion and manipulation is enormous'.* In recent years, for example, pressures to cut public expenditure have been partly sustained by a belief that UK public expenditure was far too high compared with levels in other countries. In fact using OECD standardized definitions, Britain's public expenditure/GDP ratio of 44.6 per cent in 1980 was *lower* than that of all its EEC partners except Greece.

3.2 Trends in Public Expenditure

Figure 3.1 shows the relative shares of central and local government current and capital expenditure over the decade to 1982–83. From this it is apparent that

- the share of central government in general government spending increased from 68 per cent in 1973–74 to 75 per cent in 1982–83 while that of local government declined from 32 to 25 per cent. These trends reflect the different functions of the two levels of government. For example, central government has responsibility for social security which has risen steeply in recent years with rising unemployment, and with the ageing population;

* Barnett, Joel, *Inside the Treasury*, Andre Deutsch, 1982, p. 80

Figure 3.1. Percentage of general government expenditure by spending authority.

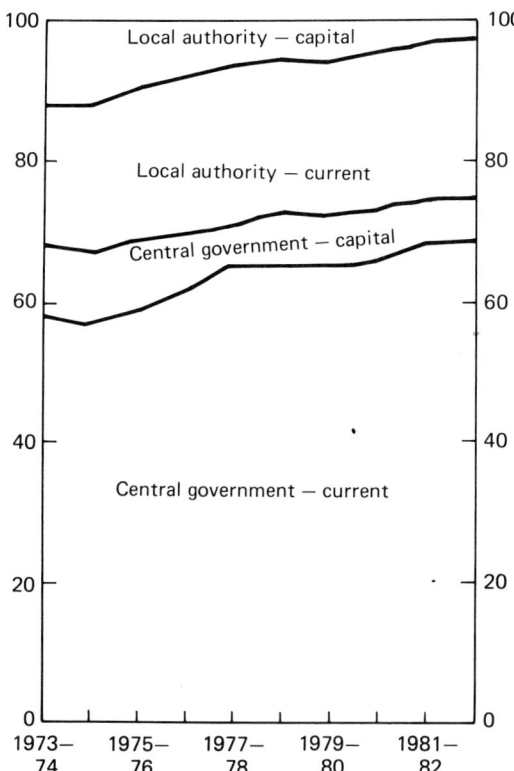

Source: Imber, Valerie and Todd, Phillipa (HM Treasury), 'Public Expenditure: Definitions and Trends', in *Economic Trends*, HMSO, November 1983.

- local government capital expenditure fell dramatically from 12 to 3 per cent of general government expenditure. This was partially due to the negative effect of council house sales.

From Figure 3.2 showing the composition of public expenditure by economic category we can see that

- current expenditure increased from 77 per cent of the planning total in 1973–74 to 90 per cent in 1982–83. Over half this was an increase in current transfers – mainly social security benefits – over the decade. Capital expenditure declined from 23 to 10 per cent of the total.

Figure 3.2.   Percentage of expenditure by economic category.

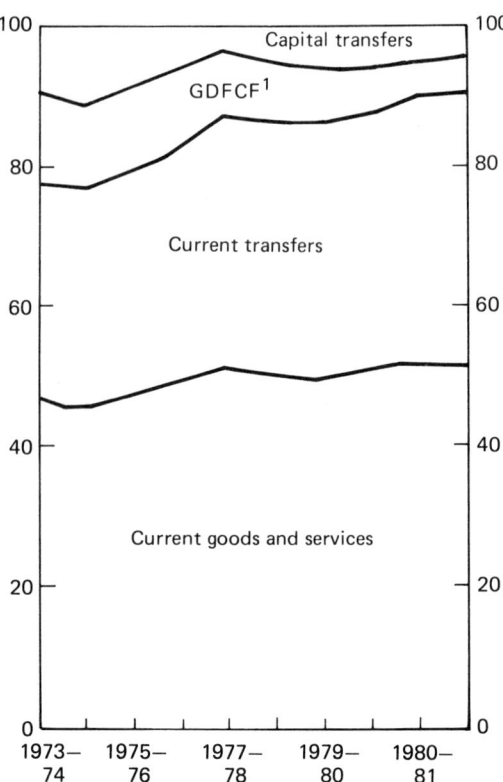

Note [1] Gross domestic fixed capital formation.
Source: Imber, Valerie and Todd, Phillipa (HM Treasury), 'Public Expenditure:
Definitions and Trends', in *Economic Trends*, HMSO, November 1983.

Figure 3.3(a) shows changes in public expenditure measured on two
definitions: that used prior to January 1977 and that used in a later white
paper (Cmnd 8789, February 1983) for the period 1963–64 to 1982–83.
From this data we can deduce that

- public expenditure (on both definitions), and measured both at constant prices and as a percentage of GDP (Figure 3.3(b)), has risen
  steadily with fluctuations around the upward trend particularly following the 'oil crisis' of 1973–74. Despite recent government efforts to
  control, this trend has continued with public expenditure 6 per cent
  higher in *real* terms at the beginning of 1984 compared with 1979–80.

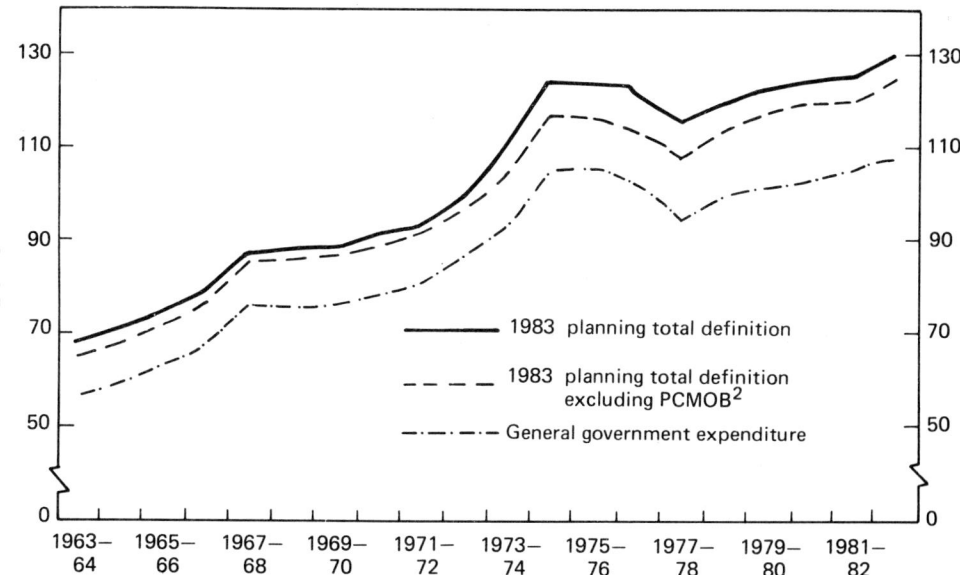

Figure 3.3(a) Public expenditure in cost[1] terms.

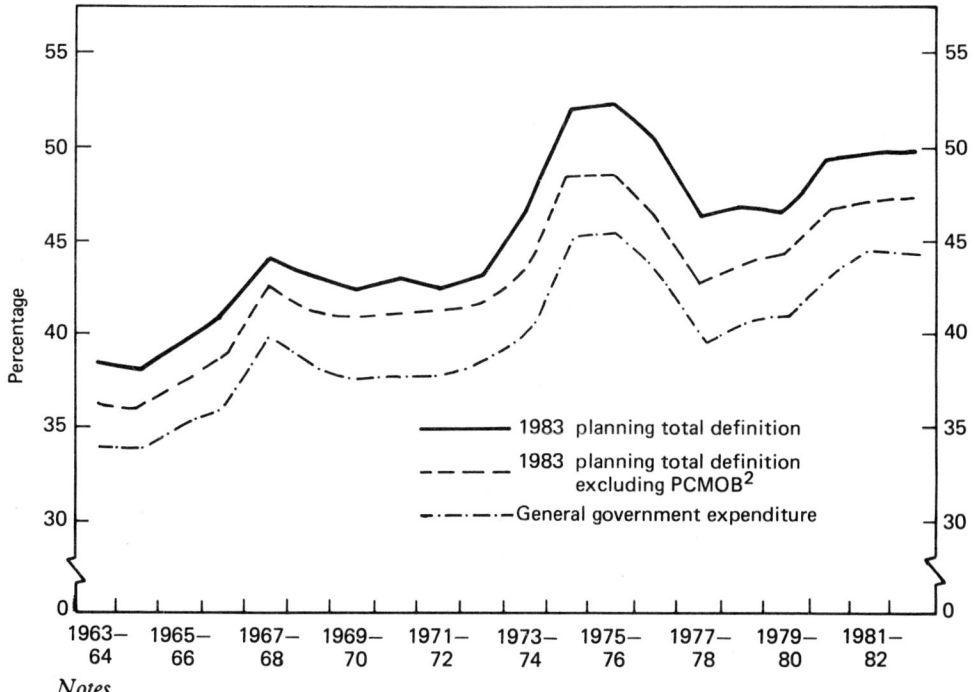

Figure 3.3(b) Public expenditure as a percentage of GDP.

Notes
[1] Cash figures at constant prices (using GDP deflator index, 1981–82 = 100).
[2] Public corporations market and overseas borrowing.
Source: Imber, Valerie and Todd, Phillipa (HM Treasury), 'Public Expenditure: Definitions and Trends', in *Economic Trends*, HMSO, November 1983.

The functional analysis of central government public expenditure (Table 3.1) shows the allocation of funds between spending programmes. Changes in the shares of the total allocated to each programme over time reflect

- changes in the social and economic priorities of different governments;
- changes and innovations in government policy;
- changes in economic conditions;
- demographic change;
- in the case of transfer payments changes in the number of beneficiaries and level of benefit as influenced by the preceding factors.

Finally, some indications of future trends are apparent in a Green Paper published with the Budget in March 1984 in which the Government set out its objectives for the long-term future of public expenditure. On the basis of assumed GDP growth rates of 2.25 per cent per annum for the next five years and of 1.5–2 per cent for the subsequent five years to 1993–94, the Green Paper makes clear that the Government intends

- to achieve a reduction in public expenditure as a per cent of GDP from its current level of 40 per cent to 32–34 per cent in 1993–94;
- despite 'strong pressures' for more public expenditure, to exercise a very tight control in order to constrain public spending at its present level.

3.3 Financing the Public Sector

The major source of public finance is taxation, which, if measured to include employees' and employers' social security contributions as well as direct and indirect taxes, finances about two-thirds of UK public expenditure. Another 30 per cent or so is financed by trading income, including nationalized industries' surpluses, and charges (for example for prescriptions or council rents). The remaining 4 or 5 per cent is financed by public borrowing.

Table 3.2 analyses taxation revenue for 1981–82. Income tax is by far the most important single revenue-raiser, supplying well over 30 per cent of the total. Indirect taxes (taxes on expenditure such as VAT and excise duties plus local rates) account for about 40 per cent. About 17 per cent is derived from national insurance contributions.

---

* *The Government's Expenditure Plans, 1984–85 to 1986–87*, Cmnd 9143–1, February, 1984

	1978-79	1979-80	1980-81	1981-82	1982-83	1983-84	1984-85
Defence	12,183	12,835	13,092	13,442	14,408	14,968	15,448
Overseas aid and other overseas services							
Overseas aid	1,162	1,090	1,037	1,022	965	988	997
Net payments to EC institutions	1,220	1,167	259	163	580	476	340
Other overseas services	615	631	603	611	619	721	734
Agriculture, fisheries, food and forestry	1,320	1,400	1,576	1,473	1,861	1,987	1,857
Trade, industry, energy and employment	6,486	5,574	6,033	7,220	5,791	5,790	5,088
Arts and libraries	553	562	560	558	616	595	544
Transport	4,342	4,559	4,687	4,561	4,395	4,343	3,966
Housing	5,803	6,286	5,228	3,336	2,640	2,629	2,264
Other environmental services	3,611	3,672	3,598	3,314	3,554	3,607	3,130
Law, order and protective services	3,306	3,585	3,703	3,979	4,174	4,459	4,446
Education and science	12,602	12,438	12,769	12,627	12,682	12,720	11,839
Health and personal social services	12,067	12,377	13,313	13,568	13,817	13,988	13,987
Social security	26,713	27,006	27,453	30,463	32,445	33,642	33,747
Other public services	1,570	1,608	1,658	1,640	1,631	1,587	1,622
Common services	1,386	1,403	1,286	1,550	1,560	905	1,002
Scotland	6,034	6,324	6,279	6,217	6,242	6,445	6,225
Wales	2,419	2,460	2,475	2,366	2,386	2,464	2,345
Northern Ireland	3,464	3,402	3,397	3,429	3,500	3,618	3,657
Local authority current expenditure not allocated to programmes (England)							599
Adjustments							
Special sales of assets		-1,389	-417	84	-488	-1,143	-1,723
Reserve						95	2,494
General allowance for shortfall						-286	
Planning total[1]	106,857	106,989	108,588	111,624	113,377	114,598	114,606

Note [1]Totals do not always add because of rounding.

Table 3.2.   Taxation and miscellaneous receipts.

	1981–82		1982–83 forecast
	Budget forecast	Estimated outturn	
TAXATION	£ million	£ million	£ million
Inland Revenue –			
Income tax	28,205	28,504	30,775
Corporation tax	4,600	4,800	4,850
Petroleum revenue tax	2,210	2,380	2,290
Supplementary petroleum duty	1,850	2,050	2,040
Capital gains tax	575	540	600
Development land tax	25	35	40
Estate duty	15	16	10
Capital transfer tax	445	470	465
Stamp duties	775	800	810
Special tax on banking deposits	400	355	–
Total Inland Revenue	39,100	39,950	41,880
Customs and Excise –			
Value added tax	12,650	12,300	14,750
Oil	4,800	4,550	5,100
Tobacco	3,220	3,325	3,525
Spirits, beer, wine, cider and perry	3,200	3,000	3,275
Betting and gaming	510	500	550
Car tax	550	525	600
Other excise duties	25	20	20
EC own resources			
Customs duties, etc.	835	920	1,060
Agricultural levies	210	210	270
Total Customs and Excise	26,000	25,350	29,150
Vehicle excise duties	1,628	1,629	1,854
National insurance surcharge	3,809	3,594	3,443
Total Taxation	70,537	70,523	76,327
MISCELLANEOUS RECEIPTS			
Broadcast receiving licences	552	603	754
Interest and dividends	222	260	321
Gas levy	–	383	512
Other	4,213	4,519	4,981
Total	75,524	76,288	82,895

Source: Financial Statement and Budget Report 1982–83, HMSO, p. 37.

3.4 Planning and Control of Public Expenditure – The PESC System

The system of public expenditure and control introduced in 1961 owed its essential features to the Plowden Report on Public Expenditure Control which recommended that:

> ... decisions involving substantial future expenditure should always be taken in the light of surveys of public expenditure as a whole over a period of years and in relation to prospective resources.
>
> (The Control of Public Expenditure, Cmnd 1432, HMSO, July 1961)

Thus the new system, which was to survive until 1981, was based on

- an annual survey of public expenditure as a whole covering a five-year period and rolled forward one year at a time;
- planning of expenditure in *volume* terms (i.e. at constant prices) in order to estimate the opportunity costs of the public sector and to facilitate Keynesian demand management policy;
- a medium-term economic assessment of trends for GDP, investment, balance of payments and so on, to provide an indication of the prospective real resources likely to be available for future expenditure.

The essential elements in the annual procedure for planning public expenditure are

- expenditure plans for the next five years (now three years) are submitted to the Treasury by spending departments;
- under the supervision of the Public Expenditure Survey Committee (PESC) consisting of the Principal Finance Officers of spending departments chaired by a senior treasury official, the Treasury collates all the information required for the annual survey and drafts a Report for consideration by the PESC;
- The PESC Report and the medium-term assessment (also prepared by the Treasury) are distributed to Departmental Ministers enabling them to see where unchanged policies will lead and the extent to which real resources are likely to be available over the years of the plan;
- in a series of cabinet discussions ministers argue the case for their own programme on the basis of submissions prepared within their own departments by civil servants in the light of the PESC Report and medium-term assessment;
- the medium-term assessment provides the basis for the calculation of next year's public sector borrowing requirement (PSBR), before deci-

sions are taken in Cabinet on the aggregate level of public expenditure and its broad functional allocation;

● the public expenditure plan is published in the annual White Paper on the government's expenditure plans for debate (and normally approval) in Parliament.

It is appropriate at this point to note the considerable influence of the bureaucracy on public expenditure decisions. Since it is Treasury and departmental civil servants who prepare submissions, brief ministers, and produce the PESC Report and the medium-term assessment, resource allocation in the public sector is far from being a purely political exercise.

CASE STUDY 3.1

Fudging the Figures

Another area where officials were quite brilliant was in the different ways they had of 'fudging' figures, particularly on expenditure decisions. It was more understandable if you started from the same standpoint as officials, which was conservative with a small 'c', although this would by no means apply to all of them.

Nonetheless, the prevailing belief among them was that our poor industrial and economic performance meant we must restrain the growth of public expenditure. Consequently, all their considerable efforts in presenting the figures would be geared to that end. My main complaint was not about the 'fudging' or, as they occasionally put it, 'massaging' (there was 'light' and 'deep' massage) of the figures, but that it should be clear to *me* just what they were doing.

I thought I had done a fair amount of juggling with figures as an accountant, but when it came to the sort of sophisticated 'massaging' and 'fudging' I learned as Chief Secretary, I realized I had been a babe in arms by comparison. It was a case of changing this and that 'assumption', and abracadabra – the Public Sector Borrowing Requirement (PSBR) is about the figure you first thought of! More seriously, lest it be thought that officials were somehow cooking the books, let me make it clear that I make no such accusation. They would not put their names to figures which, as they saw it, impugned their integrity.

The simple fact is that arithmetic and accountancy bear little or no resemblance to economics in general, and the 'art' of presenting huge public expenditure figures in particular. In the preparation of a public expenditure White Paper, a whole variety of 'assumptions' have to be made (economic jargon for 'guessing') about such matters as earnings, prices, shortfall, along with a host of other 'estimates'. Any one of these variables could ensure that the picture painted was such as to require action of the kind which officials believed to be right, and, as they were genuinely convinced, in the national interest. The trouble was that a slightly different 'assumption' or 'guesstimate' could give a rather different picture, to the tune of say £1 billion less on the estimate borrowing requirement – and therefore considerably reduce the case for an equivalent public expenditure cut.

(*Source:* Barnett, Joel, *Inside the Treasury,*
Andre Deutsch, 1982, pp. 21–22)

STUDENT ASSIGNMENT 3.1

The Influence of Bureaucracy

1. To what extent do civil servants appear to influence public expenditure and resource allocation decisions?
2. To what extent should they do so?

3.5 Weaknesses in the PESC System

In the mid-1970s conditions of 'stagflation' (low economic growth plus inflation) exposed inherent weaknesses in the PESC system which eventually led to its demise.

Planning in volume terms failed to control the level of public expenditure in cash terms, i.e. the figure which actually had to be financed by taxation or borrowing. This problem arises because the costs of public sector inputs tend to rise more rapidly than private sector costs and prices partly because the public sector is more labour intensive and it is much harder to obtain productivity increases. Whenever this **relative price effect** (RPE) is positive the ratio of public expenditure to GDP rises even though the volume of public expenditure remains unaltered.

If, for example, the pay of teachers or nurses rises faster than private sector pay should the volume of public spending be reduced or should taxpayers pay more for the same service? If the latter, then although public expenditure in volume terms does not rise, increased taxation or borrowing is necessary to finance the pay increase. Hence, given volume planning the incentive to public sector managements to control costs was weak.

In times of rapid inflation volume planning failed to take into account *financing* implications. In 1974–75 public expenditure in cash terms was about £5.8 billion more than planned in the 1971 White Paper. Nearly 70 per cent of this increase (equivalent to 5 per cent of GDP) was attributable to unforeseen increases in prices paid by the public sector relative to those in the private sector. This was largely due to huge increases in land and construction prices between 1970 and 1975.

A further problem arose from the fact that the planned growth of public expenditure was determined in the light of the rate of growth of real resources indicated by the change in GDP forecast in the medium-term assessment. If the GDP forecast was over-optimistic then, of course, the ratio of public expenditure to GDP at constant prices rises. In 1965–68 public expenditure was planned to grow in real terms at 4.25 per cent on the projection that real GDP would grow at 3.8 per cent. In fact GDP grew at only 2.2 per cent. In 1974–75 real GDP actually fell by 1.8 per cent. In both periods the relative size of the public sector increased because expenditure plans were realized but GDP forecasts were not.

3.6 Cash Limits

First introduced in 1976 in the context of a public sector 'pay explosion' cash limits set a limit on the amount of cash the government proposes to spend or authorize on certain services during one financial year. The underlying principle was that 'levels of service must be determined in the light of finances available'.

By 1982–83 cash limits had been extended to cover about 40 per cent of total expenditure. In setting limits the Treasury inevitably takes a view of the expected rate of inflation in the forthcoming year since this will obviously affect cash spending and therefore the levels of taxation and borrowing necessary to finance it. However, a problem arises because the forecast rate of inflation built into the cash limits tends to condition inflationary expectations which in turn have an important influence on the actual rate of inflation. In particular public sector unions will tend to regard the Treasury figure for wage inflation as setting a minimum acceptable pay increase.

If this is so, then in order to dampen inflationary expectations and public sector pay claims, the Treasury has an incentive to incorporate a forecast rate of inflation lower than the actual rate it expects to emerge. If public sector pay settlements in the coming year exceed the inflation rate allowed for in the cash limit, then either there must be cuts in service or large savings in non-wage costs.

3.7 Cash Planning

The decision to plan public expenditure in cash terms announced in March 1981 reinforced the government view that levels of public service must be determined by available finance rather than by the needs of particular programme objectives.

The 1982 White Paper* plans for the year ahead could for the first time be translated directly into cash limits – the control figures for the year ahead. The same White Paper made explicit government's determination to avoid a public sector 'pay explosion' of the kind which had so damaged the PESC system in 1975–76, warning that, 'excessive expenditure on pay increases reduces the cash available to finance investment or services to the public' – a clear message to public sector unions that if they pushed wage increases too hard, the consequences would be service cuts and redundancies.

3.8 Local Government Expenditure

Since social needs and problems arise in local communities it is local county or district authorities who, operating within powers given to them by Parliament and under the supervision of central government departments, administer many important social services.

Local government expenditure amounts to nearly 10 per cent of GDP though as we have seen (Figure 3.1) local government's share in general government expenditure has declined from about one-third to about one quarter over the past decade. Much of this relative decline reflects a substantial fall in local government capital expenditure due partially to council house sales which rose from £1 million in 1973–74 to £2.1 *billion* in 1982–83, but also represents a substantial reduction in investment in council housing, schools, local roads and so on. Table 3.3 which compares local capital expenditure with that in other parts of the public sector reveals the dramatic nature of this decline.**

The functional analysis of local government expenditure of Table 3.4 requires careful interpretation. Planned local authorities' current expenditure for 1982–83 was £1,300 million higher than the cash figures given in the previous White Paper largely because of 'overspending' in 1980–81 of £1,050 million, or 6 per cent more than central government planned for them. As the 1982 White Paper noted 'the new higher plans for 1982–83 are 2 per cent more than local authorities' latest budgets for 1981–82.

* Cmnd 8494, HMSO, March 1982
** Street, A., Local Authority Capital Spending on Roads, *National Westminster Bank Quarterly Review*, November 1983

Table 3.3.   Public sector capital expenditure 1976–77 to 1982–83.

	Capital expenditure in 1982–83 as a % of 1976–77 (at 1982 prices)
Central Government	91
Public Corporations	70
Local Government	28

Note Translated into cash, this means that of the £8 billion annual fall in public capital investment over the period, £5 billion was borne by the local authorities.

Table 3.4.   Public expenditure by local authorities in Great Britain.

	1982–83 outturn	*1983–84 budgets*	*1984–85 plans*	*1985–86 plans*	*1986–87 plans*
			£ million cash		
Current expenditure	25,178	28,410	27,903	28,573	29,135
Capital expenditure	3,551	3,829	3,662	3,870	4,022
Total	28,729	32,239	31,565	32,443	33,154

Allowing for pay and price increases local authorities will have to make significant real economies to keep within new plans.'

'Overspending', too, needs careful interpretation. Significant 'real economies' had in fact already been achieved by local government whose manpower had fallen by over 91,000 between June 1979 and June 1983. The lion's share of this reduction was borne by the education service whose manpower fell by 75,000 or 6.25 per cent between 1979 and 1983. And, as we have seen, local government capital expenditure fell dramatically in the same period.

The 1984 White Paper* made it clear that the squeeze on council spending was to continue as local authorities were told to cut their budgets by about 13 per cent in real terms in the three years to 1986–87. By this time **rate-capping** legislation (see Section 3.11) was before Parliament, giving Ministers more powers to enforce the planned cuts by setting limits on rate increases.

3.9 The Finance of Local Government

Local authorities finance their expenditure from three main sources:

* Cmnd 9143–1, HMSO, March 1984

- central government grants;
- rates;
- fees, charges, and rents.

In addition the Secretary of State may authorize borrowing either from Central Government or on the open market to finance capital spending. In recent years the Government has reduced the proportion of local government expenditure financed by grants so that the proportions of revenue arising from rates and charges has increased. Table 3.5 shows the ways in which local government expenditure was financed in 1981–83.

Table 3.5.   Local authorities transactions.

	1981–82		1982–83
	Budget forecast	*Estimated outturn*	*Forecast*
Receipts		£ billion	
Rates	10.3	10.9	12.2
Rate support grant	11.4	11.5	11.5
Other grants from central government	3.9	4.6	4.4
Other	4.4	4.6	5.1
Total	29.9	31.6	33.2
Expenditure			
Current expenditure on goods and services	19.5	20.6	21.5
Capital consumption	1.2	1.4	1.6
Grants and subsidies	2.1	2.6	2.6
Interest payments	4.5	4.3	4.7
Gross domestic fixed capital formation	2.5	2.2	2.5
Net lending to private sector	1.2	0.7	1.1
Total	30.9	31.8	33.8
Local Authority Borrowing Requirement	1.0	0.3	0.6
of which:			
Borrowing from central government	0.9	–1.2	–0.3
Other borrowing	0.1	1.5	0.9

Source: Financial Statement and Budget Report 1982–83, HMSO, p. 29.

3.10 Rates

Rates are a tax on domestic and business property expressed as a *rate poundage* based on the rateable value of properties determined by a rental value (last fixed in 1973). If, for example, your house has an annual rateable value of £1,000 and the rate poundage is set at 150p in the £, your rates bill will be £1,500. All houses in England and Wales receive 'domestic rate relief' of 18.5p from central government. Rates are criticized

- for being too regressive, i.e. imposed a *relatively* higher burden on lower income groups;
- providing only a weak link between consumers of local services and what they have to pay;
- high business rates contribute to unemployment (See Case Study 3.2).

Despite such criticisms, the rate system has survived, and alternatives like local income tax, favoured by the Layfield Committee* on local government finance, have been rejected. However, a government green paper published in 1985 is likely to be followed by legislation enabling the government to limit rates levied on business.

CASE STUDY 3.2

The Rate Burden on Business and Commerce

Rates are the biggest single tax to be paid by UK businesses. The CBI estimates that close to £6 billion will be paid in rates by all UK businesses, including the nationalized industries, in the financial year 1983–84. This compares with Treasury estimates of around £4 billion to be paid by businesses in mainstream corporation tax and of £1.7 billion to be paid in the employers' national insurance surcharge.

Table 3.6 compares the increase in local authority rates with the increase in other business costs and with inflation in general.

An increase in rates will either be passed forward in prices or backward in lower wages or employment; or result in lower profits implying lower dividends and less investment; or reduce the return to land or property owners; or produce a combination of these effects.

In a recession it is difficult to increase prices and the rate burden is therefore more likely to fall on wages, investment, and profit margins. Reduction of the wage bill effectively means reductions in employment itself, as the pressure to maintain wage levels per employee is high and money wage reductions are rarely achieved. Reduced investment can only lead to lower productivity and hence reduced competitiveness in the longer term which means less jobs than otherwise would have been the case. Squeezing profit margins which are already at very low levels will put the marginal firm out of business altogether which again means less jobs.

* *Alternatives to Domestic Rates*, Layfield Committee Report, Cmnd 6453, HMSO, 1976

Table 3.6. Indices of various prices and industrial costs 1979 = 100.

Year	Industrial rates	Costs of materials & fuels bought by industry	Average earnings in manu-facturing	Price of manu-facturing output	Retail price index
1979	100	100	100	100	100
1980	125	120	118	116	118
1981	152	136	134	128	132
1982	176	145	148	140	143

3.11 Central Government Grants to Local Government

Grants may be **specific**, usually in the form of a percentage of spending on a particular service such as police or housing, and **non-specific** chiefly the *rate support grant* (RSG) reformed in 1981–82 into a *block grant*.

The RSG provides local authorities with some 40 per cent of their income. It contains three components:

- the needs element, intended to compensate authorities whose expenditure is higher than average because of the socio-economic structure of the local population, e.g. the proportions of school age, elderly, population density and so on;
- the resources element, intended to offset some of the financial constraints experienced by those authorities whose total rateable value, i.e. their taxable capacity, is below national average;
- the domestic element – a subsidy to rates on domestic, but not industrial or commercial, property.

The objective of the needs and resources elements was to enable different authorities to levy similar levels of rates for similar standards of service.

From April 1981, in order to strengthen central control over local government spending the RSG was modified into a *block grant* which provided government with a mechanism for determining and controlling the expenditure of *each* individual local authority. This works as follows:

- The total of all grants paid to local authorities is cash limited.
- Grant-related expenditure (GRE) is calculated by central government for each local authority on an assessment of needs based on local socio-economic and demographic factors.
- A grant-related poundage (GRP) schedule is derived for each authority's grant-related expenditure.

Figure 3.4.   The block grant.

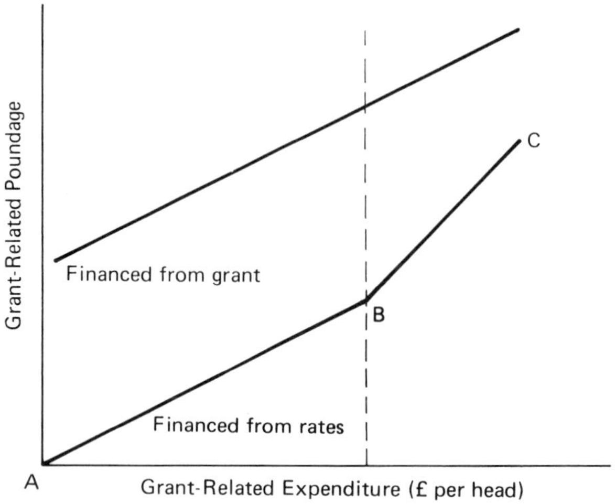

Source: Brown, C. V. and Jackson, P. M., *Public Sector Economics*, Martin Robertson, Oxford, 1982, p. 214.

- The block grant is tapered so that if a local authority exceeds its centrally determined GRE (i.e. if it 'over-spends') it will receive a declining amount of grant for each unit of excess expenditure. In some cases grant may actually fall. In Figure 3.4 the line AB shows the grant-related poundage that would have to be levied in order that a local authority be able to spend a particular GRE. At B a threshold is reached at which the Schedule tapers – the slope of BC exceeds that of AB. Thus if a local authority overspends, i.e. exceeds its centrally determined/assessed GRE, it will receive less grant. Beyond B total block grant will increase but at a decreasing rate as expenditure increases.

As a result of this system 107 English local authorities who had breached their targets in their spending plans for 1985–86 were expected to lose a total of £550 million in rate support grant for overspending their targets by £278 million, amounting to a cut of 6.5 per cent in the £8.5 billion available for block grant.

In 1981, too, central control over local government borrowing was strengthened into controls on capital expenditure resulting in a huge fall in council house building.

3.12 Conflicts between Central and Local Government

Since 1979 there have been intensifying conflicts between local authorities and central government. The way in which these conflicts have developed is well summarized in the following extract from *The Economist* (19–25 November 1983):

1) The newly elected Conservative government was eager to hold down public spending; local councils accounted for a quarter of this; and much of that came from government grants. So

2) The grant system was changed in 1981, in a way that gave Whitehall power to decide, more or less, how much each council ought to spend, and cut grants to overspenders. Control on borrowing also was strengthened into controls on capital spending – hence the big fall in council house building. But

3) Some Labour councils simply thumbed their noses at Whitehall, went on spending, lost part or all of their grants and thus

4) Had to impose huge rate increases (rates in England rose 91% on average from April, 1979, to April, 1983, far more in some areas). This aroused furious protests, which led to

5) Further controls and refinements of the grant-penalty system, and eventually, in 1983,

6) A White Paper was published saying the government would take 'rate-capping' powers to limit the rate increases of a few high-spending councils in England and Wales from April, 1985, with reserve powers to set limits for all councils. This would not apply to councils with budgets below £10m – i.e., about 275 of the 296 shire districts. The real targets were councils that had so exceeded Whitehall's targets for their spending (e.g. the GLC, 35% overspent) that they had no 'block' grant left to be cut.

Both Labour and Tory councils reacted fiercely. In the late 1970s, both had co-operated with Whitehall attempts to keep their spending down. But then they had been consulted and persuaded, not shoved.

Both objected when the shoving began in 1980–81, but (mostly) for different reasons. Labour councils were angry at being forced to cut, or not increase, local services; the loudest Tory protests came from councils that were already tight-fisted and had no room for further economy.

Tory and Labour councils united in 1983 on a basic issue: Whitehall control of their levels of service and their rates. There was fierce outcry from the three main representative bodies that Whitehall talks to, the Tory-controlled (shire) county and district council associations and the Labour-controlled one of metropolitan authorities. 'A fundamental breach of local democracy', said the district councils.

CASE STUDY 3.3

Rate-Capping Problems

Undeterred by rate-capping threats, several high-spending councils are going ahead with plans for big rate rises (1984–85).

Although the London Borough of Hackney was one of the councils on the Conservative Central Office 'hit list' drawn up the previous year, it proposed to increase its rate by 60 per cent above the present level of £2.15 in the pound.

According to the *Local Government Chronicle*, it was to spend £21 million more than its government-imposed spending target.

Hackney's Director of Finance and Borough Treasurer, Mr John Beha, said it was not possible to get down to the target and still perform statutory duties.

The council is about to embark on a court action challenging the spending target, and is expected to be joined by other Labour-controlled London boroughs.

In north London, Islington has been predicting that its rate will rise by 27 per cent from the current 204.6p in the pound, but the Director of Finance, Mr Eric Dear, said he thought the figure would eventually be reduced.

In the current year Islington received £20 million in Government grant, but expects to lose all that in 1984–85 because of grant penalties. It also expects to be included on the July rate-capping list.

In south London, Lambeth's rate is likely to rise by about 40 per cent. Sheffield's might have gone up by 20 per cent. Other councils which did not expect to avoid rate-capping as their rate increases would be well above inflation were two more London boroughs, Camden and Southwark, and also Liverpool.

> (*Source:* Jacobs, Anne, 'Olive branch for Tory rates rebels',
> *The Observer*, 22 January, 1984)

Postscript

For the year 1985–86, eighteen Labour councils were rate-capped. A number of these councils, including six London boroughs defied the Government by refusing to fix a rate, an action which would have left councillors solely liable for the consequences, including personal bankruptcy and disqualification from public office.

The rebellion did not end until July 1985 when the last of the rate-capped authorities, Lambeth, decided to set a legal rate. With thirty-two of its Labour members having been served with notices that they were to be surcharged for the delay in fixing a rate, the decision to set a rate at the maximum legal limit was taken on a one-vote majority caused by the resignation of a Labour councillor.

Lambeth Council leader, Mr Ted Knight, promised, however, that the decision would not change the borough's opposition to rate-capping; the council would carry on spending as before, whatever surcharge the Government imposed.

By September 1985, 49 labour councillors at Liverpool and 32 at Lambeth faced possible bankruptcy and disqualification from office under surcharge orders made by district auditors for refusing to set a rate in time to avoid incurring unnecessary expenditure.

STUDENT ASSIGNMENT 3.2

Westport Metropolitan District Council

Westport Metropolitan District Council represents an urban community of about a million people. Westport has suffered from long-term economic and social decline as its main industries of shipbuilding and steel have contracted. Currently Westport's unemployment rate of 18 per cent is more than twice the national average. About half of Westport's unemployed are in the under-25 age group.

In the inner-city area poor housing, over-crowded schools and a generally run-down environment have contributed to the multiplicity of social problems which are characteristic of so many of Britain's inner cities.

Over the past few years Westport Metropolitan District Council has borne the brunt of successive local government expenditure cuts as central government has tightened its grip over local authority finance. The Council is now faced with the prospect of absorbing yet another cut in its budget for the forthcoming financial year. The Council's objective is as far as possible to maintain the same level and standard of service within the constraints imposed by expenditure cuts.

Preliminary Research

1. Find out in some detail what range of services is provided by a Metropolitan District Council, and what is spent on each.
2. Find out what range of services is provided by *one* of the following Council departments: (a) Education Department or (b) Social Services Department.
3. Role-play a meeting of one of these departments to consider impending budget cuts.
4. Outline the *alternatives* which may be considered and explored by Westport's
   Education Department *or*
   Social Services Department
   each of whose budget for the forthcoming year is to be cut in real terms by 5 per cent.

(N.B. You are not required to arrive at final conclusions. Your objective is to identify the *options* facing the Council Department and explore the broad implications of each.)

3.13 The Expenditure of Nationalized Industries

Almost all the current expenditure and about two-thirds of the capital expenditure of the nationalized industries is financed by income derived from their trading activities. The remaining third of capital expenditure is externally financed from grants or borrowing and it is this which is included in the public expenditure totals.

Nationalized industries' capital expenditure is controlled in several ways:

- On the basis of annual reviews of their investment programmes and financing, the government informs each industry of the approved level of its investment programme and of its external financing limit (EFL) which constrains the industry's ability to borrow from sources other than government. The 1984 White Paper★ maintained the squeeze on nationalized industries by sharply reducing their total EFLs from £2.5 billion in 1983–84 to only £90 million by 1986–87.
- A financial target is specified for each industry.
- Rules to be followed for pricing, investment, and financial planning are set out in a White Paper dealing with the financial and economic objectives of the nationalized industries. The latest of these★★ sets out a framework covering financial targets and criteria for investment appraisals. The required rate of return of 5 per cent was set to reflect the opportunity cost of capital in the economy. The financial target which determines pricing policy was set to enable each industry to finance a higher proportion of its own investment programmes, thus reducing its borrowing requirement.

3.14 Privatization

In 1979 the newly-elected Conservative Government expressed its commitment to achieving a fundamental shift in the balance of power between the public and private sectors of the economy. In his 1979 Budget speech, the new Chancellor announced the government's proposals for privatization.

In the first four years of Mrs Thatcher's Government public sector asset sales raised some £2 billion. The 1983 White Paper envisaged raising a further £750 million (subsequently revised to £1.25 billion) in 1983–84, £1.9 billion in 1984–85, and £500 million the year after. With the sale of British Telecom expected to yield about £4 billion, these figures may be huge underestimates.

★ Cmnd 9143–1, Table 1.6
★★ *The Nationalized Industries*, Cmnd 7131 (HMSO, 1978)

Clearly asset sales on this scale not only alter the distribution of resources between the public and private sector, but also have economic implications for the control of public expenditure and borrowing. Since the assets sold off will generate future streams of costs and benefits privatization may not be an effective way of dealing with relatively short-term problems of controlling the PSBR. The proceeds of the sale of a profitable public enterprise (Amersham International, for example) may help to reduce the current year's PSBR, but assuming continued profitability, may contribute to a higher *future* PSBR as its profits no longer flow into the public purse. On the other hand, the sale of unprofitable public assets can result in a lower future PSBR as its need for public subsidy is removed.

3.15 Summary

1. The public sector consists of central and local government, nationalized industries, and other public enterprise.
2. An important indicator of the relative size of the public sector is public expenditure as a ratio of national output.
3. Because there is no unique definition of public expenditure and because there are numerous measures of national output, such ratios require careful interpretation.
4. Exhaustive public expenditure on goods and services involves government in the allocation of resources directly; in the case of transfer payments, government redistributes income from taxpayers to beneficiaries who influence the composition of final output through what they choose to spend their grants on.
5. Current expenditure on wages and salaries, fuel, materials, and so on is recurrent expenditure required for the operation of services; capital expenditure represents public investments in fixed assets.
6. Public expenditure in volume terms and as a percentage of GDP has risen steadily over the post-war period. Central government's share in the total has increased over the past decade.
7. Changes in the functional allocation of expenditure are the result of economic, demographic, and political change.
8. Taxation, including national insurance contributions, finances about two-thirds of UK public expenditure. About 30 per cent is financed by trading income and charges. The remaining 4 or 5 per cent is borrowed.
9. Under the PESC system planning was on the basis of a rolling 5 year expenditure survey in volume terms.
10. Volume planning failed to take into account the financing implications

of expenditure plans. This produced severe strains in the PESC system and led to the introduction of 'cash limits' in 1976.

11. Cash limits were extended to cover about 40 per cent of expenditure by 1982–83, much of the rest being 'demand-determined' transfer payments. From 1981 cash planning was introduced confirming the government's view that levels of public service must be determined by available finance.

12. Local government's share in general government expenditure has declined from about one-third to one quarter over the past decade.

13. Local government expenditure is financed by grants from central government; from rates; and from fees, charges and rents. Borrowing for capital projects requires authorization from the Secretary of State for the Environment.

14. The Rate Support Grant provides local authorities with about 40 per cent of their income.

15. Since 1979 relations between central and local government have been subject to increasing strains as central government has taken increasing powers to control the budgets of individual local authorities, culminating in 'rate-capping' legislation in early 1984.

16. About one-third of the capital spending of nationalized industries is externally financed and is included in public expenditure totals. Each industry is subject to an annual 'external financing limit'.

17. In order to change the balance in the mixed economy in favour of the private sector, government has embarked on a massive privatization programme.

Exercise

Review your understanding of the following:

    public expenditure/GDP ratios
    exhaustive public expenditure
    transfer payments
    current and capital expenditure
    cash limits
    rate support grant
    block grant
    rate-capping
    external financing limits
    privatization

Further Reading

Brown, C. V. and Jackson, P. M., *Public Sector Economics*, Martin Robertson, Oxford, 1982.

Heald, David, *Public Expenditure*, Martin Robertson, Oxford, 1983.

Imber, Valerie and Todd, Phillipa (H. M. Treasury), 'Public Expenditure: Definitions and Trends', in *Economic Trends*, HMSO, November 1983.

Barnett, Joel, *Inside the Treasury*, Andre Deutsch, 1982.

PART II
THE ACQUISITION OF
RESOURCES

4

Labour Markets, Recruitment and Selection

4.1 The Nature of Labour Markets

Labour markets are the mechanisms by which employers such as companies, public corporations, local authorities and so on, who seek to buy labour services, and workers who wish to sell their labour services can effect the deployment and utilization of human resources.

We can only begin to understand the considerable complexities of labour market operations when we recognize that unlike machines, raw materials, or other inputs to production, labour is not a commodity. The labour market is composed of millions of human beings whose wellbeing is of great importance.

In selling his labour a worker does not sell himself. Except for the slave economy it is the *services* of labour – the human, physical and mental effort in production – which are bought and sold in a labour market. Nevertheless the owners of labour services cannot separate themselves from their services but must accompany them.

These obvious but sometimes neglected points have widespread implications. Perhaps the most important is that labour market behaviour cannot be explained solely in economic terms. Workers are interested in many non-monetary aspects of work such as job satisfaction, good relationships with other employees, and a pleasant working environment. In some cases workers may prefer some combination of these aspects of employment to higher paid but less congenial work. Consequently, workers will not necessarily change their jobs, firms or the localities in which they live solely in response to relative improvements in pay elsewhere. Furthermore, people's beliefs about what is fair are pervasive and influential determinants of relative pay levels.

From the standpoint of the business organization, there are important differences between the acquisition and use of human resources and the acquisition and use of (say) capital. Capital investment ensures the businessman of absolute control of the assets and the returns which these yield, but in the case of his labour force no such control is possible. Expenditure on education, training and staff development programmes, investment in human capital, does not yield control of the assets embodied in employees who are free to offer their skills to other employers whenever they wish. And of course management does not have to motivate, discipline, bargain with, and otherwise manage his machines as he does his work force.

4.2 The Importance of Labour Markets in the Wider Society

Decisions taken and agreements reached in the nation's multifarious labour markets have significant effects not only for those who take or reach them, but for the entire economic system and indeed for the wider society. When at going wage rates the supply of labour exceeds demand, involuntary unemployment occurs. Prolonged high rates of unemployment can produce social tensions and political instabilities, particularly when such unemployment is unequally distributed regionally, between different social groups, and by age and sex, as it has been in recent years. For the national economy, high unemployment figures represent wasted resources, lost production, and for the Exchequer increased payment of unemployment benefit and other income support payments, as well as considerable loss in taxation revenues.

Since most people obtain their livelihoods from the sale of their labour services, unemployment results in reduced incomes and living standards as well as possible damage to physical and mental health and loss of social status for those individuals so afflicted. There is some evidence, too, linking unemployment to crime, suicide, family breakdown, and homelessness. For all these reasons, post-war British governments have seen 'a high and stable level of employment' as a major socio-economic objective, towards which much of government economic policy in recent decades has been directed.

The influence of collective bargaining (see Chapter 8) and in particular of trade union behaviour, figures importantly in most analyses of inflation. The generally accepted view that inflationary pressures emerge in the economy when aggregate earnings rise more rapidly than does aggregate productivity, has provided the rationale for incomes policies introduced in one form or another by most post-war British governments. When governments have used demand management to attack inflation, there has been a presumption that the level of pay settlements will respond to changes in the general level of economic activity, and that inflationary expectations will be revised downwards in response to tightening economic pressures.

Finally, increased labour productivity is a major wellspring of economic growth and an essential pre-condition for improvements in the nation's export performance and hence its balance of payments position.

4.3 Marginal Productivity Theory

Traditional labour market theory rests on the suppositions that small scale competitive employers bid for labour and that individual workers compete with each other for jobs in the free market. This emphasis on competitive market forces found expression in the marginal productivity theory of wages, according to which the reward to labour tends to equal the marginal revenue products of the last units employed. In its simplest form the theory assumes that labour is homogenous; that workers and employers have perfect knowledge; and that there is perfect labour mobility.

Employers are assumed to be profit-maximizers and the demand for labour is held to be derived from the demand for the goods or services which that labour helps to produce. From the technical law of diminishing returns we know that the marginal product of any given type of labour will decline as more of it is employed relative to other factors. Consequently, an increase in the supply of labour to any particular occupation (assuming other resources are constant) will, by lowering the marginal product, tend to lower the wage rate paid in that occupation. Any profit maximizing employer is interested in the marginal revenue product (MRP) found by multiplying the marginal physical product by its market price. Given the

STUDENT ASSIGNMENT 4.1

Marginal Productivity Theory

1. To what extent do you think the marginal productivity theory adequately explains the present pay levels of
   (a) teachers, social workers and policemen employed in local government?
   (b) semi-skilled and skilled manual workers employed in manufacturing industry?
2. (a) To the extent that the theory does explain current pay levels in these occupations, explain fully how this is so.
   (b) To the extent that the theory does *not* explain current pay levels in these occupations, explain what factors *do* determine these pay levels.

assumption of profit maximization an employer should continue to hire units of labour until the potential gain from hiring an additional unit is just equal to the cost of hiring that unit, i.e. when falling MRP = wage rate. (See Figure 4.1 and accompanying notes.)

Figure 4.1.   The demand for labour.

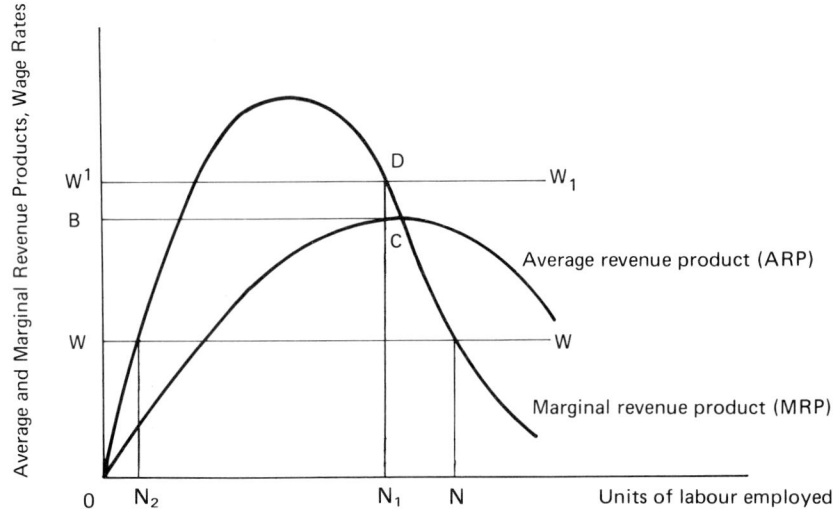

Notes
(a) Perfect competition is assumed.
(b) The average and marginal revenue product curves are given by the firm's production function subject to the law of diminishing returns.
(c) OW is the wage rate at which each unit of labour is paid.
(d) When ON units of labour are employed profits will be maximized because OW = falling MRP.

Proof
(a) The firm will not continue to employ labour if it cannot cover its variable costs, i.e. if the wage rate exceeds the value of the average product. At wage OW_1 for example, the employment of ON_1 units of labour would result in a loss represented by the rectangle W_1BCD.
(b) OW = MRP when ON_2 units of labour are employed as well as when ON units are. However, profits will not be maximized when ON_2 units are employed because it is possible to add to profits whenever the marginal revenue of employing extra units of labour exceeds the marginal cost, i.e. so long as MRP is greater than OW which it is until ON units of labour are employed.
(c) Employment of units of labour beyond ON will add more to costs than to revenue (i.e. W > MRP) and consequently reduce profits.
(d) It follows that profits are maximized when MRP is falling and is equal to OW at ON level of employment.
(e) The firm's demand curve for labour is that portion of the falling MRP curve lying below the ARP curve.

4.4 The Geographical Boundaries of Labour Markets

The majority of companies will tend to operate mostly in the external **local labour market**. Local labour markets have no fixed boundaries and there is always some overlapping between any one local labour market and those which it adjoins. One can imagine, for example, a local labour market functioning around a medium-sized town within which employers will tend to recruit from the catchment area determined largely by the ease and speed of public transport within and around the town. Though rather a vague concept, the local labour market idea has much practical importance since for any particular kind of worker there will tend to be a local 'going rate' which is the minimum wage which must be offered by any employer recruiting in that market.

Changes in the position of the boundary of the local labour market can be affected by a firm's own policies and by factors beyond the control of the firm. Thus, by offering above average earnings or by laying on special transport facilities to outlying districts a firm may succeed in extending its recruitment area. An increase in the rate of unemployment in nearby towns, or an improvement in a public transport provision or roads may induce workers from further afield to seek employment within the particular local labour market. Better information about job opportunities, whether provided directly by the firm's own advertising or through government job centres, may also widen the boundaries of the local labour market.

In some cases it may be more appropriate to regard the labour market as national in character. In particular, larger organizations will tend to recruit professional and managerial staff by means of national advertising.

A number of factors have tended to make some labour markets international or even global in character. As in recent decades big business has become more and more multi-nationalized, massive corporations recruit technical and managerial expertise from all over the world. The entry of Britain into the EEC, with its provision for the free movement of labour between member states, has led to some increase in the mobility of labour between these countries, especially of those workers possessing scarce and therefore highly valued skills. The recent extension of the EEC can be expected to add to this trend.

4.5 The Internal Labour Market

The internal labour market 'refers to the interaction of forces related to wage systems, the factory technology, the actions of management and work force, and so on, that determine utilization and deployment of

manpower within the firm itself'.* Whenever labour is supplied or
demanded within a plant or a company without direct access to the
external labour market, there is an internal labour market. Robertson sees
the conditions in the internal labour market as providing a set of rules that
influence or constrain the behaviour of business owners and managers and
of workers and their representatives. Such rules may be determined and
applied either unilaterally or joinly, and may be formal or informal (e.g.
custom and practice). The rules may originate from outside the firm, e.g.
from a trade union, an employers' association, or from the law. In the case
of large (especially trans-national) corporations, the rules may have been
made a long way from the plants which they influence. The nature and
extent of the company's internal labour market is influenced strongly by
various aspects of the company's personnel policies. The extent to which
any particular organization recruits externally, largely depends on its
recruitment, internal training, and promotion policies.

Numerous other factors will influence the scope given to the internal
labour market. These consist of the various ways of increasing the supply
of effort offered by a company's existing labour force, including

- overtime working as an alternative to recruitment;
- increases in output per man hour achieved through productivity
  bargaining (see Chapter 11);
- increases in the supply of effort achieved through the introduction of a
  payments-by-results system (see Chapter 11).

In these cases, however, offering more money *alone* is unlikely to be a
sufficient inducement to motivate workers to alter working practices and
to ensure an increase in the supply of manpower effort. Neither the
internal nor the external labour market works by cash alone. A complete
analysis of the highly complex workings of an internal labour market is
beyond the scope of this chapter.

4.6 The Mobility of Labour

Changes in the structure of demand for goods and services in the
economy, changes in technology, product innovation, company mergers
and many other aspects of the dynamic economy require the labour
market constantly to re-allocate labour between different occupations,
different localities, and different industries. In a perfect market, adjustments in relative wage rates would be sufficient to ensure that labour
moved in the ways made necessary to meet the needs of the economy. In

* Robertson, Derek, 'Local Labour Markets and Plant Wage Structures', in *Local Labour
Markets and Wage Structures*, D. Robinson (ed.), Gower Press, 1970, pp. 17–18

such an idealized world the occupational, geographical, and industrial mobility of labour would be perfect. In the real world, however, there are numerous social and economic causes and consequences of labour immobility.

GEOGRAPHICAL MOBILITY

Geographical mobility of labour is the physical movement of workers from one part of the country to another or from one country to another. For the economy as a whole, an increase in the geographical mobility of labour will be reflected in a changed regional distribution of population and employment. An examination of Table 4.1 will reveal that in the post-war period there has been a net migration of people from the north-west, where unemployment has been consistently higher and earnings lower than the national average, to the south where unemployment has been consistently lower and earnings higher, providing some evidence of market forces at work albeit quite slowly.

Despite this movement, severe regional imbalance in employment and earnings persists in the United Kingdom and many workers remain reluctant to move. From an individual's viewpoint, reasons for not wanting to move locality are not difficult to find. It may be reluctance to move away from friends and neighbours, to break strong social ties with the local church, clubs or societies. The cost of moving can be considerable. The home owner must spend a considerable sum in selling his house and seeking to buy a new one. The home owner and tenant may fear that he will not find accommodation which he can afford for his family in a new

Table 4.1. Percentage of people living in a region who were born there.

Northern	81.8
North East	79.7
North Midlands	78.3
Eastern	46.4
London	59.3
South East	50.3
South West	53.9
Wales	72.9
Midland	82.8
North West	79.2
Scotland	82.0
Northern Ireland	90.2

Source: Labour Mobility in Great Britain, 1953–63 Social Survey, London, 1966, Table 4, (quoted in B. J. McCormick, *Introducing Economics,* Penguin Books, 1978).

area. There may be loss of pension rights involved in movement. If there are children, a change of school and disturbed education will be a problem. A potentially mobile worker may quite simply lack the knowledge of job opportunities or earnings in other parts of the country. Workers too may feel uncertain about the continued demand for their skills in a new area.

OCCUPATIONAL MOBILITY

Occupational mobility of labour occurs when workers move between different job types or skill levels. Even in times of high unemployment there are skill shortages impeding economic recovery. The economic importance of occupational mobility is emphasised in one official report after another. A former Chairman of the Manpower Services Commission, for example, explains its importance as follows:

> If Britain is to compete in the world market and have an efficient labour market to cope with change it is essential for education and training to provide individuals with the means of acquiring the skills that will help them to move from one job to another.*

Lack of skills is obviously an important barrier to occupational mobility. Such lack may be due to insufficient natural ability, for example to become a brain surgeon or professor, or to lack of education and training. The latter may in turn be due to lack of finance, of time necessary to acquire the training, and to social deprivation of various kinds. In some cases, workers may feel they are too old to learn new skills, and in others trade unions or professional associations may control entry. Occupational mobility may often involve geographical mobility and/or industrial mobility. Finally, discrimination on the grounds of race, sex, or social background may prevent many workers from changing their jobs.

INDUSTRIAL MOBILITY

Industrial mobility occurs when an individual moves from one industry, say mining, to another, say manufacturing. When such mobility occurs without change in occupation and/or locality it is less difficult than when it does not. When work is closely linked to the industry concerned, a miner or railwayman for example, changing industry is really a problem of occupational rather than industrial mobility. For the economy as a whole, industrial mobility means changing the proportion of the labour force employed in different industries. As society has become more affluent in the post-war period, there has been a significant movement from primary and manufacturing industry to public and private service industries.

* *Department of Employment Gazette*, August 1981, vol. 89, no. 8

CASE STUDY 4.1

Labour Markets in the Future?

The car industry is declining because of energy costs. A car is a luxury item for city dwellers. Energy costs are likely to fall, but never back to the levels of the 1940s and 1950s in real terms. Car sales are now declining sharply, and are likely to decline for the next few years. A sharp contraction in the motor industry will hit industries like steel, rubber, and electronics. The construction industry will also be one of the major sufferers in the period ahead. There will be a protracted slow-down in building roads, shopping complexes and manufacturing plant. Service industries, like marketing, finance and banking, will suffer indirectly, influenced by the general contraction in the 'smoke-stack' industries. During a depression, retail sales suffer, and most other services contract.

Most job opportunities in the years ahead will be in science and engineering. The next generation of robots will be able to see, touch, hear, smell and even talk to you. But robots are not human. They are mechanical devices, subject to periodic mechanical failure. Industry will require highly skilled technicians to look after these robots. They will need extra loving care. It has been forecast that there will be 1.5 million jobs for robot technicians by 1990. And career opportunities for robot engineers will be bright.

The drive to become independent of fossil fuels is likely to continue indefinitely. This will mean new job opportunities as new energy sources become available. Demand will greatly exceed manpower in nuclear power stations; in the processing and distribution of solar system manufacturing, installation and maintenance; in synfuels production; in biomass facilities operations and industries involving coal, shale and tar sands extraction. 'O' levels and two years training at a technical college will be required for energy technician jobs.

(*Source:* Robert C. Beckman, *The Downwave*, Pan Books, 1983)

STUDENT ASSIGNMENT 4.2

Labour Markets in the Future?

Read Case Study 4.1. *Labour Markets in the Future?*

Assume that it is generally accepted that the predictions concerning the future of jobs are broadly correct.

1. What factors underlie the predicted changes in the structure of the labour market?
2. What is likely to happen to the inter-occupational wage structure?
3. Apart from adjustments to the wage structure what other changes will be necessary to achieve the re-allocation of manpower?
4. What policies should *currently* be adopted by
   (a) A manufacturer of gas central heating appliances using or contemplating using robot technology?
   (b) A company operating a chain of motorway restaurants?
5. What should government do now?

STUDENT ASSIGNMENT 4.3

Unemployment and Vacancies in Regions of the UK

Table 4.2.   Regional unemployment 1974 and June 1983 and vacancies[1] June 1983.

	Unemployment Average % 1974	Unemployment % June 1983	Number (thousands)	Vacancies (thousands) June 1983
South East	1.5	9.1	694.0	47.0
East Anglia	1.9	10.1	74.3	4.2
South West	2.0	10.8	180.5	11.4
West Midlands	2.2	15.1	341.8	11.4
East Midlands	2.8	11.2	179.7	8.1
Yorks & Humber	2.4	13.4	274.0	8.9
North West	3.5	15.1	418.9	15.2
North	4.6	16.6	215.8	7.2
Wales	3.4	15.3	161.6	6.7
Scotland	4.5	14.1	315.9	17.5
Northern Ireland	6.1	20.3	112.3	1.2
United Kingdom	2.6	12.4	2970.4[2]	139.3

Notes
[1] Vacancies relate only to those notified to Jobcentres remaining unfilled on the day of the count. An MSC National Survey in 1977 suggested that about one-third of all vacancies were notified to employment offices.
[2] From April 1983 unemployment figures reflect the effects of budget provisions which took over 100,000 men aged sixty and over out of the count.

Questions

1. Assuming that only one-third of vacancies are notified to Employment Offices, what reasons explain the existence of half a million job vacancies when almost three million people were registered unemployed in June 1983?
2. To what extent are UK regional differentials in unemployment rates attributable to a failure of labour markets to allocate manpower efficiently?

4.7 Differentials and the Wage Structure

Although the concept has considerable practical significance there appears to be no one universally accepted definition of the term 'wage structure'. The term is used variously to describe an observed array of wage rate or earnings differentials between different groups or individuals. There are at least six kinds of differentials to which we can apply the term wage structure, none of them very precise.

1. Inter-industry wage structure, for example the differences in average earnings between manual workers in different industries;
2. Geographical or regional wage structure;
3. Inter-occupational wage structure;
4. Inter-sectoral wage structure – the difference in pay between wage earners in the public and private sector;
5. Personal wage structures – differences in pay based on sex, age and so on;
6. Inter-firm wage structure – differences in pay between wage earners who work for different companies or establishments.

The economic or market function of a set of wage differentials is to allocate appropriate supplies of labour between different industries, occupations, regions, sectors and firms. We have already noted that this will be less than perfectly achieved because workers are interested in more than monetary rewards associated with the job and will not necessarily move in response to changes in these. Nevertheless, over a period of time there is likely to be re-allocation of labour within the economy in response to changes in the wages structure, as we saw earlier in connection with the drift of workers from the northern and western parts of Britain to the south of the country.

Apart from their market function, earnings differentials have a social significance. Income is an important indicator of status in the consumer society and people tend to measure their social position and that of others on this basis. Both market and social functions of differentials are used extensively in pay bargaining. In recent years, for example, claims for higher pay by firemen, ambulancemen, policemen, and miners have been won partially on the basis of the argument that if the significant pay increases demanded were not forthcoming, insufficient manpower would be attracted to these vital occupations. Comparability arguments used in wage bargaining rest on deep-rooted notions of fairness and on the social evaluations of the value of one kind of work relative to another.

4.8 Recruitment and Selection

Recruitment and selection are parts of the same process by which organizations obtain new employees from the external labour market. **Selection** refers to those stages having to do with choosing from among a group of job applicants using various selection techniques (See below).

Although recruitment falls within the expertise of the personnel specialist its success depends on co-operation between the personnel department and line managers. The need for such co-operation is obvious in the preparation of job descriptions, at the interview and at other stages of selection.

By getting appropriately qualified and experienced people into the correct jobs, successful recruitment will make an important contribution to the efficiency of any organization. Despite this, recruitment often occupies a low position among organizational priorities, partly, perhaps, because of a lack of awareness within management in general about its complexity, its importance to the organization, and about the professional manner in which it should be carried out.

Recruitment and selection comprises the following stages:

- preparation of job descriptions
- preparation of personal specifications
- selection of appropriate media for advertising
- placing advertisements
- processing application forms
- short-listing candidates ⎫
- interviewing candidates ⎬ these three stages together constitute selection
- testing ⎭
- placement and induction within the organization
- provision of 'main terms and conditions'
- statements to successful applicants

4.9 Choosing the Right Media

In the first place it is crucially important to *attract* candidates with the necessary qualifications, experience or attributes to do the job(s). If an

Figure 4.2. Interview plan.

Name of organization	Name		Date	
Position sought	Age	Interviewer(s)		
Current salary and other payments		Salary asked	Expenses	
Impact Physique, health Manner Communication Dress and appearance				
Education and training Qualifications and achievements Specialized training Professional institutes				
Experience Depth and variety Career progression Relevance of experience Special aptitudes and abilities				
Motivation Ambition; aims Preferences; dislikes Expectations Enterprise; resourcefulness				
Disposition Acceptability Initiative Reliability Judgement, qualities Weaknesses				
Circumstances Family, housing Mobility, transport Likelihood of acceptance Other jobs applied for				
Notice required				

organization fails to do this, then the subsequent stages of recruitment and selection are a waste of time and effort.

Hence it is very important to advertise in the correct market. This, in turn, implies careful media selection. Specialized recruitment advertising agencies can ensure placement of job advertisements in the most appropriate outlets. Cost-effective media selection does not, however, mean finding the cheapest outlet. Failure to appeal to well qualified potential recruits because of faulty media selection can cost an organization dearly. As Sir John Trelawney* of Korn-Ferry International, the world's largest executive search consultancy firm has remarked

> Finding a manager of the right calibre can mean the difference between putting the company on a firm footing or setting it on the path to destruction.

Great care therefore needs to be taken in choosing between for example press, journal, TV or radio advertising, between national, regional or local media, and between different newspapers and journals.

The recruitment market is itself 'big business' especially for the press. In 1982 expenditure on job advertisements in national daily, Sunday, and regional newspapers amounted to £131 million. Some 85 per cent of *all* classified recruitment advertising appears in the national, mainly 'quality', press. (See Table 4.3)

STUDENT ASSIGNMENT 4.4

Situations Vacant

1. (a) Examine the 'situations vacant' advertisements in a recent issue of your local newspaper. Classify the vacancies by occupation and industry.
   (b) What sorts of information are provided to prospective job applicants?
   (c) What does your analysis tell you about the current state of the local labour market?
   (d) To what extent are job advertisements placed in your local paper for vacancies elsewhere? What sorts of jobs are these?
2. (a) Examine the 'situations vacant' advertisements in a national daily (e.g. *Times, Daily Telegraph*) or Sunday newspaper (e.g. *Observer, Sunday Times*). Classify the vacancies by occupation and industry.
   (b) Why do you think the organizations advertising their vacancies have chosen the particular newspaper in which to advertise?

* Quoted in *Personnel Management*, August 1983

(c) Select what you consider to be (i) the most effective and (ii) the least effective job advertisement. In each case give reasons for your choice.

(d) What proportion of the recruitment takes place through recruitment agencies?

Table 4.3. Percentage share of recruitment advertising in quality newspapers, May 1983.

	% share		% share
Daily Telegraph	33.6	Sunday Times	16.0
Guardian	26.9	Observer	1.6
Times	12.3	Sunday Telegraph	0.4
Financial Times	9.2		

Source: Media Expenditure Analysis Ltd for *The Guardian* 'Recruitment Monitor', *Personnel Management*, August 1983.

Apart from press advertising, employers fill many vacancies by making use of various private and public employment agencies. In 1982, Manpower Services Commission (MSC) Jobcentre network placed more than 1.5 million job seekers. The MSC estimates that it only has about one quarter of the job-placing market, suggesting that well over 6 million jobs were filled in the UK in 1982 indicating considerable recruitment activity even at the depth of an economic recession.

The MSC also operates the Professional and Executive Register, a computerized service specializing in helping to match the supply and demand for management and other professional staff.

In the private sector, employment bureaux and agencies assist organizations seeking particular kinds of labour to be put in touch with jobseekers. Employment bureaux tend to specialize mainly in secretarial and office employment, or in the recruitment of scientific or technical expertise.

In larger organizations, personnel departments will keep in touch with other potential sources of recruits such as the Youth Employment Service, training and re-training centres, schools, colleges, and universities.

4.10 The Job Advertisement

Designing and wording the advertisement ranks almost as important as selecting the appropriate advertising media. A well designed advertisement will both attract attention and help to confirm a good organizational image. The written content of the advertisement demands an equal amount of care. Not only is it important to offer an accurate summary of (a) the nature of the work to be done derived from a well prepared job description, (b) the experience and qualifications required for the job, and (c) particulars of the physical and social environment of the work, but also to ensure that the advertisement complies with various legal rules governing recruitment advertising.

Certain provisions of the following Acts are relevant in this context:

- Equal Pay Act, 1970.
- Sex Discrimination Act, 1975.
- Race Relations Act, 1976.
- Fair Employment (Northern Ireland) Act, 1976.
- Employment Protection (Consolidation) Act, 1978.

If the necessary legal expertise does not exist within the organization, advice can readily be obtained from the Equal Opportunities Commission and the Commission for Racial Equality.

4.11 Interview and Selection

When the organization has attracted suitable applicants, the personnel and line manager will co-operate in drawing up a short-list of candidates for interview and/or selection procedures. The objective is to predict the success or otherwise of an applicant for a job. By far the most commonly used selection technique is the interview.

In many organizations interviewers use some form of standard interview plan designed to give structure to an interview and ensure that a given range of relevant issues are covered. An example of a six-point interview plan is given in Figure 4.2.

Exclusive reliance on the interview has long been criticized for being too subjective. There is serious doubt about the ability of the interview to identify candidates who will succeed in the job. For these reasons, especially for the higher management and professional posts, many larger organizations have placed increasing reliance on the use of various kinds of selection tests to complement or replace the interview. Such tests may attempt to assess the candidate's skill, aptitude, intelligence or 'trainability'. In some cases various psychological and personality tests may be used.

4.12 Internal Sources

The internal labour market can be an important source of manpower both to meet current requirements and to fill future vacancies. An 'internal search' offers several benefits:

- Responsible jobs may be filled by people who are known to be capable and reliable, and who are familiar with the organizational structure, communication systems, and management style.

- Internal promotion contributes to employee motivation. (The preparation of an internal 'succession plan' can also be important in meeting unforeseen contingencies.)
- Cross fertilization between departments, divisions, and companies within an organization can help prevent what has been called 'functional parochialism'.

Effective use of internal labour market in these ways depends upon:

- a well-understood and equitable promotions policy;
- the provision of appropriate training and re-training as required;
- a (preferably computerized) set of up-to-date, well designed, and easily accessible personnel records.

STUDENT ASSIGNMENT 4.5

Trends in the Demand for Executives in Great Britain

(Table 4.4 is based on an analysis of job advertisements for managerial and technical appointments in *The Times, Daily Telegraph, The Guardian, The Economist, Sunday Times* and *Financial Times*.)

Job Category	Job Advertisements 2nd Qtr 1983*	% Increase or Decrease compared with 2nd Qtr 1982
Research Development & Design	1752	+ 83
Marketing and Sales	1576	+ 35
Production	1443	+ 49
Accounting	1267	+ 35
Computers	738	+ 42
General Management	334	− 7
Personnel	249	+ 139
Miscellaneous	981	+ 71
TOTAL	8340	+ 49

(*Source: Personnel Management*, August 1983)

* Due to industrial action the *Financial Times* did not appear throughout June 1983.

1. What does the table above say about the state of demand for executives between the second quarters of 1982 and 1983?
2. Look up the *New Earnings Survey* and find out what happened to salaries for these job categories.
3. At a time when unemployment has risen continuously to unprecedented post-war levels why in your opinion has the demand for personnel executives risen by 139 per cent? And why has demand for executives in general risen by almost 50 per cent?

STUDENT ASSIGNMENT 4.6

Albion Mail Order Limited

Due to an upturn in the economy, both the demand for consumer goods and services in general and the overall level of employment in the economy are rising. In the north west of England unemployment has fallen dramatically from 10 per cent to only 2.5 per cent.

In these conditions, Albion Mail Order Limited, located in Oldchester, a medium-sized industrial town in the North West, wish to expand their operations and consequently wish to recruit increased supplies of (mainly unskilled) labour. The problem is that most other firms in and around Oldchester are also benefiting from the improved economic conditions and are seeking to recruit similar kinds of labour.

What can Albion Mail Order do in order to attract the additional labour it seeks?

4.13 Summary

1. Because it is composed of millions of human beings labour market behaviour cannot be explained solely in terms of money.
2. Labour market behaviour has important impacts on the level of employment, the rate of productivity change, the pace of inflation and on the economic and social wellbeing of the nation's people.
3. Marginal productivity theory predicts that the wage rate paid by a profit-maximizing employer for any particular kind of labour will be determined by its marginal revenue product i.e. the employer will equate the cost of the last unit of labour with the increase in total revenue resulting from its employment.
4. Firms may succeed in extending the boundaries of local labour

markets by offering pay above the 'going rate', laying on transport, or supplying better information about job opportunities, pay and conditions. Unemployment in neighbouring areas or improved transport facilities may also extend an organization's catchment area for recruitment.

5. The markets for skilled technical, professional and managerial grades are often national or even international in character.

6. The internal labour market may be an important source of labour supply. Its nature and size will depend on organizational personnel policies especially those relating to recruitment, internal training, promotion, and productivity bargaining.

7. The geographical and occupational mobility of labour required by the continuously changing economy is subject to numerous social, economic and institutional constraints.

8. These constraints often prevent wage differentials from achieving their market function of allocating appropriate labour supplies between different industries, occupations, regions, sectors and firms.

9. Although successful recruitment and selection can make a highly significant contribution to the achievement of organizational goals, it often is low on the list of organizational priorities.

10. In order to attract suitable candidates it is essential to advertise in the most appropriate media. Failure to do so can mean the loss of well qualified recruits with adverse effects on organizational efficiency.

11. The recruitment market is itself 'big business'. The vast bulk of classified recruitment advertising appears in the national 'quality' press.

12. MSC Jobcentres and private recruitment agencies are other important sources of recruitment.

13. Well designed job advertisements attract the attention of potential recruits and confirm a good organizational image. Such advertisements must comply with certain legal requirements.

14. The interview is the most commonly used selection procedure. Despite this it is of highly doubtful effectiveness and other 'selection tests' are sometimes used especially when highly paid managerial and professional staff are recruited.

15. Internal recruitment may have the advantage of improving employee motivation, cross-fertilization between departments or divisions of an organization, and of appointing staff who are familiar with organizational structure and style.

Exercise

Review your understanding of the following:

marginal productivity theory
local labour market
internal labour market
geographical and occupational mobility
wage structure
stages in recruitment and selection

Further Reading

Pratt, K. J. and Bennett, S. G., *Elements of Personnel Management*, Gee & Co. Ltd., 1979.

Ungerson, B., *Recruitment Handbook*, 2nd ed., Gower Press, 1975.

Braithwaite, R. and Schofield, P., *How to Recruit*, British Institute of Management, 1979.

Hunter, L. C. and Robertson, D. J., *Economics of Wages and Labour*, Macmillan, 1969.

Rowland, K. M. and Ferris, G. R., *Personnel Management*, Allyn & Bacon Inc., 1982.

5

Raw Materials, Commodity Markets, and Materials Purchasing

5.1 Introduction

Production in every sector of the industrial economy relies directly or indirectly on inputs of raw materials produced in the extractive industries or agriculture and subsequently partially processed for use in the production of goods and services. Such materials may be

- foodstuffs   – maize, rice, wheat, cocoa, coffee, tea, beef, and sugar, for example;
- natural fibres   – mainly cotton, wool, and jute;
- metals   – iron, copper, nickel, tin, lead, aluminium, zinc, and many others;
- non-food products of agriculture   – such as natural rubber, tobacco, timber, and hides and skins.

According to a recent Census of Production the cost of purchased materials (including semi-finished or finished components as well as raw materials) in British manufacturing industry accounts for 55.5 per cent of the gross value of output. In several major industries – cars and chemicals, for example – the figure is nearer 70 per cent. Consequently the factors affecting the costs of materials are significant determinants of total manufacturing costs and hence of the profitability of many business organizations.

5.2 The International Character of Commodity Trade

The fact that commodity markets are international in character has many important implications, the most obvious of which from a business perspective is that raw material supplies and prices are subject to fluctuations in world supply and demand conditions and currency exchange rates over which individual business enterprises are likely to have little control.

Industrial nations and regions are heavily and increasingly dependent on the rest of the world for their supplies of essential industrial materials and foodstuffs. In the mid-1970s Britain, for example, imported 100 per cent of its nickel, zinc, and manganese requirements; nearly 90 per cent of its iron ore; 82 per cent of its copper; roughly two-thirds of its tin and aluminium; and half its lead. The EEC's dependence on metal imports is similar. A net exporter of raw materials until 1950, the United States recorded a deficit of $4 billion due to its materials imports in 1970, which according to the U.S. National Commission on Materials Policy is projected to rise to $60 billion by 2000 AD when the US will depend upon the rest of the world for 80 per cent of its raw materials. Clearly, this magnitude of increase in US demand can create enormous problems of supply and cost for the rest of the industrialized world.

5.3 The Organized Commodity Markets

Much of the trade in raw materials is conducted through the highly organized commodity markets which emerged during the 19th century in the context of an enormous expansion of newly-industrialized Britain's import and export trade. This explosion of international trading activity established London as the world's chief commercial centre and port, through which commodities such as tea, sugar, wool, and so on, were imported from other continents and re-exported to West European countries. It was this large *entrepôt* trade which led to the development of highly organized and internally regulated commodity markets which have survived to the present time.

Today London is famous for its Metal Exchange where copper, tin, lead, zinc, and silver are traded and for its Commodity Exchange which deals in cocoa, coffee, tea, and sugar. Similar exchanges exist in Liverpool with its Cotton and Grain Exchanges and in other parts of the world – wool exchanges in Australia and New Zealand, for example.

Only accredited dealers buy and sell on the organized markets which are strictly regulated by their management committees. An important feature of these markets is the provision of a facility to fix the price of transactions at some future date. The operations of the 'futures markets' are analysed in Section 5.10.

5.4 The Volatility of Raw Materials Prices

The prices of raw materials are from time to time subject to substantial and often sudden fluctuations, with far-reaching effects on costs and profits not only for those firms directly using large quantities of the price-affected materials but also for other enterprises using components or products embodying the materials whose price has varied.

Thus, during the commodity price boom of 1973–74, the increase in the price of copper on the London Metal Exchange from £450 per ton in January 1973 to £1,400 per ton in April 1974 and its subsequent decline to £600 by September 1974 not only affected the costs of companies manufacturing power cables who directly used the metal, but also the costs of car assembly firms, house builders, domestic appliance manufacturers and many other indirect users of copper.

Furthermore, there may be considerable secondary effects on costs as the increased price of copper and other raw materials pushes up the prices of manufactured goods in general, triggering compensatory wage claims from trade unions seeking to defend the real living standards of their members. This 'primary price/industrial price/money wage' spiral will tend to increase in momentum as inflationary expectations are built up.

5.5 The Economics of Raw Materials Price Fluctuations

Because raw materials producers must plan their production a number of years in advance, increases in the supply of industrial raw materials and foodstuffs take considerable time to effect. For this reason production decisions cannot be adjusted suddenly in response to changes in market demand. The interval between planting and harvesting crops of coffee, cocoa, or rubber for example is one of several years. Producers of food and agricultural raw materials are at the mercy of weather conditions. Drought, flood, or unseasonal frost can destroy their crops; bumper harvests may result when the weather is exceptionally favourable. The investment decisions of mining companies normally require planning between twenty and thirty years ahead of any mineral production. Frequently raw materials have still to be produced and sold even when their prices are insufficient to cover costs. In short, the supply of raw materials of all kinds tends to be highly inelastic in the short and medium term.

In the short term, too, demand for raw materials tends to be equally inelastic. The consumption of most foods, for example, does not increase significantly even when prices are driven down to low levels in periods of good harvests. Nor does food consumption fall enough to prevent prices from surging upwards at times when poor harvests create shortages. Similarly the overall level of world industrial activity which determines the demand for raw materials, does not tend to adjust rapidly in response to changes in commodity prices.

Figure 5.1.   The supply and demand for cocoa.

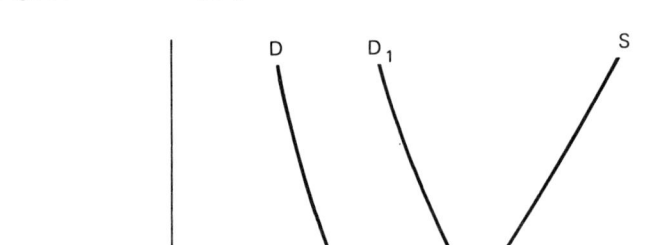

Quantities of cocoa supplied and demanded (tons)

Since both the supply and demand for raw materials tend to be relatively unresponsive to price in the short term, market imbalances – shortages or surpluses – can only be accommodated by large price changes. The typical case is illustrated in Figure 5.1.

The original market demand and supply are indicated respectively by the curves *DD* and *SS* yielding a price per ton of *OP*. An upturn in industrial activity in the world economy shifts the demand curve for copper to the right to DD_1. At the current price to *OP* there is a shortage of NN_1 tons of copper. Because supply is relatively inelastic price shoots up by 66 per cent to OP_1 inducing a less than proportionate extension of supply of NN_1 tons. The extent of the price change will vary with the elasticity of demand. The more elastic is the demand for copper, i.e. the more horizontal is the demand curve, the less will be the price increase.

This simple economic analysis is, however, only the beginning of the story of commodity price fluctuations. Underlying changes in world supply and demand are a whole complex of economic and non-economic factors which jointly determine the availability and prices of raw materials.

5.6 Environmental Effects on Materials Supplies and Price

Environmental effects can be classified into

- natural environmental influences – crop diseases, drought, floods, and pests, for example, can result in poor harvests and large price increases for food and agriculturally produced raw materials. The unusually severe frost of 1975, for example, resulted in a massive fall in world coffee production and an immediate increase in the world market price which shot up by around 600 per cent from 50¢ a lb to over $3.00 a lb;
- man-made environmental effects – crops and farmland can be destroyed by over-cropping or over-grazing; over-fishing can exhaust fishing grounds; industrial pollution may destroy forests, aquatic life, and disrupt ecological balance.

5.7 The Politics of Raw Materials

We have already referred to the large and growing dependence of the industrialized nations on supplies of vital materials from the rest of the world. An implication of this dependence is that material and fuel supplies and prices are subject to numerous political influences.

In 1975, for example, when frosts destroyed so much of Brazil's coffee crop, civil war in Angola and internal upheaval in Amin's Uganda exacerbated the supply disruption and helped to push up the price of coffee to unprecedented levels.

Undoubtedly the most significant political influence on the supply and cost of a raw material emerged in the early 1970s when the political unity and grip on world oil supplies of the OPEC countries enabled them to deny or determine the availability and price of the most crucial raw material used in the industrialized world.

The initial impetus to OPEC unity was the West's support for Israel in the Arab–Israeli Yom Kippur War of 1973. As a result of OPEC control over supplies and prices of oil to the West, the world price of crude oil shot up by more than 400 per cent from $2.10 per barrel in October 1973 to $9.84 per barrel in October 1974.

Thus in the early 1970s a combination of **political** factors (the support by Western governments for the Israelis in the Yom Kippur War), **geological** factors (the concentration of a high proportion of the non-Communist world's oil reserves in a few Arab countries, Saudi Arabia alone accounting for around 40 per cent of these), and *economic* factors (inelastic demand for oil in the industrialized world) provided the OPEC nations with a power base which established them as a new force in the world economy. It was this above all that engendered a more political view of resources based on the changed relationships and potential conflicts between user and producer nations.

The political view recognizes that there may be threats to the supply and price of a wide spectrum of non-fuel minerals as well as to oil. Of particular concern (as Case Study 5.1 shows) is the concentration of a number of important minerals in potentially unfriendly or unstable countries.

CASE STUDY 5.1

Britain's Supplies of Strategic Metals

The USSR and South Africa account for about 95 per cent of world output of the platinum group of metals, which include palladium and rhodium. It is therefore logical to assume some sort of price collaboration.

This concentration of the production of a strategically important group of metals, widely used in the oil and electronics industry, makes the West feel extremely vulnerable.

One of its suppliers is potentially unfriendly and the other potentially unstable. But platinum and its companions are not the only strategic metals and minerals that the West is deficient in and whose supply lines could be put in jeopardy.

Aware of the threat to their supplies, several Western governments have begun taking out insurance policies against disruption.

It was revealed earlier this year that the UK, prompted by assessments of requirements triggered by the Falklands conflict, had joined the US, France and West Germany in building up its own stockpile of strategic metals. Many of these are used in the manufacture of special steels, with important military applications, particularly in the aerospace industry.

Chromium, manganese and cobalt headed the British shopping list. These three, like platinum, highlight the West's dependence on just a few sources of supply, and their vulnerability.

Nearly 65 per cent of non-Communist chromium production comes from just two countries – South Africa (54.8 per cent) and Zimbabwe. Of total world output, the Eastern bloc accounts for nearly 40 per cent.

Zaire alone produces roughly 55 per cent of the West's cobalt, with a further 11–12 per cent coming from other southern African countries.

When guerrilla activity back in 1978–79 temporarily cut off Zairean supplies, buyers panicked and the price shot up tenfold. The US, the EEC and Japan have at best only negligible indigenous reserves of cobalt – and of manganese; some 45 per cent of the world's manganese output is in the Communist bloc, and the bulk of the rest concentrated in South Africa.

These facts and figures are culled from the *World Index of Strategic Metals*. The authors, David Hargreaves and Sarah Fromson, have set themselves the task of evaluating the risks to supplies of 37 strategic metals and minerals, ranging from antimony to zirconium.

For each mineral studied, the authors calculate its 'total strategic factor', which is based on all the perceived risks relating to supply.

The highest risk minerals, according to this system of calculation, are precisely those sought by the British Government earlier this year: chromium, manganese and cobalt.

(*Source:* Stainer, Robin 'Strategic metals get South Africa and the USSR talking', *The Guardian*, 9 August 1983, p. 19)

Postscript

In November 1984 the government announced its intention to dispose of its stockpiles of chrome, manganese, cobalt, and vanadium which it had acquired in 1983 at a cost of £45 million. By July 1985 it had become clear that the intention was to offer the material (at that time estimated to have risen in value to about £63 million) for sale by tender, a decision that was criticised by metal traders and industry who argued that the timing was most unfortunate; the argument for strategic reserves to ensure independence from vulnerable supply sources such as South Africa was borne out by the country's at that time state of emergency.

STUDENT ASSIGNMENT 5.1

Politics and Purchasing

The following remarks were made by James Kelly, a chief purchasing manager of Imperial Metal Industries in an interview with *Procurement*, November 1974:

> In procurement terms we didn't have great problems over raw materials because they were within the British Empire and produced by British or US companies. When we lost the Empire things became more difficult and since then enormous changes have been taking place in the developing countries who own these natural resources. They have been buying and nationalizing the mines and other natural resources and saying, quite naturally I suppose: 'No longer will foreigners be permitted to exploit our birthright'. Therefore a lot of raw materials are now state owned and run by state corporations. We as buyers are no longer talking to commercial operators in commercial language only but we must also talk to states in political language. It is not so much that we are in a bad negotiating position, but we have to recognize we are in a totally different one.

Asked if he saw industrial companies getting together in large consortia as being the key to ensuring that the UK gets its share of resources, Mr Kelly replied:

> Yes, if this small island is going to survive when all it has left is the skill and character of our people then that survival rests primarily on

our ability to secure a portion of the world's natural resources sufficient to maintain our industrial production.

International politics and the growing interdependence of national economies makes it no longer possible or logical for individual industrial concerns to undertake long term procurement in isolation in a purely commercial aspect.

1. Mr Kelly argues that we must 'also talk to states in political language'. Explore the meaning of the term 'political language'. What are the implications for management and business education?
2. Write a short report for circulation to other companies using similar raw materials to your own company, arguing the case for joining together in order to purchase raw materials as a consortium.

5.8 The Role of Transnational Corporations

Thirty mining corporations, in many cases closely allied with each other, account for about 45 per cent of the West's output of non-fuel minerals. Through ownership and other forms of control, these transnational mining groups exert a dominant influence on the other 120 mining enterprises which account for the remaining 55 per cent of world output.

In the case of most agricultural raw materials and foodstuffs, production and distribution is in the hands of even fewer global corporations. In the case of coffee – the most valuable agricultural commodity traded internationally – two giant corporations General Foods and Nestlés dominate the manufacture and marketing chain in both producer and consumer nations.

Unilever controls through its plantations and other operations about 80 per cent of the world's trade in palm oil – an important ingredient of margarine.

In the majority of developing countries transnational corporations control agricultural inputs (fertilizers, pesticides, and farm machinery) as well as agricultural production and marketing. These 'agribusinesses' often operate as capital-intensive enclaves of production, largely segregated from the country's economy, and with the co-operation of the local governments, use vast tracts of best farming land for export production.

The effects of transnationals on materials markets cannot be analysed fully here. However, it may be safely assumed that their operations have a powerful influence on the price of many raw materials.

5.9 The Impact of Changes in the Global Economy

The demand for primary materials is strongly influenced by changes in demand from the industrialized nations who are the major consumers. Such changes may be both result and cause of cyclical changes in the level of world industrial activity. Thus in the world boom conditions of the mid-1970s the demand for raw materials increased sharply throughout the world forcing up prices and generating pronounced increases in the rate of inflation which in turn checked the boom. Hence, for example, the large fluctuations in the price of copper referred to above, and in the prices of virtually all other raw materials.

Such fluctuations can place enormous strains on both producer and user nations. Thus, even before the impact of the OPEC oil embargo and oil price increases of 1973–74, Britain's import bill for metals alone was rising rapidly, amounting in 1974 to roughly double the 1972 figure. Over the same period the price of imported foodstuffs rose by 245 per cent to treble Britain's food import bill.

Many developing countries are heavily dependent on export earnings from a single raw material. Ghana, for example, relies on cocoa exports to provide approximately 60 per cent of its foreign exchange earnings. Similarly Ethiopia relies on coffee (70 per cent of export earnings); Zambia on copper (80 per cent or more); Zaire on cobalt (46 per cent); and Sudan on cotton (60 per cent). Recession in the industrialized world which reduces demand for these commodities causes very severe problems for such countries not only in terms of foreign exchange earnings and capacity to import capital or manufactured goods, but also equally severely in terms of effects on employment and income levels.

STUDENT ASSIGNMENT 5.2

Commodity Price Fluctuations

1. Using supply and demand analysis and appropriate diagrams show the effects of the following events on the world prices of the raw material(s) concerned:

   (a) The severe frosts of 1975 which destroyed a large proportion of Brazil's coffee crop;
   (b) A decision in 1974 by Saudi Arabia, the largest OPEC producer, to cut its crude oil production by 5 per cent;
   (c) The internal political unrest in Zaire in 1978–79 and the consequent effect on supplies of cobalt;
   (d) The onset of recession in the world economy and its impact on the markets for metals and other industrial raw materials.

2. In each of the above cases attempt to analyse the effects of the changes in price and supply (a) on British business, and (b) on the producer countries in the developing world.

5.10 Spot and Futures Trading

Most commercial organizations concerned with basic raw materials which are traded internationally attempt to insulate themselves against risks of losses which can arise from unpredictable price fluctuations by buying and selling through a commodity market which provides a facility to fix the price at some future date rather than be caught with high priced stocks when prices fall. Transactions in raw materials tend to be conducted by dealers or merchants who have developed special expertise in trading in one particular commodity. When commodities are purchased for immediate delivery this is referred to as a 'spot' transaction, for which a 'spot' price is quoted. However, in many cases raw materials are 'bought' in the present for delivery at an agreed future date and at an agreed future price.

The general purpose of this 'futures trading' is to reduce the uninsurable risks of heavy losses for both producers and users of raw materials which may result from largely unpredictable fluctuations in price.

For a commodity to be dealt with on a futures market a number of conditions must be satisfied, important among which are the following:

- the commodity must be durable so that stocks can be held;
- it must be of a standard quality, which implies it must be possible to grade the commodity by tests. On the London Metal Exchange, copper is required to be of a quality of not less than 99.9 per cent purity of an accepted brand to be delivered to an authorized warehouse;
- it must be subject to price fluctuations

Only a small fraction of the base metals and an even smaller fraction of agricultural commodities traded on London's futures markets actually involve the delivery or receipt of a product. The objective of risk-reduction is achieved by 'closing out' futures contracts by making exactly opposite transactions before the delivery date arrives. How this works is seen in Case Study 5.2.

CASE STUDY 5.2

The Futures Market in Copper

Suppose a copper producer ships 100 tons of copper to a British cable manufacturer. The goods will take three months to reach Liverpool and will be priced at the London Metal Exchange (LME) settlement price which applies on the day of arrival. On the day the goods are shipped from the country of origin, the producer hedges his position by selling

100 tons of copper futures at the ruling price, say £800 a ton, the spot price being £750 at that date. Three months later prices have declined by £100. On arrival at Liverpool, the copper consignment realizes only £650 a ton. But on the same day the shipper 'buys back his futures' for £700 a ton, thus closing out his hedging operation. The 'loss' due to the decline of £100 a ton between shipping and arrival is exactly compensated (in this simplified example) by the profit of £100 a ton on the futures transaction, and the net realization is £750 a ton. If price had moved the other way and increased by £100 a ton, the consignment would have realized £850 a ton on arrival at Liverpool, but this would be reduced by a loss of £100 a ton on the futures transaction so that the net realization would again be £750 a ton. The producer is removing the uncertainty from his transaction, the risk of making either more or less than expected.

Meanwhile, let us suppose that the cable manufacturer sold to a European customer a quantity of cable requiring 100 tons of copper to complete. The price is based on the spot price of £750 a ton ruling at the date the contract is signed. Between this date and delivery of the cable three months later, the manufacturer is at risk; so he hedges his position by buying 100 tons of copper futures at £800 a ton. If price increases by £100 a ton, the manufacturer 'loses' £10,000 on the physical transaction, but makes a compensating gain by selling his futures for a £100 a ton profit. If price falls by £100 a ton, the loss on the futures transaction is compensated by an equal gain on the physical transaction. Again, the uncertainty has been removed.

(*Source:* Bailey, P. J. H. and Farmer, D. J. *Purchasing Principles and Management*, 4th (revised) ed., Pitman, 1981)

The purchasing controller of a large group of British companies has listed some of the valuable services provided to business by the operation of futures markets*, including:

- A measurable standard of quality acceptable in most producing and using countries, with rules and arbitration procedures for settling quality and packaging disputes.
- A firm price in the currency of the buyer's country – which is protected from currency devaluations.
- The acceptance of responsibility by the dealer or merchant for honouring his contract with usually only a delay in delivery liable to *force majeure*. Shipping delays, dock strikes, and other delay hazards do not

---

* Lloyd, F. S., 'Commodities or Cash', *Procurement*, November 1974

release the dealer from ultimately delivering in the quality and at the price agreed.

- In many commodity markets there is a facility to trade in alternative grades or qualities at appropriate discounts or premiums, offering genuine buyers of the physical materials an opportunity of hedging the differences between the standard grade and the alternative required, at those times when changes in supply or demand make such differentials unrealistic.
- Futures markets are without exception international markets set up by agreement between producers and consumers in all major non-socialist countries, and the standard of integrity in trading should be the envy of politicians and idealists who are still searching for satisfactory means of international co-operation in other fields.

Despite these many advantages some larger raw material users tend to negotiate direct fixed-price contracts with producers, or their agents or shippers. However, if world prices rise much above or fall much below the 'fixed' price of the contract there are enormous pressures to renegotiate it. As a result the prices for individually negotiated contracts are strongly conditioned by the prices established by the commodity markets, and price stability therefore is only possible if and when world market commodity prices can be stabilized.

5.11 International Commodity Agreements

The common objective of the various international commodity agreements which have been established is to stabilize commodity price within mutually acceptable narrow limits in order to ensure producers' income and users' supplies thus reducing the risk of economic loss to both which arises from large price fluctuations.

The essential features of such agreements are:

- a governing body, representing producers, or producers and consumers;
- the finance of a buffer stock;
- the appointment of a buffer stock management;
- an upper and lower commodity price between which the buffer stock management is to operate;
- purchases for stock when prices are falling and sales from stock when prices are rising in order to stabilize world price.

In practice the operation of commodity agreements is more complex than this, often involving a system of annual export quotas determined by the governing body for each producer.

5.12 Materials Purchasing

In a purchasing context 'materials' usually refers to supplies bought from outside which a manufacturing business transforms into outputs of finished products. In this sense the final product of one company (electric cable, for example) may be the material input of others (domestic appliance manufacturers, for example). From the perspective of a manufacturing concern, therefore, purchased materials may be classified into

- raw materials
- partly manufactured parts
- finished components.

In common usage even 'raw' material has come to mean a material which needs to be further worked upon by a business in order to become its final product. Thus flour produced by milling companies will be looked upon as a raw material by a bakery or confectionery firm.

Defined in this way materials are the lifeblood of industry. Without continuous supplies of materials of the correct quality no industry can continue to operate. Consequently purchasing, just as much as marketing or finance, is an integral and vital part of business management. The central task of purchasing management is to ensure that materials of adequate quality are available in the correct quantities at the right price and in the right place at the right time in order to ensure that production can proceed smoothly and as planned.

Since for many businesses bought-out materials costs account for between 50 and 60 per cent of total costs the efficiency with which purchasing management carries out its function has a significant impact on an enterprise's cost-structure and hence its profitability.

We may begin to see the inter-relatedness of materials purchasing when we set it within the wider function of materials management which co-ordinates a number of related activities throughout the materials cycle, including

- production planning and control
- purchasing
- planning and control of stocks
- storekeeping
- internal transport and materials handling
- external transport.

The materials cycle in manufacturing begins at the product design stage. The simplified version of this cycle presented in Figure 5.2 indicates the pervasive nature of materials management.

Within this framework the role of the purchasing specialist is to:

Figure 5.2 The materials cycle in manufacturing.

Design R&D	Sourcing	Production planning	Receiving	Stores	Stock control	Materials handling
Determines combinations and qualities of materials required	Decisions made about choice of supplies	Determines the way in which materials purchase orders are scheduled from external and internal sources	Checks on specified quality standards	Provision of adequate suitably designed warehouse or stores capacity	Quantity control to ensure supply is available and to minimize costs	Physical distribution of supplies at all stages of the materials cycle

- ensure an uninterrupted flow of materials timed for delivery to meet production schedules;
- purchase materials at the 'right' price – efficient buying involves obtaining the best value for every £ spent. Buying at the right price and ensuring continuity of supplies both require continuous monitoring and interpretation of changing market conditons;
- manage stock levels in such a way as to minimize the costs of stock-holding consistent with ensuring sufficient stocks to meet production needs;
- ensure materials are of the necessary minimum quality to perform their functions satisfactorily;
- to develop and maintain good and durable vendor relationships so that potential problems which may arise between buyer and seller can be readily ironed out, and to ensure continuity of supply;
- to develop reliable alternative sources of supply, with the same objective of ensuring continuity of supply;
- to provide purchasing staff with appropriate training (including schemes designed by the Institute of Purchasing and Supply) and to develop staff procedures and policies in order to achieve the foregoing objectives;
- to integrate as fully as possible with other departments or functions.

Added together these components of efficient materials purchasing constitute a formidable task for the purchasing staff. Yet the costs of failure can be very high. Failure to ensure continuity of supplies, for example, can mean disrupted production and an unreliable service to customers who may be lost, perhaps permanently, to rival businesses. If materials are of less than adequate quality, a company's reputation for a reliable product may suffer with consequent market decline. Buying at the 'wrong' time, misjudging price, or carrying 'excess' stocks will all escalate costs, resulting in damage to market competitiveness and potential profits.

5.13 Some Issues in Materials Purchasing

A manufacturing business is faced with a number of key questions, each of which requires careful evaluation and answer if the materials purchasing objectives of the enterprise are to be efficiently achieved. Among these the question of 'make or buy' has obvious implications for the form of materials to be purchased. Should the business buy components from outside or manufacture them within?

The advantages of buying components derive mainly from the economies of scale available to an external high volume supplier, which often makes it cheaper to buy than to manufacture parts. For this reason manufacturing industry tends to rely on a high and rising proportion of bought-out components produced by specialist high volume external component manufacturers. Whenever this is the case it is the job of purchasing specialists to keep suppliers' costs to a minimum, to ensure technical standards and quality of the components and to manage delivery schedules in order to meet internal production schedules.

Further crucial questions relate to efficient 'sourcing' i.e. the choice of supplier and the development of supplier goodwill. The choice of materials suppliers will be influenced by many considerations such as the suppliers reliability for continuous supply, low prices, delivery times, and accessibility. If suppliers were rated equally for quality, delivery, and service, the lowest bidder will tend to be accepted. In practice, however, those variables are likely to differ in which case it is necessary to choose suppliers who offer the best combination of price, quality, delivery, service, and so on. In large organizations this choice is likely to be assisted by a continuous computerized process of 'vendor-rating'.

Should a single supplier or a number of suppliers be used? Concentration on a single supplier can yield benefits if it is known that the lone supplier will look after the company in times of scarcity, and that he can offer a more competitive or larger discount for bulk-buying. In addition dealing with one supplier yields savings in administration and paperwork costs. However, if the single supplier faces disruption for example by industrial action, his customer may not readily be able to attract alternative suppliers. Such risks to supply may be lessened when several suppliers are used.

It is sometimes suggested that for firms using large quantities of bought-out materials, two suppliers should be used in a roughly 70:30 ratio. The 70 per cent supplier is assured of profitability and has the incentive to offer extra services such as warehousing and special deliveries when required. The 30 per cent supplier is kept on his toes by the potential for increasing his market share, which provides him with incentives to match the larger supplier.

All these questions are more complex when, as is often the case, materials are bought internationally. Risks of supply disruption, delivery delays, political uncertainty, the actions of overseas governments or transnational corporations and the changing relationship between developing and industrialized nations as we have already seen greatly magnify the problems of purchasing wisely.

5.14 Information Technology as an Aid to Purchasing

As with all other business functions, materials purchasing and management can be significantly assisted by the introduction and use of electronic

STUDENT ASSIGNMENT 5.3

Eastern Electric Ltd

Eastern Electric Ltd, a manufacturer of domestic electrical appliances, purchases its electric cable as a finished component. With a view to exerting greater control over its selling prices the company has ascertained from its cable suppliers the separate costs of the copper and of cable manufacture in order to use an accredited dealer in the metal market to 'hedge' the price of copper. Hitherto Eastern Electric has bought its cable from four different suppliers each of whom charges a different price ranging from £925 to £975 per ton.

1. What benefits may be available for Eastern Electric from 'hedging'?
2. What are the advantages and disadvantages of Eastern Electric's policy of purchasing in rotation from four different suppliers?

information technology. This point was stressed by Monty Burton, newly-appointed President of the Institute of Purchasing and Supply in his inaugural address of October 1983. Mr Burton emphasized both the opportunities and importance for *using* micro-electronic information technology in purchasing management and the need for purchasing management to *buy* such technology effectively. Although 'the paper-less office' may never be a total reality, he said, the 'less-paper office' was already available though we were totally ill-equipped to handle the impending marketing onslaught of information technology manufacturers.

STUDENT ASSIGNMENT 5.4

Roadworthy Cycles Ltd

You have recently been appointed as purchasing manager for the Roadworthy Cycle Company, a manufacturer of high quality bicycles. During recent years the company has experienced several disruptions of its production due to sudden shortages of one or two raw materials used by its component suppliers.

You are asked to write a short report indicating the steps you would take in order to minimize such risks to Roadworthy's production in the future.

Pointing to some of the potential benefits of the 'less-paper office', Burton referred to office space used for paper storage at £20 per square foot in London at an estimated cost of £100 million per annum. In addition to savings from this source, the opportunities for improved stock control with use of the new technology were enormous. It had been estimated that for three large UK companies an improvement in stock turnover ratio from 3 to 12 would lower the value of their stock-holdings by £680 million and increase profit by up to 90 per cent.

5.15 Summary

1. Production of goods and services in every sector of the economy depends upon a continuous supply of diverse raw materials.
2. Most raw materials are traded internationally. Britain and other industrialized nations are heavily dependent upon materials imported from the rest of the world.
3. Much of the trade in raw materials is conducted through the organized commodity markets which developed in London with the expansion of international trade which accompanied the Industrial Revolution.
4. The prices of raw materials upon which industry depends are sometimes subject to sudden and substantial fluctuations in price, with widespread effects on business costs and profitability, and on producers' income.
5. The reasons for price volatility in the world's commodity markets are economic, environmental, political, and institutional.
6. Because the production of metal and foodstuffs must be planned often years in advance, the supply of materials tends to be inelastic in the short and medium term. Demand for such materials also tends to be inelastic in the short term with the result that market imbalances can only be met by large price increases.
7. A variety of 'natural' forces – crop diseases, floods, frosts, or droughts can destroy or damage food and other agriculturally produced materials. Over-cropping, over-grazing, and the effects of industrial pollution can destroy the fertility of the land.
8. Wars, revolutions, government changes, or political unrest in producer countries affect the supplies and prices of raw materials.
9. The supply and cost of raw materials are subject to political influences because deposits of essential minerals are unevenly distributed between nations. For example, reserves of a number of vital minerals upon which the West depends are concentrated in southern Africa and the Soviet Union.
10. Since the OPEC-engendered 'oil crisis' of the early 1970s there has

been increasing concern about the security of supply and prices of a wide range of non-fuel minerals as well as oil.

11. The demand for raw materials is strongly influenced by cyclical changes in the level of industrial activity in the world economy.

12. Many developing nations are dependent on one or a few raw materials for most of their export revenue and much of their employment. Consequently, commodity price fluctuations can seriously hamper production, investment, and in some cases the entire development plans of such countries.

13. 'Futures' trading on commodity markets provides a facility for both producers and users of raw materials to reduce the risk of heavy losses which may result from large and unpredictable fluctuations in price.

14. A number of international commodity agreements have been negotiated with the objective of price stabilization within narrow mutually acceptable limits. The governing bodies of such agreements finance a buffer stock. In order to stabilize world prices, stock is bought when world prices are falling and sold when world prices are rising. Annual export quotas for each producing member-state may also be set in order to help stabilize prices.

15. In manufacturing, bought-out materials (including raw materials, partly-manufactured parts, and finished parts) often account for between 50 and 60 per cent of total costs. Efficient materials purchasing can have significant effects on manufacturing costs and profits.

16. Materials purchasing as part of the wider function of materials management is a pervasive and integral part of business management. The purchasing function is responsible for buying materials of the necessary quality at the 'right' price; ensuring continuity of supplies in order to meet production schedules; cost effective stock control; and for efficient 'sourcing' and maintaining good vendor relationships.

17. When the crucial 'make or buy' decision has been reached, purchasing management must decide which supplier(s) to use, and whether to use a single supplier or more than one.

18. The efficiency of materials purchasing and management can be greatly assisted by the introduction of micro-electronic information technology.

Exercise

Review your understanding of the following:

raw materials
commodity markets
a 'political view' of resources
futures trading
materials purchasing
materials management
sourcing

Further Reading

Bailey, P. J. H. and Farmer, D. J., *Purchasing Principles and Management*, 4th (revised) edn., Pitman, 1981.

Lomax, D. 'Commodity Markets in a Fragmenting World Economy', *National Westminster Bank Quarterly Review*, May 1980.

Mattadeen, A. C. 'Reflections after a Decade of OPEC Pricing Policies', *National Westminster Bank Quarterly Review*, May 1983.

6

Capital Markets and the Acquisition of Finance

6.1 Introduction – The Need For Business Finance

All business enterprises need finance for two broad purposes:

- working capital is required to finance stocks and work in progress, to bridge the period between delivery and receipt of payment, and for the general financing of fluctuations of trade in marketable goods;
- funds are needed to replace plant, machinery, and equipment as they wear out.

Both kinds of expenditure are necessary for every type of enterprise and irrespective of whether the business is expanding or not. In times of inflation the amounts needed by businesses just to keep going inevitably increase. Thus, whereas about one third of company finances paid the costs of simply keeping going in the 1960s and early 1970s, just over one half was required for this purpose in the inflationary conditions of the mid and late 1970s as the costs of raw materials, fuels, and services soared.

For expanding enterprises concerned to increase their productive capacity, additional funds are needed to finance investment in new and more up-to-date plant, buildings, and machinery (or to pay for the takeover of other businesses if this is the chosen form of expansion) and to pay for increased stocks, new marketing expenditures, and more trade debtors associated with the expansion.

6.2 Sources of Company Finance

In this section we focus on the finance requirements of industrial and commercial companies for the most usual purposes of investment in fixed assets, acquisitions, and for stocks and other working capital. By far the most important source of company finance is retained profits.

Figure 6.1. Main types and sources of finance for UK industrial and commercial companies.

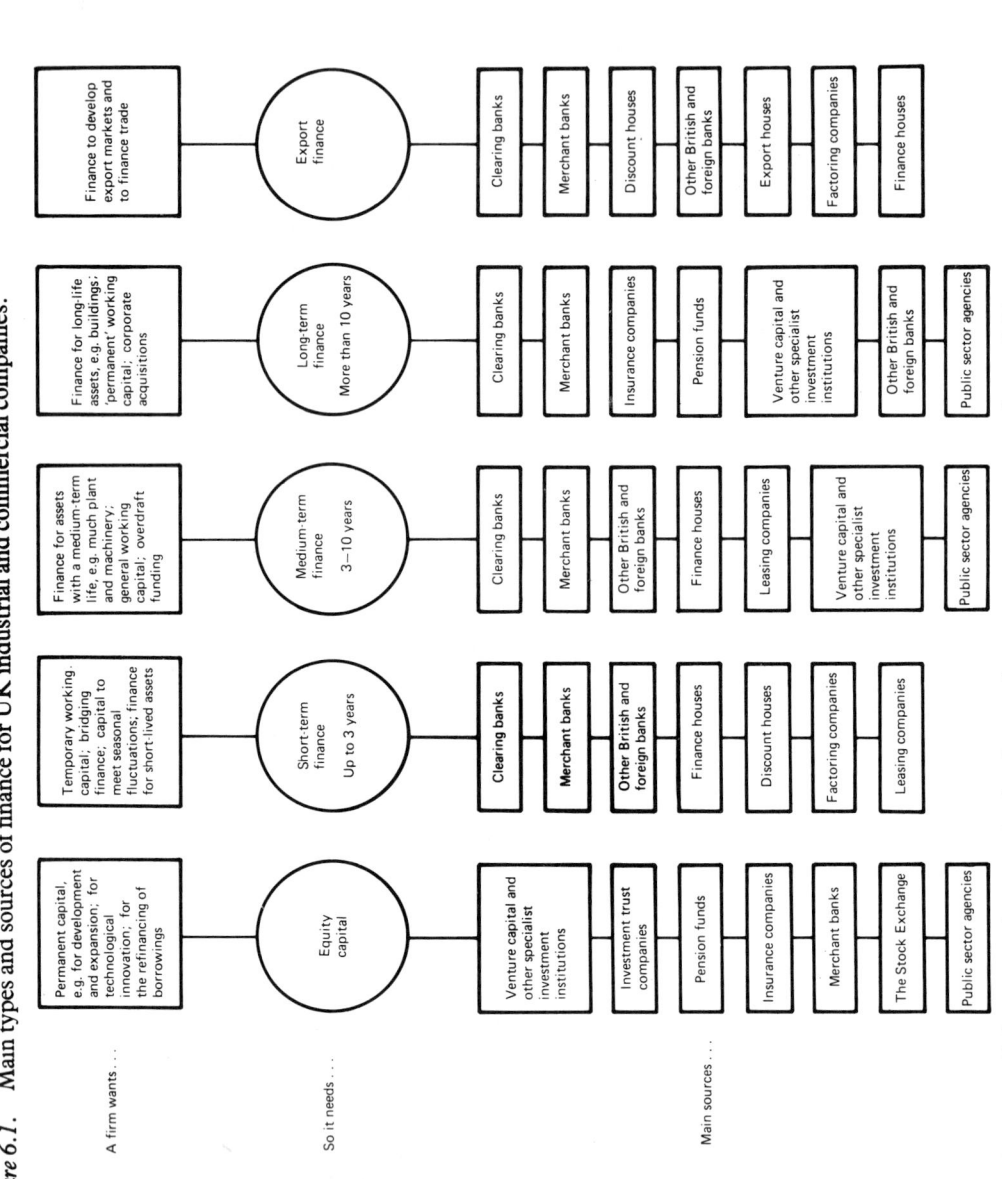

Note Interest relief grants on loans, and other forms of government support, may by available.

Though the self-financing ratio (i.e. the ratio of internally generated funds to total funds employed) varies from year to year with levels of profitability and capital investment, internal finance provided an average of around 70 per cent of companies' requirements in the 1970s. In 1983 undistributed profits provided no less than £26,543 million out of an estimated total of £35,048 million of finance required by UK industrial and commercial companies.

External finance is either share capital or borrowing of one kind or another. Government grants and allowances provide a third important source of external finance for companies. Figure 6.1 summarizes the main types and sources of external finance.

6.3 Share Capital

A company's share capital is capital authorized by the Memorandum of Association to be divided into shares of different classes. Persons who acquire shares in a company are recognized at law as being the proprietors of the company. The sub-division of capital into shares of small denominations enables the company to attach different rights to different classes of share and as a result to appeal to different classes of investors, thus broadening the market from which it may acquire its capital.

The vast majority of companies are formed with limited liability, so that shareholders are not liable to lose more than they have put in or promised to put in to the business. Because the liability of shareholders is limited in this way, companies are able to amass large sums of capital by attracting the small savings of many individuals. Limited liability shares are of two main classes:

Ordinary shares represent the risk capital of the business and tend to carry voting rights conferring control over the company's affairs through the right to elect and dismiss its directors and to vote at general meetings. Ordinary shareholders have the right to all the company's property once the special rights of all other classes of security-holder have been met. Thus, they share in the profits only after interest has been paid to debenture and other debt-holders and after dividends have been paid to preference shareholders. The percentage dividend on ordinary shares is recommended by the Board of Directors to shareholders at the company's annual general meeting, and paid after it has been approved by a vote. Ordinary shareholders may expect high percentage dividends when profits are high, but little or even no dividend when profits are low.

Since each ordinary share provides an equal share of available profits, they are often called equities and the capital raised from their issues is known as equity capital. Because they carry the greatest risks, ordinary shares tend to be bought by wealthy investors prepared to gamble for a large return and by institutional investors such as insurance companies and investment trusts seeking high profit in a balanced portfolio of securities.

In recent years, some companies have issued voteless ordinary shares in order to retain control by the original ordinary shareholders.

Preference shares carry preferential rights in the distribution of profits, in the repayment of capital if the company is to be wound up, or in both. Typically, preference shares carry the right to a fixed percentage dividend before other classes of shareholders receive any return at all. It is this prior claim on profits that makes them less risky than ordinary shares.

Part of the shareholders' funds are represented in the company's balance sheet as reserves which arise chiefly from any premium on the issue of shares at a price above par value; from any accounting surplus arising from a revaluation of assets; and from accumulated undistributed profits. Because reserves are merely an accounting concept they do not always represent finance available for investment. However, in two respects reserves may be seen as a source of finance – first, retained profits increase the amount available to finance expansion; and second, since reserves may be a significant element in capital structure, they may help to determine the amount a company can borrow.

6.4 The New Issues Market

A public limited company (PLC) may choose one of a number of methods of raising capital from the public by means of a new issue of shares. Most of these will involve the company in employing the specialist services of a financial institution known as an issuing house. The issuing house will investigate its client company's operations in order to assess whether its prospects are sufficiently promising to justify the public issue. The investigation will be comprehensive, involving examination of audited accounts, past profit and turnover records, sales trends, capital structure, investment plans, and management efficiency. If, after investigation, the issuing house is satisfied with the company's prospects it will proceed to act on behalf of its clients, offering advice on the most appropriate type and class of security to be issued and analysing financial markets in order to pitch the terms of the issue correctly. This latter function of the issuing house, i.e. deciding what prospective dividend is needed to float the issue, is of vital importance because if shares are issued at prices lower than the market is prepared to pay, amounts considerably below potential may be raised. An important function of the issuing house is to underwrite the issue by guaranteeing to take up any unsold shares.

The ways in which a new issue may be placed before the general public include:

- an invitation by prospectus. The Companies Acts require certain information to be disclosed in the prospectus concerning the terms of the offer, the number of shares of each class, and the class rights attaching to them; details of any company contracts which would be of interest to a prospective investor, and the directors' interests in these; reports from the company's auditors on results over the last five years; and the minimum subscription necessary for the issue to be viable;
- an offer for sale involves the company in selling the complete issue to issuing houses, stockbrokers, or other institutions, who then re-sell the shares to the public at a higher price. This method is most favoured by the Stock Exchange Council and is one of the most commonly used methods of issuing shares. An offer for sale still requires the publication of an original prospectus disclosing the statutorily required information;
- when its issue is relatively small and/or unlikely to attract much public interest, a company may arrange with an issuing house for a placing. In this case the public is not invited to buy the offered shares. An issuing house or stockbroker purchases the shares, which are placed in blocks with other selected financial institutions such as insurance companies or investment trusts. Since this method tends to be cheaper than the first two, it tends to be attractive to smaller companies;
- a rights issue is the predominant method for companies who already have a good spread of shareholders. This differs from other methods of issue in that it is possible to by-pass the external capital market altogether. Equity shares are first offered to existing shareholders in proportion to their current holding, e.g. one new share for four existing shares. This option is usually made on favourable terms. For a company with existing shareholders this is the least costly of all methods of issue. Only in the fairly unlikely event of the shares not being fully taken up by existing shareholders is there an invitation to the public to subscribe. Shareholders may sell their allotted quota if they so desire.

6.5 The Stock Exchange

Although the Stock Exchange is not involved in the issue of new shares it provides an important market for second-hand shares and debentures and for government securities. The advantage for a PLC in having its shares traded on the Stock Exchange is that the liquidity and marketability that this confers on its shares makes the company more attractive to private and institutional investors, with the result that it is easier and cheaper for the company to raise new capital.

A PLC wishing to enhance the marketability of its shares by having them traded on the Stock Exchange must apply for listing. Such a company will undergo searching enquiries and must satisfy the Stock Exchange requirements by subscribing to the listing agreement which requires them to disclose fuller information than unlisted companies. At least 25 per cent of the listed company's shares must be held by the public and the public and the aggregate value of its shares must be no less than £500,000 at the commencement of dealing.

The government levies a capital duty of one per cent on the proceeds of a new issue. Other costs may include a Stock Exchange initial listing fee or for the Unlisted Securities Market (see Section 6.6 below) a small annual charge; commissions payable to the issuing house or stockbrokers which may amount to 2 per cent or more; professional and advertising fees; and the costs of printing the prospectus. In all, expenses are likely to amount to between 5 and 10 per cent of the amount raised.

6.6 The Unlisted Securities Market

In its Interim Report* of March 1979 the Wilson Committee, set up in 1976 to review the functions of Britain's financial institutions, made several recommendations to improve the financial provision for small firms, including the establishment of an Unlisted Securities Market (USM) which would improve the supply of equity to small and growing companies. The USM created in 1980 on the basis of modified Stock Exchange proposals, offers many of the benefits of listing and is now a thriving and quite rapidly growing market which by 1983 involved over 150 PLCs. Participating companies are required to disclose less information than listed companies, and the costs of entry to the market, especially for advertising and publication of a prospectus, are lower than for a Stock Exchange listing.

The Stock Exchange requires evidence of a satisfactory prior trading record of at least three years, though in certain circumstances it will allow entry to a new company.

In all cases at least 10 per cent of the company's shares must be held by the public before dealing starts in the USM or 25 per cent of an issue taking the form of placing must be placed with the Market.

In order to safeguard shareholders and to ensure a free and orderly market, companies are required to sign a general undertaking (similar to the listing agreement) imposing obligations concerning disclosure of information to investors.

A company seeking either a quotation for its shares on the USM or a Stock Exchange listing will need a sponsoring organization and an official

---

* *The Financing of Small Firms*, Cmnd 7503, HMSO, 1979

stockbroker as a channel of communication with the market. Often the official stockbroker acts as sole sponsor and financial adviser, ensuring that legal and Stock Exchange requirements are met, advising on any capital reorganization that may be necessary, and determining the price at which the issue can be made.

6.7 Loan Capital

The second major way in which a company may acquire funds to finance investment is through long-term borrowing for periods in excess of ten years. Such borrowing is invariably secured against the company's assets and may be negotiated at fixed or variable rates of interest.

Long-term borrowing takes a number of forms including borrowing by the issue of debentures. A debenture may be defined as 'a secured transferable loan stock'. Like shares, debentures may be listed or unlisted and may be bought and sold in capital markets.

As creditors of the company, debenture holders are entitled to payment of their fixed rate of interest before dividends are paid to any class of shareholder (and regardless of how satisfactory the company's trading position appears to be). In this sense they represent a prior charge on a company's post-tax profits.

Over the past decade borrowing by means of fixed interest debenture issues has suffered a considerable loss of appeal as in conditions of declining profits, high inflation, and associated high and volatile interest rates of the 1970s, companies were more and more reluctant to borrow in this way. By 1980 this trend had led to the virtual closure of the corporate bond market.

Apart from debentures, firms may borrow for the long- and medium-term by conventional term loans which are chiefly provided by banks and which may be negotiated for periods of up to twenty years at variable rates of interest. Bank lending and especially term lending to industry and commerce grew rapidly in the late 1970s as companies turned away from the debenture market. Thus, whereas in the 1960s banks provided less than half of companies' external finance, in the 1970s they contributed some 60 per cent and often more. In the 1970s, too, the structure of bank lending changed with a relatively smaller proportion being in the traditional form of short-term overdrafts for working capital and a growing proportion of total advances taking the form of term loans which by 1980 accounted for some 40 per cent of total bank lending.

Because the future is very uncertain, lending money long-term is always risky. The degree of risk varies of course from firm to firm. A small fledgling company with no past trading record is seen as being more risky than a large well established firm with a proven trading and profits record.

The differential risk will be reflected in the cost of borrowing which each will have to pay. The lender's risks are reduced when a loan is secured, and long-term loans in whatever form and from whatever source will almost without exception have to be secured on the company's property or fixed assets. Indeed, if a loan can be secured it is often both easier and cheaper to borrow the required amount for whatever period.

Before granting term loans, banks may carry out a thorough investigation of its potential client's activities and business record. In the case of small companies the owners may be asked to offer personal assets, such as their houses, as security for the loan.

Large institutional investors, in particular the insurance companies and pension funds, are major providers of long-term loan finance both as debenture holders and through negotiated mortgage loans for periods of twenty years of more.

Long-term funds can also be raised by sale and leaseback, which involves a company in selling part of its property, usually to an insurance company or pension fund who desire the asset as a long-term investment rather than for occupation. The company then leases the property back from the purchaser at a favourable rent, usually for periods of up to 25 years. Again, the purchaser will want to be assured of the rent income from the investment and will carry out thoroughgoing investigations into the company's past record and future profit potential as well as an independent valuation of the asset, the costs of which are paid by the seller together with legal and accounting fees. The benefits of this method of borrowing will depend largely on the tax aspects of the transaction which should be investigated thoroughly.

Many bank loans are tailored to meet the needs of particular enterprises, with repayments geared to the forecast earning capacity or estimated cash flow of the business. 'Balloon loans' allow for repayments to begin after a long period of grace; 'bullet loans' defer the whole repayment until the end of the agreed loan period.

6.8 Leasing

This increasingly popular form of financing business assets involves a leasing company – usually a bank or other finance house – in buying plant, equipment, or small industrial buildings required and selected by an industrial or commercial company. The leasing organization then leases the asset to the business at an agreed rental payable over a specified period of up to ten years either at regular intervals or under other arrangements.

In recent years, as low levels of profitability have significantly lowered industrial companies' liability to corporation tax, many companies have been unable to benefit from Britain's generous investment allowance system which allows companies to 'write off' against their potential corporation tax 100 per cent of the cost of new plant in the year of purchase. However, for a company whose capacity to offset tax has been exhausted, leasing assets enables it to benefit from the leasing organization's tax capacity. This is because the leasing organization claims any available investment incentives, e.g. grants or tax allowances, on the purchase of the asset over which it retains ownership while its client enjoys its possession and use. Since the investment allowances are reflected in the terms of the lease the lessee can gain the use of needed equipment at a relatively low rental.

Stemming in a large part from this situation, leasing has become established as a vast and growing industry on Britain's financial scene. A Bank of England estimate suggests that the total value of leased assets in Britain nearly quadrupled between 1977 and 1981 from £930 million to £3,300 million.* The same source suggests that about one-third of the equipment used in British industry is now leased rather than bought. In his budget statement of March 1983, however, Chancellor Lawson announced the phasing out of the generous system of accelerated investment allowances which were to be reduced in annual steps first to 75 per cent, then to 50 per cent by March, 1985 and finally abolished the year after. These changes have removed many of the former advantages of leasing.

6.9 Short-term Funds

Companies raise short-term loans chiefly for financing fluctuations in stocks of raw materials or components; increases in the value of trade debts; for ironing out seasonal fluctuations in trade; and for investment in short-life equipment and vehicles. Short-term funds may also be needed at times when a temporary decline in sales revenue produces a tight cash flow position, and companies whose sales are liable to seasonal peaks and troughs tend to make extensive use of short-term loans. The banks are by a large margin the principal suppliers of short-term loans, which may be negotiated either at fixed or variable rates of interest.

Among the many ways in which short-term finance may be raised are:

- the overdraft which, of the almost infinite number of ways in which banks lend, is the most widely used and most flexible way in which businesses can borrow short-term funds. Since the borrower pays interest only on the amount outstanding on a daily basis, an overdraft is also one of the cheapest forms of borrowing. It is this feature that makes

---

* *Bank of England Quarterly Bulletin*, September 1981

the overdraft especially useful to firms whose production or sales fluctuate seasonally and whose need for short-term finance consequentially varies considerably. It is usually possible, subject to appropriate personal guarantees or other security, for businesses to arrange a bank overdraft fairly quickly and at low cost. Within the agreed limit, money can be withdrawn or repaid without prior notice. The chief disadvantages of the overdraft are that they are repayable on demand (though this is rarely enforced) and are subject to interest rate fluctuations;

- short-term loans are straightforward bank loans sought for a specific period and for a specific purpose (e.g. the purchase of a small computer) rather than for working capital in general, with repayment of capital and of fixed or variable interest in equal instalments at agreed regular intervals over the period of the loan;
- trade credit – in the course of its operations a firm will find itself both owing and being owed money by other businesses for purchases and sales yet to be paid for. The excess of the latter over the former may be considerable and provide a substantial amount of short term finance. However, this tends to be expensive when cash discounts are lost;
- bill finance – a bill of exchange is a short-term (typically 30 to 91 days but sometimes for 180 days) post-dated IOU that can be realized by selling it at a discount. Bills are extensively used in international trade, enabling an exporter to get cash for his goods soon after despatch and allowing an importer to delay payment until he has processed and resold them. Bills are not confined to export trade and can be used to settle any transaction providing that they are drafted in accordance with the Bills of Exchange Act 1882.
- factoring and invoice discounting – factoring is an arrangement whereby the factoring company buys the trade debts of a business firm in return for a fee normally expressed as a percentage of the debts purchased and usually in the range of 0.75 per cent to 2 per cent. Debtors then deal directly with the factor who is now effectively running the firm's sales ledger as well as relieving it of the costs of debt collection, bad debts, and of extending trade credit to its customers. The factor will provide up to 80 per cent on the spot against the value of each new sales invoice as it is raised, with the balance minus the fees payable when the invoice is settled.

For well established companies many factors also provide an invoice discounting service, whereby a company can generate cash by selling a selection of invoices for an agreed proportion (up to 75 per cent) of the total amount due. Subsequently, the factor pays over the balance, less charges, in accordance with an agreed schedule. In this case, however, the business retains responsibility for debt collection and bad debts.

Despite economic recession, factoring has shown considerable growth in recent years. In 1983, for example, the amount of funds made available by members of the Association of British Factors to client firms against their invoiced sales rose by 28 per cent to a total of £232.7 million. Much of this new growth has come from successful expanding companies for whom factoring can be a very important means of finance. The reasons for this are highlighted in the case of Bishopsgate Terminals (Case Study 6.1) a company which supplies the essential components of custom-built viewdata services; the keyboards and the intelligent terminals that pull in data from different sources and manipulate it for display on screen.

CASE STUDY 6.1

Bishopsgate Terminals

'When we realised a couple of years ago that we were in the process of doubling our turnover, from £1.7m to £3.7m, we knew we had to use factors. If we had not done so, we would probably have gone out of business,' says Ian Craig-Wood of Bishopsgate Terminals.

The business is fast-growing because Bishopsgate has carved out a niche in the UK market for private viewdata systems and at present claims a technical edge over US rivals Micrognosis.

Yet if Craig-Wood, whose family interests are major shareholders, had agreed to accept his bank's conventional overdraft ratios, the working capital required to power this growth just would not have been available. 'The trouble with the conventional approach of the clearing banks,' says Craig-Wood, 'is that their analysis of your business is based on audited accounts; these are by definition several months out-of-date. In a fast-growing, technology-based industry, you either have to find a bank that will finance you (along US lines) with a level of funding based on current trading levels or you have to turn to factors. It is quite a simple issue, really. If you double your turnover, you are going to increase the level of outstanding debts by a similar amount.'

(*Source:* Jones, David 'Cash-flow factors', *Banking World*,
March 1983, p. 31)

6.10 Export Finance

The Export Credit Guarantee Department (ECGD) of the Department of Trade and Industry offers insurance to exporters against the major risks of non-payment by their overseas customers, providing up to 90 per cent cover for commercial risks including insolvency or protracted default on payment by the importer and up to 95 per cent for political risks of wars, revolution, and transfer delays. Although the government does not itself provide the export finance, an ECGD insurance policy usually makes it much easier to obtain bank finance for exports.

A second important form of export finance is factoring. Factors provide a service which, as well as supplying funds, offers information on overseas customers, markets, and terms of business, as well as underwriting and collecting debts. A recent journal report* suggests that exporters may find that factors compare favourably (on cost and time) with the traditional mechanisms of ECGD guarantees, bank finance, and the use of a local agent.

STUDENT ASSIGNMENT 6.1

Farm Machines PLC

As a result of a successful overseas marketing and promotion exercise, Farm Machines PLC is about to enter the export market. It has just obtained several large export contracts which require additional stock and work-in-progress to be carried for a period of about twelve months. The company has estimated that this will requie additional finance of £1 million.

At present the company has net assets of £3 million; an average annual pre-tax profit of around £500,000; and no debt.

Carry out thorough investigations and advise the company on possible ways of:

(a) raising the necessary finance, and
(b) reducing the risks of non-payment by its overseas customers.

6.11 Loan Versus Share Capital

Every company will need to make careful decisions about its desired capital gearing as measured by the ratio of borrowed funds to equity capital. A closely related decision concerns the desired ratio of fixed return 'priority' capital (debentures and preference shares) on the one hand and equity on the other. Many factors will influence the optimum financial mix in a company's capital structure.

* *Banking World*, March 1984

The major attraction of loan capital is simply that debt interest (unlike share dividends) is tax-deductible against corporate profits, so that provided a company earns taxable profits borrowing can offer a relatively cheap source of finance in comparison with equity. However, if a company allows itself to become too highly geared, i.e. borrows excessively in relation to its equity base, it exposes itself to numerous risks including:

- the risk that the burden of interest and repayments of debt may become too great relative to the company's available earnings and cash flow. As a useful rule of thumb, it has been suggested that for most businesses the ratio of estimated trading profits (before interest and tax payments) should be at least twice the amount necessary to cover all interest charges;
- the risk that should there be insufficient cash to meet interest or capital repayment, the company's creditors who are likely to include one bank or more can call in the Receiver or start proceedings to have the company liquidated. Were this to happen, the costs of liquidation would tend to be borne largely by the shareholders as residual claimants. Other things being equal, the greater the debt the greater the risks of default and the greater the costs of insolvency to shareholders;
- the more highly geared the company, the more the dividend return of ordinary shareholders tends to fluctuate. Because interest charges represent a prior claim on profits, the more risky the nature of the business the greater the danger of a high capital gearing policy based on raising large amounts of priority capital;
- the risk that too large a proportion of company profit is pre-empted for interest payments and that insufficient remains for retention in order to finance planned expansions.

All these risks are magnified in times of declining industrial profitability, especially if a large proportion of past borrowing has been at varying interest rates. Paradoxically, in the recent years of recession many companies have been forced to borrow more heavily merely in order to survive, and it becomes increasingly questionable whether companies can generate sufficient cash flow to meet interest repayments.

Each type of debt will vary in its tax and risk characteristics and in its interest charges. In deciding which kinds of debt to use, a company finance manager must investigate the tax advantages, interest rates, and risk characteristics of each. The optimal *mixture* of debt will be that which offers the lowest expected cost (net of tax) for a given acceptable risk to the company.* The choice will seldom be clear-cut, and the services of an

* Rutterford, Janette 'The UK Corporate Bond Market: Prospects for Revival', *National Westminster Bank Quarterly Review*, May 1984

expert financial adviser should be sought before any decisions are made.

All companies will need an adequate equity base of permanent risk capital if only to attract additional funds from the investing public when required. By reference to the general practice in the particular industry of which it is part, a company should be able to establish within what range its capital gearing ratio should normally fall. As we have seen, the more risky the business the lower the desirable gearing ratio should be. For the majority of companies a Bank of England guide* suggests that as a rule of thumb capital gearing should be around 1 : 2, i.e. equity should be twice the level of company borrowing, with a maximum ratio of 1 : 1 as a limit which should not be exceeded other than in very exceptional cases and then only for very temporary periods. The need for an injection of additional equity is signalled whenever the higher end of the capital gearing range is approached.

6.12 Interest Rates

To the tune of several billion pounds annually, industrial and commercial companies taken as a whole are net borrowers of savings made in other sectors of the economy. These savings, coming largely from the personal sector, are channelled sometimes directly but more usually by various financial institutions to provide a massive flow of funds to meet a large proportion of business investment needs. The strength of corporate and government demand for loanable funds will vary mainly with changes in income and in the economic outlook, as too will the strength of the flow of savings from the rest of the economy – the supply of loanable funds. Such variations in demand and supply conditions in the markets for finance will partially both determine and be determined by the general level of interest rates prevailing at any given time.

The act of saving implies a sacrifice of current consumption in the expectation of higher consumption at some future date. The payment of interest is the lender's reward for the sacrifice of liquidity during the currency of the loan. The pre-eminent determinant of the level of savings is the level of income, but at any given level of income, the rate of interest will have an important effect. Rising interest rates will tend to induce a higher ratio of savings to income and vice versa.

The demand for funds by companies depends upon a large variety of factors, important among which are the general economic outlook and the expected market prospects for its products. If business takes an optimistic view of the future, demand for funds will obviously be higher than when it

* *Money for Business*, a guide prepared by the Bank of England and the City Communications Centre, 4th ed., 1983

Figure 6.2.   The determination of interest rate.

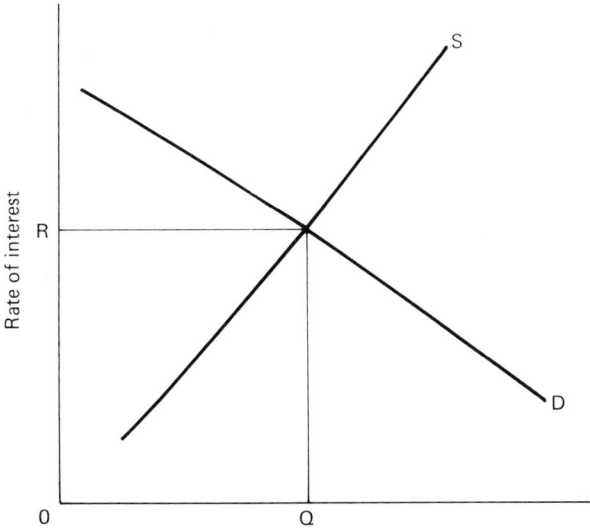

Demand for funds (investment) and supply of funds (savings) per time period

expects economic stagnation or decline. From this it may be argued that for any given set of business expectations the demand for funds to finance capital investment will be strongly influenced by the level of interest rates – since, for example, at low interest rates it becomes more profitable to borrow than at high interest rates. Because the costs of borrowing are lower, more investment projects are likely to yield returns sufficient for capital and interest to be repaid. The market forces model of interest rate determination is illustrated in Figure 6.2.

6.13 Government Influence on Interest Rates

Central government and local authorities borrow enormous sums in order to finance the nation's social capital – roads, schools, hospitals, and so on – which cannot be financed from current revenue from taxation and rates. Though the public sector borrowing requirement (PSBR) has tended to decline in recent years, it still represents a massive government contribution to the demand for funds exerting an upward pressure on the level of interest rates.

In the context of its monetary policy brought to bear against inflation, the manipulation of interest rates may be used to restrain monetary growth with a direct and immediate impact on the costs of business borrowing. The effects on small businesses – local farmers and other small traders who may depend heavily on borrowing and who cannot usually pass along the higher interest charges in the form of higher prices – are likely to be much greater than on large companies whose self-financing ratio is higher and whose greater control over market price allows them to pass along higher rates to their customers.

In theory, high interest rates should make individuals and companies less willing to borrow, especially when rates are high in not only nominal but in real terms, i.e. in relation to the expected inflation rate. However, in the recent years of recession the intended effect has been swamped by other pressures. Many firms have been forced to continue or even increase borrowing merely to survive (distress borrowing) and even to finance high interest payments. In the latter event the effect of high interest rates has become the opposite of that intended. Nevertheless, real interest rates were added to the Government's battery of monetary targets in the Budget of March 1983.

Interest rates can also be affected by governments who use a more Keynesian approach combining fiscal demand management and incomes policy. To the extent that such policies are seen to be succeeding, there will be an improvement in inflationary expectations resulting in a stimulus to savings and a consequent fall in interest rates. Conversely, an expansionary fiscal policy designed to stimulate spending will tend to push up public sector borrowing and, by improving the business outlook, induce a higher level of investment with a consequent increase in demand for funds and upward pressure on interest rates. Finally, government may use interest rates to protect the foreign exchange rate of the pound.

6.14 The Importance of the Institutional Investors

Within Britain's ever-changing financial system, much of it concentrated in the City of London, there is a wide range of specialist institutions, most of whom help to channel a large proportion of the nation's savings into productive investment in commerce and industry.

At the heart of the financial system are the high street banks whose traditional role has been one of money transmission and of channelling personal savings into the provision of working capital for trade and industry. However, since the demise of the debenture market, banks have offered more and more diverse forms of loan with an increasing proportion of their total lending being in the form of tailor-made term loans. Banks are also important providers of leasing finance, having either established or taken over equipment leasing subsidiaries. As Figure 6.3 shows, the banks increased their share of commerce and industry's external finance from rather less than half the total in the 1960s to 60 per cent and often more in the 1970s.

Figure 6.3. Industrial and commercial companies: external finance.

£ billions: annual averages

	1963–66	1967–70	1971–74	1975–79
Bank borrowing	0.5	0.7	3.2	2.7
Other loans and mortgages	0.1	0.2	0.3	0.4
Ordinary shares	0.1	0.2	0.2	0.9
Other capital issues	0.3	0.3	0.1	–
Overseas finance	0.2	0.3	0.8	1.2
	1.2	1.7	4.6	5.2

Source: National Income Accounts.

By 1980, 79 per cent of British companies' total new external finance came from the banks, and by February 1983 all banks in Britain had a massive £88 billion on loan to UK companies.

The capital of Finance For Industry (FFI) is subscribed by the banks and the Bank of England. The FFI provides medium-term loans to industry at both fixed and floating rates. Its subsidiary, Industrial and Commercial Finance Corporation (ICFC), makes funds, including equity finance, available to small firms.

Today, the clearing banks are involved in almost every aspect of company finance, providing business with loan and equity capital and offering many services such as financial advice and investment management.

The major beneficiaries of the dramatic post-war rise in personal savings have been pension funds and life assurance companies. Since life assurance and pension contributions are now far and away the most important ways in which individuals save, these institutions have become pre-eminent in the provision of long-term funds for industry and commerce.

Both insurance companies and pension fund managers invest huge sums of money in a number of directions, including company securities. The majority of pension funds are managed by financial institutions, mainly merchant banks, insurance companies, investment trusts, and stockbrokers. In addition, the nationalized industries, many of the large local authorities, and large companies operate self-managed funds.

Though exact figures for their investment of contributions and insurance premiums are not available, the pensions funds and life companies own a significant proportion of British industry. At the time of the Wilson Committee Report* it was estimated that there were about 11.5 million

* Report of the Committee of Enquiry to Review the Functions of the Financial Institutions, Cmnd 7937, HMSO, 1980

employee members of occupational pension schemes. The assets of the self-administered funds were estimated at £31.1 billion at the end of 1978 with an annual in-flow of £3.7 million, to which externally managed funds had to be added. By March 1983 the pension funds (self-administered and managed) amounted to well over £100 billion, with an annual in-flow of about £9 million or some 3 per cent of GDP

In recent years an increasing proportion of pension funds has been invested in companies, and in particular into the ordinary shares of larger companies.

In the mid-1970s the great upsurge of long-term personal savings flowing into life assurance and pension funds produced a dramatic change in the ownership of company shares, with financial institutions steadily increasing their share at the expense of individuals whose ownership became indirect. As a result of this trend the proportion of listed shares owned by individuals declined from 59 per cent in 1963 to only 32 per cent at the end of 1978, as the proportion owned by the institutions rose from 28 per cent to 58 per cent in the same period. By the end of 1978 the pension funds and insurance companies jointly owned well over one-third of UK listed ordinary shares. This massive concentration of investment power (pension funds alone owned around 20 per cent of listed ordinary shares) caused former Prime Minister Harold Wilson to remark; 'The pension funds are so powerful they don't know how powerful they are'.

Many anxieties and criticisms have been expressed about the rise of the institutional investors who by virtue of their holding can exert effective if indirect influence over the running of companies in which they invest. It is argued, for example, that because their primary legal concern is to safeguard the long-term interests of their members they are reluctant to invest in high risk or unusual projects.

6.15 Some Recent Innovations

Following a recommendation of the Wilson Report, an experimental loan-guarantee scheme was launched by the Finance Act 1981. The scheme was intended to help finance small businesses that would not normally be able to raise funds elsewhere. This help was to be made available by the removal of constraints imposed by the security requirements of lenders which had restricted bank lending to small firms, by getting the government to underwrite loans provided by the financial institutions within an overall limit of £50 million. As demand rapidly exceeded initial expectations, the limit of £50 million was raised a number of times. By mid-1983 Government had guaranteed loans amounting to around £350 million to some 10,000 businesses. In the same year the scheme was extended to 1987, with a raised limit of £600 million. Firms borrowing under this scheme are enabled to offer the lenders complete security for 80 per cent of the amount owed. The lender, invariably one of the high street banks, will carry out an initial appraisal of the firm.

Despite the success of the loan-guarantee scheme in supplying funds to more and more small businesses, a more recent DTI-commissioned report expressed considerable disquiet concerning the high failure rate of the loans which by 1983 amounted to one in five. The report argues strongly that the banks should be much tougher on appraising loan applications under the scheme.

Furthermore changes to the original scheme introduced in May 1984 (a) raised the cost of borrowing on the government guaranteed portion of the loan and (b) reduced the proportion of the overall loan guaranteed from 80 to 70 per cent. As a result the number of loans drawn under the scheme fell dramatically in 1984–85 chiefly because (a) potential applicants faced increased costs and an unattractively high burden of repayments, and (b) potential lenders were less ready to approve applications under the scheme. Consequently both loan applications and approvals fell.

Under the Business Expansion Scheme (BES), introduced in 1981, individuals who supply finance for business start-ups either directly or indirectly through specially created funds, can deduct the sums invested from their taxable income. The capital has to be committed for at least five years and any subsequent realizations are subject to capital gains rather than income tax. Initially the scope of the scheme was very restricted, but the 1983 Budget extended the arrangements to existing as well as new businesses, providing an important new way for small firms to raise risk capital and to achieve a more satisfactory capital gearing position. By March 1983 an estimated £80–£100 million had been invested under the new scheme.

The tax advantages for the investor are considerable. For example, a top rate taxpayer can reduce the cost of a £10,000 investment to £4,000, though the base cost for capital gains purposes is treated as the gross cost, i.e. £10,000.

Only qualifying companies are enabled to benefit from the BES. Such companies must be incorporated in the United Kingdom and their shares must be neither quoted on the Stock Exchange nor dealt with in the USM. The company must not control or be controlled by another company or be controlled by an individual who also controls another company carrying on some other trade.

If the company has not begun trading at the time the shares are issued, it must begin within two years. Investment must be in 'eligible' shares, i.e. newly issued ordinary shares, for five years with no preferential rights to dividends, or on a winding up, or for redemption.

Finance for Management Buy Outs is concerned with firms whose owners wish to sell, e.g. parent companies wishing to divest themselves of subsidiaries. Alternatively, buy outs may arise from receivership or intending retirement of the owner. In recent years, as economic recession has often forced companies into selling off subsidiaries at a time when potential buyers have been few, managers have often been able to acquire the companies for discount. Financial institutions have been quick to seize the opportunity to provide finance to managers on favourable terms. For these reasons the number of management buy outs, previously rare in Britain, increased significantly in the early 1980s. Typically, a management buy out is financed by a combination of loan and equity funds with the majority of equity shares lying with the management.

In December 1983, when the Midland Bank launched its Business Advisory Service (BAS), it followed Barclays and Lloyds who had already established similar services offering a wide range of useful services to support new business enterprises.

Specially trained regional advisers will spend four or five days visiting an enterprise in order to analyse objectives, products, and markets, together with the present financial and management structure and future requirements. Following the visit, a confidential report containing recommendations for future action will highlight areas of potential improvement. In addition, guidance on expansion and how it should be financed will be offered, and available government and EEC grants will be identified.

The banks have introduced many other services to business in recent years. The National Westminster Bank computer services subsidiary, Centrefile, for example, offers a tailor-made accounting service for businesses of all types. Accounting systems are designed on the basis of the bank's analysis of business needs. The service may be offered by the installation of a complete computer system in the firm's office; a mini computer terminal in the office linked to Centrefile by telephone; or sending all its documents direct to Centrefile for processing. The services are backed by ongoing support training and comprehensive documentation.

6.16 Presenting the Case for a Loan

An application for a loan to a bank or other investing institution needs very careful preparation. The method of approach will vary with the type of finance, the history and current position of the applicant's business, and the requirements of the finance provider. Advice on preparing a case for a loan is available from lending institutions. Figure 6.4 lists some important 'do's and don'ts' for raising finance.

Figure 6.4. Quick check-list of opportunities and pitfalls.

DOs	DON'Ts
• Do appoint an expert financial adviser and, if possible, one or more good non-executive directors with a financial background.	• Do not delegate too much responsibility to your advisers – you yourself must be able to represent your firm in discussions with potential financiers.
• Do consider all sources of finance and try to identify the best.	• Do not try to use facilities from too many sources, or to play one off against another.
• Do make a detailed assessment of your financial needs over the period for which you are raising finance. Be clear how much you need and what you need it for, and allow a margin for error.	• Do not take on commitments that are not supportable given the size and cash flow of the business.
• Do ensure that you have adequate financial controls, and that your management information takes into account the effects of inflation. You should know clearly how you are doing and how much money you are using. Provide your financiers with full information on your business.	• Do not be reluctant to share information with your financiers and backers, both at the outset and subsequently. They will welcome frankness and an early indication of potential difficulties.
• Do try to understand the worries and concerns of potential financiers; and consider how you can provide them with greater security.	• Do not limit your opportunities by refusing to part with equity. Do not be reluctant to give reasonable security as evidence of your personal commitment.

STUDENT ASSIGNMENT 6.2

Flexible Plastics

Flexible Plastics, a successful private company manufacturing specialist plastic containers, has recently expanded rapidly with assistance from the company's bank which has provided large overdraft facilities. Profits are of the order of £200,000 per year before tax. The business is at present financed by shareholders' funds (principally retained profits) of £350,000 and by bank overdrafts of £250,000.

The company wishes to exploit a new process (the development of which is complete). This entails equipping a new factory (to be leased from the Department of Trade and Industry in an assisted area) at a cost of £250,000 (net of Regional Development grant) and providing for associated working capital and start-up costs estimated at £450,000.

The new development is forecast to yield profits of £100,000 a year before tax. On this basis the maintainable pre-tax profits of the company are considered to be £300,000 a year.

The present financial position of the company is shown below*:

		£000
Fixed assets		200
Current assets: stocks and debtors	550	
Less Current liabilities:		
Creditors	150	
Bank overdraft	250	
	400	
Net current assets		150
		350
Financed by		
Share capital	50	
Reserves (including share premium)	300	
Shareholders' funds		350
Medium-term bank loan		–
Long-term fixed-rate loan		–
		350
Debt/equity ratio		0.7 to 1

Identify and evaluate alternative ways in which the company might acquire the necessary finance for modernizing and expanding its operations. Consider the effects of your alternative proposals on the company's capital structure.

* Adapted from *Money for Business*, a guide prepared by the Bank of England and the City Communications Centre, 4th Ed., 1983

6.17 Summary

1. All businesses require short-term working capital to finance stock and outstanding debts; and medium- and long-term finance to pay for replacement of worn-out plant and machinery.
2. Expanding firms need additional finance to pay for new capital equipment and buildings. Funds may also be required to adjust a firm's capital structure.

3. In the recent past, retained profits have provided for up to 70 per cent of industrial and commercial companies' financial needs.

4. External finance may be share capital, loan capital, or government grants and allowances.

5. Shareholders are the legal owners of a company and have many statutory and common law rights in and against the company.

6. Ordinary shares – or equities – represent the risk capital of the business and normally carry voting rights at company meetings. Ordinary shareholders share in any profits only after interest has been paid to debenture holders and after dividends have been paid to preference shareholders. For this reason the return on equities tends to fluctuate with the company's profits performance and may in some cases be zero.

7. Preference shares carry preferential rights in the distribution of profits and in repayment of capital if the company is wound up. Preference shares may be cumulative or non-cumulative.

8. Shareholders' funds are represented as reserves in a company's balance sheet.

9. A new issue of shares may be floated by an invitation to subscribe by prospectus; by an offer for sale; by placing; or by a rights issue to existing shareholders.

10. The Stock Exchange provides a market for secondhand shares and other securities, thus giving shares the important advantages of liquidity and hence greater marketability.

11. A company wishing its shares to be dealt with on the Stock Exchange must satisfy rigorous enquiries and conditions in order to become listed.

12. The introduction of the USM in 1980 filled an important gap in the provision of risk capital for small and medium businesses on the London Stock Exchange.

13. Once an important means of long-term borrowing, debentures are loan stocks secured against a company's assets. Debenture holders are entitled to payment of their fixed interest before dividends are paid to any class of shareholders. In conditions of inflation and interest rate volatility in the 1970s companies turned away from this form of finance, preferring to borrow medium- and long-term from the banks.

14. Companies borrow extensively from banks by means of term loans which may be negotiated for up to twenty years at fixed or variable interest rates. Term loans are normally secured against the fixed assets of a company. Banks will invariably carry out thorough investigations of a company before granting term loans.

15. Other forms of long-term borrowing include mortgage loans from large institutional investors, and sale and leaseback which involves a

company in selling part of its property to an institutional investor and leasing the property back on rental.

16. Until recently, leasing was an increasingly popular form of acquiring plant, equipment, and small industrial buildings. Because the leasing company can take advantage of 100 per cent investment allowances, leasing provided a relatively cheap means of acquiring fixed assets for companies whose capacity to offset taxes has been exhausted.

17. Businesses require short-term funds to finance working capital such as stocks and debtors and for smoothing out fluctuations in trade or to provide cash flow.

18. Short-term finance may be raised in many ways, important among which are overdrafts, short-term loans, trade credit, bill finance, factoring and invoice discounting. The banks are by far the most important source of short-term loans for business.

19. The ECGD offers an insurance service to exporters against the commercial and political risks of non-payment by their overseas customers. Factoring is also an important form of export finance.

20. In deciding how to raise additional funds a business will need to consider the effects on its capital gearing, i.e. the ratio of borrowed funds to equity capital. An excessive gearing ratio exposes companies to greater and more numerous financial risks.

21. The cost of capital – the rate of interest – varies with the liquidity and duration of the loan; the riskiness of the project for which the money is required; and the track record of the borrower.

22. In the exercise of its monetary and fiscal policies, government exerts a powerful direct and indirect influence on the level and structure of interest rates.

23. Of the many specialist financial institutions that channel some of the nation's savings into productive investment in commerce and industry, this chapter has concentrated on three of the most important – banks, pension funds, and insurance companies.

24. The Business Expansion Scheme allows individuals who supply finance for company start-up to deduct sums invested from taxable income provided certain conditions are met. In 1983, the BES arrangements were extended to existing as well as new qualifying companies.

25. By guaranteeing 80 per cent of the value of eligible term loans, the government through its Loan Guarantee Scheme helps small businesses who are unable to raise funds elsewhere.

26. Through their Business Advisory Services the major banks offer financial and management advice and reports which can help improve the financial aspects of business operations.

7

Business Location and the Use of Land

7.1 Land

Theoretically all land in Britain is owned by the Crown. Organizations and individuals cannot own land, but may own a *legal estate* in land. The estate measures the interest an organization or individual has in a piece of land in terms of how long the land is held for. Legal estates in land may be either freehold or leasehold estates.

The owners of freehold estates effectively own the land and are entitled to use it for ever. A leasehold estate entitles the leaseholders to exclusive possession of the land for some fixed period of time, for example 99 or 999 years, after which the land reverts to the lessor. Short-term leases are usually referred to as tenancies.

The lease itself is a written document which creates an agreement between the lessor and the lessee (tenant) by which the tenant is enabled to exclude all other parties from the land. The lease will invariably place a number of specific dates on the two parties.

Legally a freehold estate and more than one leasehold estate can co-exist for the same piece of land. For example, an organization owning the freehold may grant a lease for say 99 years to another organization which in turn may re-lease the land to a third party for any shorter period.

Principally because the ways in which land is used is a matter of public concern, the freedom of both freeholders and leaseholders to use their land in the way they please is constrained by certain statutory common law and other restrictions (see Section 7.3).

Both freehold and leasehold estates (as distinct from land itself) can be bought and sold, given away, or bequeathed, without affecting the use of land or its possession.

As well as the two forms of legal estate in land which give rights to land itself, there are many legal and equitable 'interests in land' which give rights to a claim of some kind against another's land. *Legal* interests in land are enforceable rights against the land itself, for example landlord's right of entry to inspect a leaseholder's property, rights of way, fishing rights, etc. *Equitable* interests are enforceable only against the person who grants them.

7.2 The Acquisition of Land

A business will normally acquire land by negotiating a contract for purchasing the freehold or leasehold estate in land or for renting it. If the land in question is *unregistered* the title to it is proved by a set of documents known as the *title deeds* which show a chain of title dating back over the past 15 years down to the present owner. In this case the contract is performed by the seller executing a deed which he transfers to the legal estate of the buyer. The deed transferring unregistered land may be in the form of:

- a deed of conveyance transferring a freehold estate to the buyer;
- a grant of lease creating a leasehold estate in favour of the buyer; or
- a deed of assignment of a lease transferring an existing lease to the buyer.

Most land, however, is *registered* land for which evidence of title is simply an entry in a register held at the appropriate Land Registry. Title to registered land is guaranteed by the state and its transfer is easily effected by completion of a short and simple Land Registry form.

Freehold estates are normally purchased with a capital sum which may be paid by mortgage arrangement. In the case of leasehold estates payment will be monthly or annual rental for the duration of the leasehold period. Leasehold estates are commonly subject to quite frequent reviews and rents may be adjusted to take account of inflation and changing land values.

The acquisition of a freehold estate gives a business the security of knowing that it can continue to use the land and premises thereon indefinitely. In the case of leasehold estates, however, at the expiry of the leasing period the land will revert to the landlord in the absence of a renegotiated lease.

7.3 Controls on the Use of Land

The uses to which land can be put are subject to numerous controls. Under the Town and Country Planning Acts of 1971–74, for example, local planning authorities are responsible for the day-to-day administration and the Department of the Environment for overall control of the land use planning system which provides the legal framework within which the development of land can be controlled in the wider public interest. 'Development' is defined in the 1971 Act as 'building, engineering, mining, or other operation in, on, over or under the land or any material change in the use of any building or other land'.

Thus, for example, a company considering particular sites for development or expansion will require planning permission from the local authority planning department (or from the Secretary of State for the Environment on appeal) who will grant permission only if the proposed development conforms with the objectives of the planning department as expressed in its plans for the future. For example, if parts of the area are intended for housing development or recreational use the planning authority may restrict industrial or commercial development in these parts. Before applying for planning permission the company should also check the local planning authority register of planning applications and their results. This will indicate to the company whether the planning application is likely to succeed. Also prior to planning applications the company must first have notified its intentions to those owning interest in the land or property and advertise its application where the proposed development may offend neighbouring land or property owners.

At common law restrictions on the use of land may arise from agreements made when the title to land is transferred by deed. The deed may include covenants (i.e. promises in the deed) for example, not to develop the land for particular purposes. Covenants may bind both outright purchasers of freehold land as well as lessees.

The common law of torts imposes further constraints on land use. For example, the tort of trespass prevents a landowner erecting buildings which intrude onto, above, or below another's land. Similarly, the tort of nuisance prevents a landowner from unreasonably using his lands in ways which interfere with his neighbour's enjoyment, for example by the discharge of industrial waste into a stream flowing through his neighbour's land.

Two major controls on land development have been applied at national level – Industrial Development Certificates (IDCs) and Office Development Permits (ODPs). The IDC system introduced in the Town and Country Planning Act of 1947 required companies proposing to build or extend factories in excess of 5,000 square feet to obtain an official licence – an IDC – as well as planning permission before proceeding. In prosperous regions such as Greater London and South East England the issue of IDCs was highly restricted, whereas in assisted areas they were readily obtainable. The severity with which IDC controls were applied has varied considerably with the economic situation. In the 1960s, for example, controls were applied vigorously but as unemployment rose in the 1970s the system tended to fall by the wayside. At the end of 1981 IDC controls were suspended altogether.

ODPs were introduced in the mid-1960s with the objective of restricting office development in London and later Birmingham in order to disperse office employment away from these highly congested city centres to less congested provincial cities. Two major effects of ODPs have been to encourage the redevelopment of provincial city centres and to push up London and Birmingham office rentals to astronomical figures.

7.4 Historical Reasons for the Location of Industry

Historically the main factors determining the location of Britain's major industries were:

- access to raw materials;
- availability of suitable power supplies;
- availability of skilled labour;
- proximity to major markets.
- transport advantages, e.g. nearness to canals, railways, or ports

The proximity of iron ore deposits to Britain's coalfields was an important reason for Britain's early industrialization. It also explains why Britain's great nineteenth-century staple industries – coal itself, iron and steel, shipbuilding, metal, engineering, and textiles – tended to locate on coalfields in South Wales, the Midlands, North West and North East England, and the Central Lowlands of Scotland. The production of steel, upon which the metalworking and engineering and shipbuilding industries depended, required iron ore, coked coal, and limestone, and the relative transport costs of obtaining these raw materials was an important locational pull.

With the concentration of the staple industries on or near the coalfields a number of so-called 'external economies of scale' became available to individual business firms locating in those areas. These economies, i.e. savings in unit costs of production, deriving from factors external to any individual firm itself included:

- the development of a pool of skilled labour;
- the possibilities for inter-firm technical or buying co-operation;
- the growth of a number of ancillary firms providing components or materials to the firms in the major industry;
- the development of service firms offering technical or specialized financial or managerial consultancy services to the main industry;
- the development of good transport and communication systems with markets;

- the association of quality with the particular location, e.g. Sheffield for cutlery, Stoke for pottery;
- the gearing of local further education and training to the needs of the industry.

All these advantages make it difficult for new entrants to an industry even to consider locating elsewhere.

7.5 Central Government Influences on the Location of Industry

Ever since the 1930s British governments have tried to influence the location of industry. A central feature of locational policies has been the designation of assisted areas of one kind or another with a range of financial inducements offered to firms who move into or expand in these areas. The government's present method of influencing the location of industry include:

- The Assisted Areas – consisting of Special Development Areas, Development Areas, and Intermediate Areas in which regional development grants, regional selective assistance, and various other incentives to firms to locate or expand are available.
- Enterprise Zones – see Section 7.8 below.
- Urban Aid – this may be available in cases where local authorities and private enterprise jointly co-operate in urban investment projects.
- Steel Closure Areas – help in these areas is available from the British Steel Corporation and the European Coal and Steel Community to compensate for large-scale redundancies in the steel industry.
- Freeports – in the summer of 1983 the Treasury invited applications for status as freeports where goods can be imported, stored, processed, manufactured, and exported free from customs duty. Duty would only become payable if the goods were moved elsewhere in the UK
- ODPs – these have been discussed above. See Section 7.3 above.

7.6 UK Regional Policy

Regional policy is mainly concerned with tackling the wide disparities that exist between the different regions of the United Kingdom in terms of income per head, unemployment, and economic growth. This regional imbalance of prosperity is generally held to originate in the twentieth-century decline of Britain's old staple labour-intensive industries which for reasons already explained tended to locate on or near the coalfields in the North of England, Central Scotland, and South Wales. As early as 1934 the government introduced its first experiment in British regional policy with the Special Areas Act which defined West Cumberland, North

Figure 7.1. Summary of incentives for industry.

REGIONAL AID	Special Development Areas (SDAs)	Development Areas (DAs)	Intermediate Areas (IAs)	Other areas
Regional Development Grants Available for capital expenditure:				
a on new building works (other than mining works);	22%	15%	NIL	NIL
b on new plant and machinery – provided chiefly for manufacturing industry.	22%	15%	NIL	NIL
Regional Selective Assistance				
i *For manufacturing, mining and construction industries* Section 7 or Project Grants based on the fixed costs of a project.	Negotiable as the minimum necessary for the project to proceed			NIL
ii *Office and Service Industries Scheme* Grants based on the number of jobs a project is expected to create over three years.	Negotiable as the minimum necessary for the project to proceed within the following maxima: £8,000 per job £5,000 per job £2,500 per job			NIL
iii *In-plant Training Scheme* Grants towards training costs.	80% of eligible training costs			NIL
iv *Loans from Europe* Fixed interest loans from the European Investment Bank (EIB) for projects creating or safeguarding jobs.	Available in all Assisted Areas			NIL
Similar loans from the European Coal and Steel Community (ECSC).	Available in all coal and steel closure areas			NIL

v *Exchange Risk Guarantee Scheme*
Covers firms against the exchange risk on foreign currency loans.

Available on loans from the EIB and ECSC

NATION-WIDE AID

i *Support for Innovation*
To encourage industrial research and development and the application of new technologies in products and processes.

Up to 33⅓% in all Areas

ii *National Selective Assistance (Section 8)*
Available to manufacturing industries for major projects involving new investments of at least £0.5 million.

Negotiable as the minimum necessary for the project to proceed

iii *Coal-firing Scheme*
Assistance is available in the agricultural, manufacturing and most service industries towards the cost of switching gas and/or oil fired industrial equipment to coal-firing.

Up to 25% in all Areas

Loans are also available from the ECSC. Borrowers can be covered under the Exchange Risk Guarantee Scheme against exchange rate fluctuations.

Up to 50% of project costs in all Areas

East England, South Wales, and Central Scotland as areas in need of special assistance. The assistance offered, however, was slight.

In the post-war period government has introduced more and more regional policy and other measures designed specifically to influence the geographical distribution of economic activity by attracting firms to move or expand into areas designated for assistance.

As a result of successive Acts of Parliament, by the early 1980s a range of incentives was available. A summary of current regional incentives and of nationwide aid available is presented in Figure 7.1.

Regional selective assistance is designed to bring forward worthwhile projects which would not otherwise go ahead and which provide more productive and more secure jobs. The criteria for such assistance available under Section 7 of the Industry Act of 1972 are as follows:

- Projects must have good prospects of viability.
- Projects must create new jobs or safeguard existing ones.
- The greater part of the project costs must be financed by the applicant or from private sector sources.
- Applicants must show that without assistance the project will not take place either at all or on the basis proposed.
- Projects should strengthen the regional and national economy, e.g. by improving efficiency or by introducing new technology or products, and thereby provide more productive and more secure jobs.
- Assistance will not normally be given for projects which have already begun. The amount offered is the minimum necessary for the project to go ahead, and takes account of other assistance from the public sector (such as regional development grants).

7.7 The Effectiveness of Regional Policy

There have been many criticisms both of the content and administration of regional policy. The extract from the British Institute of Management (BIM) Report reproduced below as Case Study 7.1 points out the difficulties of assessing regional and other locational policies and pinpoints some of the criticisms from a business perspective. The same report also itemizes the advantages of regional and locational policies claimed by its supporters.

7.8 Enterprise Zones

Initially introduced for a 10-year experimental period, enterprise zones represent an attempt to encourage companies to locate by removing major administrative and fiscal barriers which can so often prevent a company's

CASE STUDY 7.1

BIM Report (1983) on The Importance of Regional Policy

Effectiveness

It is difficult to assess the effectiveness of these policies. Amongst the main problems are:

- finding appropriate periods or areas, free from the influence of locational policy, to make comparisons;
- identifying the effects of any one instrument of change. Several changes are usually introduced together;
- distinguishing between additional investment and investment which would have taken place elsewhere in the absence of policy;
- measuring the social and political costs and benefits.

There is, however, some evidence to suggest that between the mid-1960s and mid-1970s, locational policies increased jobs and investment in assisted areas. By the late 1970s, however, the impact appeared to have become weaker. This could reflect a decline in the volume of mobile investment or the reduction in the strength of regional policy incentives which took place in 1979.

The overall cost of regional policy is also difficult to calculate. As well as the gross cost to the Exchequer, items such as unemployment benefits saved by the creation of new jobs should be included. Many of the benefits of locational policy are very long-term which makes the problem even harder.

Critics of locational policy have claimed:

- that it has lowered national efficiency by making companies locate in inappropriate places;
- that it is inappropriate in the present climate of widespread unemployment and spare capacity;
- that it may harm local communities in the long-term by encouraging overdependence on large branch factories;
- that frequent changes to policy instruments weaken the impact;
- that it has not responded adequately to changes in circumstances such as the decline of the West Midlands;
- that so many places are still eligible for some type of aid that its impact is diluted;
- that policies run by different government departments are insufficiently coordinated.

On the other hand, supporters of locational policy point out:

– that economic activity can be encouraged by directing activity to areas where resources, particularly labour, are underused;
– that it can reduce the social and political problems arising from an unbalanced distribution of growth and unemployment;
– that housing and labour market problems hinder workers moving to the work to obtain a less unsatisfactory distribution of unemployment, so work has to be moved to the workers;
– that they are required to attract internationally mobile projects to the UK;
– that they give access to the EEC Regional Development Fund.

(*Source:* Harris, Stanley (ed.) 'BIM Report – The Importance of Regional Policy', *Management Today*, November 1983, p. 145)

STUDENT ASSIGNMENT 7.1

Regional Policy Issues

The BIM Report referred to in Case Study 7.1 went on to identify a number of questions for discussion. These included:

1. Should there be a shift away from the present concentration on capital-intensive industries towards job-intensive industries?
2. Should the present bias in policy towards support for manufacturing be changed to give more help to the service and commercial sectors, small firms, and new business?
3. In view of the difficulties involved in correcting regional problems with regional policy should more emphasis be placed on encouraging greater labour mobility?
4. Should regional policy concentrate more on seeking improvements in local business environments rather than subsidizing private investment?
5. Should regional aid be more concentrated with assistance targeted on specific localities rather than broad regions?
6. Are decisions about regional policy too centralized or could local authorities have a greater part to play?

Hold small group discussions on these questions and report back in plenary session. Write a short report summarizing the discussion. Consider carefully the economic, social, and political implications of your conclusions.

expansion. Eleven sites were designated as enterprise zones in 1980 and a further twelve were announced in November 1982. Geographically these zones are very small; most, but not all, are located in the inner areas of large cities such as Glasgow, Liverpool, Newcastle, and Swansea. Others are located in smaller towns such as Londonderry and Wakefield. The attractions of the zones for industrial and commercial businesses are

- one hundred per cent capital allowance on buildings;
- complete exemption from local authority rates;
- one hundred per cent relief from development land tax;
- a drastic reduction – or the complete waiving – of various regulatory controls and bureaucratic procedures;
- quick decisions from local authorities;
- special customs arrangements.

Much anxiety has been expressed by local authorities and business firms located outside the enterprise zones regarding what they see as unfair competition. Undoubtedly some firms have relocated to take advantage of enterprise zone benefits, and it seems likely that much of any success the zones may have enjoyed has been at the expense of adjacent areas.

7.9 The Management of Relocation

Within a time span of a couple of decades, about one company in every three undertakes a major locational project in the form either of redevelopment of its existing site; the rationalization of several dispersed sites and concentration in a central location; or a major relocation in an entirely new area.

According to Roy Brown,* Head of Capital Projects Division at PA Management Consultants, the management of relocation is likely to fall into three main phases:

- fact-gathering – the acquisition and analysis of basic information relating to the main locations under consideration;
- decision-making – the choice of location together with the acquisition of land and buildings;
- a final stage concerned with setting up project resources and controls; managing construction and fitting out; and the move itself.

At the fact-gathering phase the company will assemble a wide range of information relating (a) to each potential relocation site and (b) its own

* Brown, Roy, 'Motive Power for Moving Parts', *Management Today*, Supplement on Industrial Relocation, September, 1983

activities and situation. Much of the latter information will be readily available from internal company sources and will include

- staff/labour data;
- locations of major customers;
- a schedule of specialist bought-out services employed;
- the state of the product market, including competitors' activities and intentions;
- a calculation of present and projected spatial needs for office and industrial use.

On the basis of this information the company should be able to identify clearly the resources upon which it depends in terms of:

- manpower and specialist services;
- key proximity requirements relating to suppliers and customs;
- the amount and kinds of space required.

An analysis of this information should also help to determine the optimum timing of the move; the risks of loss of staff or business associated with the move; and the acceptability or otherwise of these.

This internal information probe might well be allied with staff consultation.

The second kind of information needed concerns the availability and quality of possible locations and will include:

- the availability and cost of skilled or trainable workers;
- the extent of government assistance available;
- transport and communications facilities available;
- the availability of industrial or commercial buildings for purchase or lease or of land suitable and available for development (and relevant cost data);
- data on housing and schools in the areas;
- other socio-environmental factors.

The assembly and analysis of relevant information is itself costly and time-consuming and due allowance should be made for this in the location project appraisal. Conversely, failure to obtain accurate and relevant information can be even more expensive.

The Institute of Manpower Studies affirms the importance of labour market analysis in location decisions. According to the Institute's John Atkinson its files bulge with cautionary tales of relocating companies who have either moved back within a very short time or struggled for many years with labour problems which with an analysis of the local labour market could have been foreseen and avoided.

7.10 The Importance of Labour in the Relocation Decision

The availability of suitable labour will often be an important consideration in the location decision. Historically, the concentration of firms in the same regions partially resulted from the attraction of an available pool of skilled labour – motor manufacturing in the Midlands, textiles in Lancashire and Yorkshire, for example. Currently, however, employers may see the existence of an available pool of skills as a negative factor, regarding people trained in traditional methods as more of a liability than an asset. Many companies may also be sceptical about the unemployed as potentially good quality workers believing that it is the least competent who are shaken out in redundancy situations. Alternatively, given ongoing and rapid technological change a pool of available skills could suggest a pool of obsolete skills. Companies will also be concerned about the climate of industrial relations which has grown up around a particular occupation or district.

For these reasons the key requirement today is more likely to be the availability of *trainable* labour rather than a pool of traditional skills. Are there people of the right calibre capable of being trained in the specific skills required by an incoming company? The calibre of a potential workforce is, however, difficult to assess. Some information will be available from local CBI offices, Chambers of Industry and Commerce, and the Manpower Services Commission (MSC).

A thorough going labour market analysis will require:

- an analysis of the local unemployment figures, by age, sex, and occupation;
- demographic data including assessments of the extent to which the area is gaining or losing population;
- knowledge of forecast school rolls for the future.

Much of this information is available from the Department of Employment, local JobCentres, and MSC offices, and from the 1981 Census of Employment. The local authority planning department may also be a useful source.

There are several ways in which manpower costs can be saved by the selection of sites that offer the best combination of grants and incentives which include:

- assistance with the training costs of modernization or job-creating projects available in all the assisted areas under S.7 of the Industry Act;
- under the Department of Trade and Industry Office and Service Industries Scheme (OSIS) a special feasibility study grant of 25 per cent (to a maximum of £10,000) towards the consultancy costs of investigat-

ing the potential of an assisted-area location — part of the investigation could be an assessment of the labour market;

- also under OSIS, employee removal grants to assist with removal costs of essential workers moving with a company to a new area;
- special grants varying in scope and amount offered by many areas.

7.11 The Acquisition of Industrial Buildings

In the assisted areas and New Towns a wide range of new and second-hand factories, warehouses, offices, and shops are available on attractive leasehold terms, through the development agencies. Low rent modern factories and workshops are available in many estates within the assisted areas and these are usually ready for immediate occupation. Where there is a need, discretionary rent-free periods may be available on long rental leases, in the light of market conditions. Detached factories may also be available for sale with payment spread over a period. Land may also be available for businesses to build their own specialized industrial premises. In Special Development Areas and Development Areas regional development grants are available for capital expenditure on new building and new plant and machinery (see Figure 7.1).

Outside the assisted areas the cost of property will be determined by market forces which will vary between areas. Negotiating the purchase of suitable commercial or industrial premises will require patient and skillful negotiation and hard work. The company may decide to buy-in the specialist services of one of the number of firms of property consultants to advise on negotiation and on such questions as whether to buy or lease.

The company must also consider whether its needs will be better served by the acquisition of primary or secondary industrial property. Schiller* describes the difference between the two as follows:

> A primary building can be defined as a modern single-storey structure of 15,000 square feet with a portal steel or concrete frame, concrete floor, cavity brick or block walls to a height of 8 feet, and an insulated, top-lighted roof. The eaves height should be of a minimum of 18 feet, and there should be good access, loading and manoeuvring space together with adequate vehicle parking and all the usual main services.
>
> Secondary property is older property built between 1945 and 1965 – and would have been reckoned prime property during that period. There would be a site cover of up to 75%, which is high by modern standards. Single-storey construction and good road access would be typical, together with a steel frame, an eaves height of approximately 12 feet and a total area of some 10,000 square feet. Obviously, secondary buildings are very different from the multi-storey

---

* Schiller, R., 'Sluggish Rents Favour Tenants', *Management Today*, Supplement on Industrial Relocation, September 1983

vacant mills left over from the last century, which can still be seen over much of northern England. Secondary property, in other words, may be fairly versatile in use and of quite a respectable standard.

Secondary rents tend to vary by about 50p per square foot lower than primary rents in the same location. Secondary rents also tend to be higher relative to primary rents in regions, such as London and the South East, where primary rents are highest, and relatively low in areas of lower primary rents. In general (with the notable exception of Scotland) the regional pattern of secondary rents is similar to the pattern of primary rents, but slightly more exaggerated.

Between May 1979 and September 1983 secondary rents grew by only 8 per cent compared with a 30 per cent growth in primary rents, thus widening the differential between secondary and primary rents. The highest industrial rents (about £4 per square foot) are payable in the West London and Thames Valley area. From this peak rents tend to fall with distance from London. Similarly, rents in large provincial cities tend to be higher than in the surrounding smaller towns, though there are many exceptions to this rule.

In recent years rents in high-rent areas have grown more rapidly than those in low-rent areas, widening the rent differential between areas where property is in highest demand and the more depressed areas. In general, and quite surprisingly, rents in western parts of Britain have grown faster than in eastern parts. For example, rents have grown faster in West London than East London; in the West Midlands than in the East Midlands; and in north-west England. In every case average rents for industrial and commercial property in 1980 were higher in the western area than in its eastern counterpart.

STUDENT ASSIGNMENT 7.2

Investigating the Location Decision of General Foods

General Foods Ltd, an international food processing company specializing in canned fruits and vegetables, has announced its intention to establish a large new factory in Britain. It has not yet considered alternative potential sites for locating its new plant. Investigate and report fully to the Board of General Foods on:

(a) why the new plant should be located in your area or
(b) why the new plant should be located in some other part of UK which you have selected.

7.12 Summary

1. All land in Britain is owned by the Crown, but organizations and individuals may own a legal estate in land.
2. Legal estates in land may be either freehold or leasehold.
3. The owner of a freehold estate effectively owns the land; a leaseholder has exclusive possession for a fixed number of years.
4. The uses to which land can be put are controlled by a complex body of statutory and common law restrictions.
5. Historically the availability of power and raw materials were important determinants of industrial location in Britain. The staple industries of the nineteenth and earlier twentieth centuries tended to locate on or near coalfields.
6. Governments exert a powerful influence on business location. Regional policy offers a wide range of financial and other incentives for firms who locate in the designated 'assisted areas'.
7. The effectiveness of regional policy is very difficult if not impossible to assess.
8. In the 1980s enterprise zones were introduced in an attempt to remove administrative and financial obstacles to enterprise for firms locating in the zones.
9. The management of relocation is a complex operation involving the three phases of fact-gathering; decision-making; and the setting up of resources, management of construction and fitting out, and the move itself.

Exercise

Review your understanding of the following:

> freehold and leasehold estates
> planning applications
> external economies of scale
> regional policy
> enterprise zones
> phases in the management of relocation

PART III
CONSTRAINTS ON RESOURCE
ACQUISITION AND UTILIZATION

8

Personnel Constraints

8.1 Trade Unions

The Trade Union and Labour Relations Act (TULRA), 1974, defines a trade union broadly as 'an organization consisting wholly or mainly of workers whose principal purposes include the regulation of relations between workers and employers and employers' associations'. Unions are required to submit annual reports and accounts to a Certification Officer appointed by the Secretary of State for Employment.

Under the Employment Protection Act (EPA), 1975, trade unions may apply for listing. A listed union acquires certain tax benefits, and only a listed union may make an effective application to a Certification Officer for a certificate of independence. To be successful in this a union must satisfy the Certification Officer that it is not under the domination or control of employers and is not liable to any kind of interference by employers. A certificate of independence confers considerable legal advantages on a union.

Britain has about 480 listed trade unions with total membership numbering over 11 million. The degree of organization (i.e. the proportion of unionized to total employees) varies considerably. Engineering is more highly organized than distribution, for example. In coal, railways, and docks membership is virtually 100 per cent.

Unions fall broadly into three main categories:

- craft unions which organize workers belonging to the same trade or having the same skills;
- general unions which allow unrestricted entry;
- industrial unions which restrict entry to all grades employed within a particular industry.

In practice these distinctions are blurred. Union mergers in the present century have produced multi-craft unions such as the Electrical and Plumbers' Trade Union. The Amalgamated Engineering Union now functions as a general and industrial union recruiting all grades within engineering industries and as a craft union representing skilled engineering workers in other industries.

At workplace level elected shop stewards handle negotiations over a myriad of day-to-day issues that inevitably arise in any workplace. Shop stewards may call in full-time officials when procedure requires this or when their expertise is required. In establishments of any size negotiations will often be conducted by a multi-union shop stewards' committee whose elected chairman becomes convenor. Shop stewards have statutory rights to time off for training and to carry out their industrial relations duties.

8.2 The Functions of Trade Unions

The broad functions of trade unions can be summarized under three headings:

- representation
- regulation
- participation

The most important function of a trade union is to represent its members' interests to managers, employers, employers' associations, and even governments. Although pay and conditions of work are important union objectives, at a more fundamental level unions are concerned to uphold the dignity of employees as individuals. If a union fails in its fundamental task of representation, it no longer serves its purpose. Thus, like companies, professional bodies and most other organizations, trade unions exist to promote a sectional interest.

The means by which unions seek to represent their members' interests is collective bargaining which is essentially a rule-making process, i.e. the rules are seen in the contents of collective agreements. The effects of this regulation is to limit the independent decision-making freedom of employers in order to protect or enhance the pay, conditions, security, status and self-respect of employees. For example, a collective agreement secures certain rights for workers, for example to certain rates of pay, not to have to work beyond a certain number of normal hours, not to be arbitrarily sacked or disciplined and so on.

Finally, unions are structured to encourage member participation so that through his union a worker can exercise an influence on the rules that are made and how they are applied. Typically this works as follows.

Union members belong to branches based on geographical area or workplace. Branches elect delegates and send resolutions to the union's annual national conference, the supreme policy-making body of the union. Between conferences, executive power is vested in the national executive committee which consists of full-time officers of the union and elected lay members and which is accountable to conference. In larger unions there is usually a regional and/or district structure staffed by full-time officers responsible variously to national officers or to regional or district lay committees (see Case Study 8.1).

CASE STUDY 8.1

Democracy in Trade Unions

On 12 July 1983 Mr Norman Tebbit, Secretary of State for Employment, announced the government's legislative proposals for greater democracy in trade unions in three important areas.

- Elections for the governing bodies of trade unions
- Strike ballots
- The political activities of trade unions

The legislation will require elections to the governing bodies of unions to comply with the following principles:

- Voting must be secret and by ballot paper
- There must be an equal and unrestricted opportunity to vote
- Every union member should be able to vote directly for members of the governing body

In the case of union 'authorized or endorsed' industrial action, immunity in tort will be conditional on the support of union members concerned being tested in a secret ballot. In other words when a trade union calls or endorses a strike it will either have to ballot its members who are being called out to retain immunity or accept that calling or endorsing a strike without a ballot forfeits immunity. Without immunity the trade union would be at risk of being sued for an injunction and its funds would be at risk of an action for damages.

The government accepts that a trade union should be able to adopt political objectives and to set up political funds. However, the authorization of a political fund should be subject to review by a periodic ballot of the membership. The present members of trade unions should not be bound forever by a ballot that may well have been taken before any of them were born. The 1913 Trade Union Act would be amended to require that political objectives and funds should be submitted to ballot at least every ten years. The Trade Union Act embodying the government's proposals on industrial democracy received Royal Assent in July 1984.

(*Sources: Employment News*, 10, Department of Employment, July 1983. Department of Employment *Press Notice*, 12, July 1983)

STUDENT ASSIGNMENT 8.1

Trade Union Democracy

1. Read Case Study 8.1.
2. Consider the following comments on union democracy and then answer the questions at 3 below:

Unions are established to protect and improve the living standards of their members; the only criterion of leadership effectiveness relevant for their members is the extent to which they achieve this end. Autocratic leaders are democratic in so far as they represent the interests of their members *vis-à-vis* the employers. Union elections are unimportant because incumbent office-holders can always secure their re-election given rank and file indifference.

V. L. Allen

Our trade unions claim to be democratic institutions and indeed the claim must be allowed if trade unions are compared with many other institutions that make the same claim.

H. A. Clegg

A strong and sustained effort on the part of the membership of any union can change policy and leadership. If such efforts are rarely made it may be assumed that the membership is tolerably contented. To those who argue that the explanation is apathy rather than contentment, the reply may be made that union members can still vote with their feet.

H. A. Clegg

Those who complain about lack of democracy when they don't like what union leaders are doing are often the first to complain about lack of leadership when they don't like what the members are doing.

Democracy at Work, BBC Publications, 1977

At workplace level democracy is easier to ensure. Shop stewards are elected annually. Members are represented by fellow workers who share their problems and are in touch with their members.

Democracy at Work

Non-elected union officials does not necessarily imply lack of democracy if those officials are under the control of lay committees which in turn are freely elected by the membership.

Democracy at Work

Postal ballots increase the rate of participation in trade union elections, increasing the *quantity* but doing little for the *quality* of involvement. The press and other media use this as an opportunity to influence opinion by the selective publicity given to different candidates.

3. (a) Compare and contrast union democracy with the essential features of democracy relating to some of the following:

    (i) a local government authority (e.g. county council);

    (ii) a political party;

    (iii) parliamentary democracy;

    (iv) a public limited company;

    (v) a multinational corporation.

Consider, for example, the levels, frequencies, and methods of participation.

(b) Why, in your opinion, are trade unions required to be more democratic than most other representative bodies?

(c) In your opinion will the government's legislation succeed in making unions more democratic?

8.3 Collective Bargaining

Collective bargaining covers 'any negotiations in which employees do not negotiate individually and on their own behalf but do so collectively through representatives. The object of collective bargaining is to reach a voluntary agreement about terms and conditions of work and pay'.[*] British industrial relations have evolved on the basis of a general consensus that voluntary (i.e. not legally imposed) collective bargaining is the most effective way of regulating relations between employees and employers. Today the pay and conditions of the majority of British employees are fixed by voluntary collective bargaining.

A number of pre-conditions are necessary for effective collective bargaining:

[*] *Report of the Royal Commission on Trade Unions and Employers' Associations (The Donovan Report)*, HMSO, 1968

- there must be a willingness on the part of both sides to negotiate;
- workers must be involved in the settlement of pay and conditions as a group which implies they are organized and represented by a trade union which has gained recognition by the employer to negotiate for them;
- there must be a sufficient degree of organization among workers and, if employers are to act collectively, among employers. Otherwise agreements may not command adequate support.

As a form of *joint* decision making collective bargaining may be distinguished from *joint consultation* which involves finding out and perhaps taking into account employees' views but which leaves decision making power with management. Joint decision making can only take place where there is an *independent* union representing employees.

8.4 Industrial Conflict

Whilst it is true that workers and employers have a common interest in ensuring the success of the organization, the implicit basis of collective bargaining is that there are also conflicts of interest between them.

The most manifest conflict is about pay or more broadly about the division of the proceeds of production between labour and capital. In a company, for example, conflicts arise because there is no commonly accepted formula for allocating the firm's revenue between, say, wages, profits, and investment. Unsurprisingly, Department of Employment returns show overwhelmingly the major causes of strikes are disputes about pay.

Conflict also arises over job security. When, for example, technological innovation or market decline throw up the question of redundancies, the values and goals of employers and workers will diverge. The efficiency-centred outlook of management will clash with the security-centred values of workers who do not wish to be forced out of their jobs.

Evidence of such conflict was seen in the growing number of industrial actions over redundancies in the late 1960s and in the 1970s and more recently in the prolonged miners' dispute of 1984–5 over the closure of 'uneconomic' pits. It has even been argued that the increasing concern of employees (and governments) with the defence of jobs has constrained managements' abilities to respond to structural and technological change. 'Fear of the dole is the biggest obstacle to industrial change in Britain.'*

Yet further conflict derives from the division of authority stemming from the primacy of management or organizational objectives, i.e. there is

---

* Hawkins, K., *The Management of Industrial Relations*, Penguin Books, 1978, p. 14

conflict about the limits of management's right to make decisions. The frontiers of management prerogative have been pushed back as more and more issues have been brought within the scope of collective bargaining. Before World War II, for example, managements usually claimed the rights to 'hire and fire', to discipline employees as they thought fit, to decide annual holidays, to impose health and safety standards, and so on. Today all these and many other issues are often jointly regulated in collective bargaining. It is nevertheless still true that many fundamental decisions e.g. plant location, closures, mergers, and long-term investment plans, remain firmly within the discretion of managers.

Technological innovation is often an element in conflict both in terms of the insecurity it breeds about future job prospects as well as in terms of losses of job satisfaction in those cases where employees are relegated from skilled craftsman status to mere machine minders. In certain industries the extreme fragmentation of tasks and the control systems this involves often engender industrial disharmony. In his account of industrial relations in the Ford Motor Company, for example, Beynon* writes that 'the history of the assembly line is a history of conflict over speed-up – the process whereby the pace of work demanded of the operative is systematically increased'.

8.5 Regulating Conflict

Acceptance of the view that conflict is inherent in modern industry does not imply that it is necessarily damaging. According to Hawkins 'the acid test of good management is the extent to which conflict can be predicted and controlled' or directed towards constructive ends.

The most important way of regulating conflict is to provide for its expression in jointly agreed, clear, and comprehensive disputes procedures established through collective bargaining. In this way collective bargaining allows for the peaceful resolution of conflict rather than its suppression or denial.

Faulty or inadequate communication can be a major background cause of industrial conflict, especially in larger organizations. It follows that a further way of regulating conflict is by improving communications within the organization. The importance of this was emphasized by the CBI in its evidence to the Bullock Commission on Industrial Democracy. Among detailed objectives listed by the CBI are:

- to ensure all employees are aware of reasons for major decisions which affect them and the factors taken into account by management in

* Beynon, H., *Working for Ford*, Allen Lane, 1975, p. 178

arriving at these decisions, and to ensure that management is aware of the views of all employees before taking the decision;

- to ensure all employees are aware of the business situation of the enterprise;
- to inform all employees of the enterprise's forward operating plans and to provide for discussion of these.

8.6 The Levels of Bargaining

In most sectors of employment bargaining takes place at more than one level. Almost all industries have some kind of industry-wide bargaining machinery for settling basic terms and conditions of employment. Until the mid-1960s the industrial relations system was essentially one of industry-wide agreements negotiated in National Joint Industrial Councils (NJICs) between unions and employers or employers' associations.

Many larger multi-plant firms – Ford, for example – have developed their own bargaining machinery modelled on the NJIC system. The National Coal Board, British Rail, and other public corporations as well as the National Health Service and Local Government also have national bargaining arrangements. The majority of small firms frequently follow NJIC pay and conditions irrespective of whether their workers are unionized or not.

National agreements have rarely attempted to regulate the many issues that arise at the workplace which it was traditionally assumed could be safely left to management decisions at that level. This arrangement worked well until the advent of full employment during and after the Second World War. In the changed labour-market conditions workers increasingly rejected and challenged unilateral managerial decision making, and over post-war years a second tier of collective bargaining has evolved at company and especially at plant level.

By the time the Royal Commission on Trade Unions and Employers' Associations reported in 1968 there were 'two systems of industrial relations operating side by side but almost completely divorced from one another. The formal system operated at national or industry level . . . and . . . . The informal system, functioning at the level of the plant or firm, largely in the hands of shop stewards and local managers'.

By 1975 a study* of manufacturing establishments employing more than 200 workers showed that by a considerable margin the workplace was the most important level of bargaining in British manufacturing industry. Most workplace bargaining was carried out by teams of shop stewards independent of the official union organization. The full-time union officer

* Daniel, W. W., *The Next Stage of Incomes Policy*, PEP Report 568, 1977

was typically only brought in when negotiations were deadlocked.

Nevertheless the importance of industry-wide agreements and their influence over earnings in particular should not be underestimated. In 1976 further research** suggested that the decline of the formal (NJIC) system had been less than hitherto thought and that the regulative importance of industry-wide agreements had increased.

8.7 Bargaining Sanctions

Trade unions possess a range of sanctions which they can use to exert pressure on management to achieve bargaining objectives. Of these, the most commonly reported is the strike. However, strikes are not the only available sanctions and it would be misleading to assess the state of industrial relations by examining only the strike trends. Sanctions may take the form of overtime bans, go-slows, work-to-rule, lack of co-operation, all of which have the advantage from the union's viewpoint of imposing costs on the employer without excessive losses to the union or to employees. Poor employee relations may be reflected in high rates of

STUDENT ASSIGNMENT 8.2

The North West Division of T. W. Gates Ltd

The North West Division of T. W. Gates Ltd, a large ice-cream manufacturing and distributing company, has three wholesale depots each controlled by a Depot Sales Manager and each serving one of the three areas within the Division (Merseyside; Greater Manchester; and the North Lancashire/Cumbria area). In all there are 120 'rounds' each operated by a van roundsman whose job is to deliver a variety of ice cream products to various retail shops, hotels, restaurants, and so on. The roundsmen are all members of the General Workers' Union (GWU) and are represented by shop stewards who negotiate at Divisional and Depot levels.

The roundsmen are paid a flat hourly wage rate (estimated to be 10 per cent lower than the 'going rate' in the local labour market) but with a high percentage bonus payable when a certain 'difficult' sales target is achieved. Opportunities for overtime working (paid at a 25 per cent premium) vary with seasonal fluctuations in product demand and with weather conditions.

** Elliot, R. F. and Steele, R., 'The Importance of National Wage Negotiations' *British Journal of Industrial Relations*, March 1976

It is thought that many enhance their weekly earnings by operating a variety of 'fiddles' either at the expense of their employer or their customers. It is rumoured that the company 'turns a blind eye' to these practices which are less costly than paying extra money on a regular basis.

The recruitment and selection of van roundsmen is organized by Depot Sales Managers, who are also responsible for training which consists of each new recruit spending their first week accompanying one of the existing salesmen on his round.

The job of the roundsman is often tedious and demanding, particularly during summer peaks, when in the words of one roundsman, 'It's like being a character in a silent movie that's been speeded up'. Each roundsman is responsible for selecting the range and quantities of each of over 100 products for each day – which means he has to predict what his customers will demand. Amongst his other duties are loading and unloading the vehicle; driving, often in heavily congested city traffic which makes delivery to busy city shops very difficult; maintaining the vehicle; invoicing and cash collection; daily stock and cash balancing. Since the roundsman is the link between the company and its customers he is expected to be smartly turned out and courteous, and generally to maintain good customer relations.

The morale of the van roundsmen is at a low level, absenteeism has risen, and labour turnover has been running at the rate of 36 per cent. Customer relations have deteriorated considerably, with more and more complaints about the quality of service. Monthly sales figures are falling and the North West Division's financial position has worsened with little prospect of achieving its annual target rate of profit.

Divisional management is increasingly concerned about the poor performance. Management, aware that no progress can be made without a substantial improvement in employee relations, invite the GWU shop stewards to meet them in order to consider ways of dealing with the problem. The stewards agree to this, on the understanding that all aspects of pay and conditions are negotiable.

The student group divides into 'workers' and 'management' to consider the following questions. Questions 2 and 3 should be dealt with by respectively 'management' and 'worker' students.

1. Identify the personnel problems at T. W. Gates Ltd, North West Division. What are their causes?
2. As Divisional Personnel Officer prepare a list of bargaining objectives you would set out to achieve.
3. As convenor of the shop stewards prepare a similar list of bargaining objectives.
4. To what extent are the objectives in harmony or in conflict?
5. Identify alternative courses of action to deal with the problems and select those most likely to achieve the objectives.

STUDENT ASSIGNMENT 8.3

T. W. Gates – A Negotiating Exercise

The student group is divided into 'management' and 'workers'. 'Management' students should appoint a Divisional Personnel Officer and his three-man negotiating team. 'Worker' students should elect a convenor and three other shop stewards to negotiate with management.

Act out the negotiations and record the outcome in the form of a collective agreement.

Students not directly participating in the negotiations should attempt to evaluate critically the performance of the negotiating teams.

labour turnover, absenteeism, poor morale. By the late 1970s the overtime ban had become the most common form of industrial action.

Employers' sanctions include lock-outs and in extreme cases dismissal, though the latter is subject to legal constraints.

8.8 Incomes Policy

The main purpose of incomes policies is to curb inflation by controlling collective wage bargaining. Incomes policy challenges and constrains the freedom of managements and unions to conduct their business in their own way regardless of wider consequences. Every British post-war government has introduced some form of incomes policy. Whether voluntary or statutory the main elements in incomes policy are:

- a percentage or flat rate limit on allowable pay increases i.e. the 'norm';
- criteria (if any) for exceptions to the norm;
- a mechanism for monitoring pay settlements.

CASE STUDY 8.2

Cabinet Set 3pc Target

Unions attack 'cut in pay'
By James Wightman, Political Correspondent
The Cabinet agreed speedily yesterday to try to limit pay rises in the public sector to 3 per cent for 1984–85 as a principal part of attempts to

contain Government spending in the coming financial year.

The target, half a per cent below last year's and the lowest since the Conservatives returned to office in 1979, will affect more than 2 million State employees, mainly in the Civil Service, Armed Forces and National Health Service.

It will not apply to local authorities and nationalized industries, although Ministers are hoping for similarly low pay increases in those areas of the public sector as well.

Ministers also hope that the figure, although not being projected as 'a norm', will help to induce further pay moderation in the private sector.

(*Source: Daily Telegraph*, 17 September 1983)

In the Spring of 1985, as government ministers repeatedly emphasized the importance of wage restraint as a means of creating more employment and of containing inflation, a number of 'market-orientated' incomes policies were being advocated including a proposal from Professor Richard Layard of the London School of Economics under which employers would be taxed for excessive wage increases, and the proceeds recycled to the better-behaved firms or to those less able to afford increases.

Despite their popularity with governments, the application of such policies has resulted in numerous personnel policy difficulties for private and public employers. Among these have been:

1. THE EROSION OF DIFFERENTIALS

Whenever flat rate norms or exceptions for low pay have been allowed earnings differentials – e.g. between skilled and semi-skilled grades – have been narrowed. The compression of differentials not only creates inefficiency by distorting the allocation of labour, but can also harm employee relations and trigger industrial action. For example, the flat rate norms of 1975–77 phases of incomes policy contributed to a substantial narrowing of differentials in car assembly firms. This provoked a series of strikes by small groups of skilled workers who demanded restoration of traditional differentials and separate negotiating facilities. Finally when incomes policy ends, in the scramble to restore eroded differentials wage inflation tends to rebound, offsetting any temporary gains achieved.

2. PAY INCREASES NOT LINKED TO PRODUCTIVITY

The 'norm' comes to be regarded as an entitlement irrespective of the fortunes of the employer or productivity changes. Consequently groups, who in the absence of controls may have settled for increases below the norm now demand the full increase allowable under the policy. Pay increases unrelated to productivity improvements raise unit costs of production and may make the organization less competitive, particularly in export markets.

3. ATTEMPTS TO EVADE

Unwarranted job-regradings, 'phoney' promotions, mushrooming over-time, and extra fringe benefits all provide evidence of attempts by management and unions to evade incomes policies. Employers who are unable to recruit additional skilled labour or reward increases in produc-tivity may be particularly tempted.

4. PAY ANOMALIES

The timing of incomes policies can create pay anomalies with groups of workers doing similar jobs, perhaps even within the same organization, getting different rates of pay because of annual pay settlements occurring just before or after the date of application of a new phase of policy. Such anomalies may produce much discontent, poor morale, and possibly unrest.

5. DISTORTED PAY STRUCTURES

Pay structures designed to achieve certain objectives will be distorted if, for example, employers are unable to pay 'merit' increases linked to individual performance.

STUDENT ASSIGNMENT 8.4

The Influence of Incomes Policy on Personnel Management

Faced with rapidly rising inflation, the Government has announced the immediate introduction of a statutory incomes policy for the coming twelve months with a 5 per cent norm and no exceptions. Consider the effects of this on the following organizations:

1. Company A, a large domestic electrical appliance manufacturer, has been negotiating with its unions on the introduction of robot technology. The unions fearing redundancies and a downgraded

status for many members have been highly resistant to management proposals. Hence negotiations have been long and difficult. However, it now seems that the company is on the verge of a settlement involving, *inter alia*, pay increases for different grades of staff of up to 15 per cent. At this point the Government announces its policy.

2. Company B, a processed food manufacturer, has just settled a pay increase of 10 per cent for its semi-skilled shopfloor workers. Pay negotiations are about to commence with skilled craftsmen when the Government policy is announced.

3. Company C, an electronics manufacturer, has plans to expand over the next two years. The expansion will necessitate an increase in their computer technician staff who are known to be in short supply. The Government's pay policy has just been announced.

In each case, what, if anything, can the company management do to deal with the problems?

8.9 Employment Law

Almost every aspect of the employment relationship is subject to statute and case law. In the last 25 years or so more than a dozen Acts of Parliament have considerably widened the scope of employee rights extending them into areas which were already covered in many other European countries. Many of these rights were brought together in the Employment Protection (Consolidation) Act (EPCA) 1978, subsequently amended by the Employment Act (EA) 1980. Those concerned with health and safety (e.g. the Factories Act 1961 and the Office, Shop, and Railway Premises Act 1963) are being progressively superceded by Regulations issued under the Health and Safety at Work Act 1974. Although not law in themselves, the many codes of practice associated with the legislation can have important effects.

In 1982 a further Employment Act increased protection for non-trade union members in a closed shop; provided for regular secret ballots on closed shop agreements; removed certain legal immunities enjoyed by trade unions who organize industrial actions; and encouraged employers to develop arrangements for consulting and involving their employees.

The Trade Union Act 1984 carried forward the government's programme of union reform by requiring secret ballots before strikes, for elections to union executives and on political funds.

Among the statutory individual employment rights (and, of course, corresponding obligations on employers) are the rights

• not to be directly or indirectly discriminated against on grounds of sex or marital status. Direct discrimination consists of treating a person on

grounds of sex or marital status less favourably than others would be treated in the same circumstances. Indirect discrimination consists of applying a requirement or condition which (intentionally or not) adversely affects women more than men and cannot be justified on grounds other than sex or marital status (Sex Discrimination Act 1975).
- not to be directly or indirectly discriminated against on grounds of race, colour, nationality, or ethnic or national origins (Race Relations Act 1975)
- not to be unfairly dismissed (EPCA 1978 and Employment Act 1980)
- to redundancy pay (Redundancy Payments Act 1965)
- to a written statement of the main terms and conditions of employment (within thirteen weeks of starting) (EPCA 1978)
- to minimum periods of notice (EPCA 1978)
- to equal pay for men and women doing 'broadly similar' or equally rated work (Equal Pay Act 1970)
- to guaranteed payment if the employee is not provided with work (EPCA 1978)
- for expectant mothers the rights not to lose their jobs, to return to work after the baby is born and to maternity pay from her employer (EPCA 1978 and Employment Act 1980)
- not to be victimized for trade union activities.

Some of these rights are subject to a qualifying period of continuous employment with an employer, others are not available to part-time workers. In some cases stringent tests or conditions are required to establish entitlement to the right. All the rights are complex and subject to modification by decisions of industrial tribunals or courts. One example, the law on dismissal, will suffice to indicate this complexity.

Except in the case of dismissal for union activity which is automatically unfair, the right not to be unfairly dismissed does not apply to:

- employees with less than two years continuous service with the same employer;
- most part-time employees (unless they have worked at least eight hours a week for five years or more).

A claim for unfair dismissal must be submitted to an Industrial Tribunal within three months of the date of the end of employment.

Under the EPCA 1978, as amended by the EA of 1982, dismissal will be unfair when workers are dismissed

- for union activity;
- for pregnancy;
- when unfairly selected for redundancy.

In deciding whether a dismissal is fair or not the Tribunal will ask (a) did the employer have a fair reason for dismissing the worker? and (b) did the employer act reasonably in dismissing the worker? The Tribunal will assess the latter on the basis of an examination of the employer's behaviour and see how it compares with standards laid down in the ACAS Code of Practice *Disciplinary Practice and Procedures*. Finally, if a claim succeeds the Industrial Tribunal may order financial compensation or (less usually) reinstatement or re-engagement of the employee.

In addition to the provisions of the EPCA 1978, under the Sex Discrimination and Race Relations Act it is also unfair to dismiss employees on grounds of sex, marital status, race, colour, or ethnic origin. Under the EA 1982, it is unfair to dismiss an employee who does not belong to a union in a closed shop.

Employment law is a highly complex and continuously changing specialism. It is inappropriate to do more than introduce the subject here. Enough has been said to indicate the extent to which the law constrains personnel policies.

STUDENT ASSIGNMENT 8.5

Employment Law – Discovery Exercise

You have recently been appointed personnel manager in an engineering company employing about 1,000 people. There is a union membership agreement in operation which means that all employees are union members.

In order to survive in the face of strong international competition your company must introduce new technology which will automate many of the production processes. It is anticipated that about half the present jobs will disappear over the next two or three years.

Find out:

1. Which legislation is relevant in this situation?
2. What precise provisions are laid down?
3. What would you need to do to comply with the requirements of the law?

8.10 The Miners' Strike of 1984–85

What happens in the field of industrial relations may both strongly influence and be strongly influenced by events and changing conditions in the wider society. Nothing in recent industrial history has demonstrated this more powerfully than the year-long miners' strike of 1984–85 which has had and continues to have profound and ongoing impacts on the wider labour movement, on British politics, on the economy and economic policy, on the level of social harmony, as well as on the bargaining climate itself.

Competing analyses of the miners' dispute currently on offer tend to vary with the political perspectives of the analysts. A commonly held view from the Left, for example, is that the miners' strike was deliberately provoked by a government determined to weaken the strongest section of the British trade union movement. According to this view Mrs Thatcher, having already weakened organized labour by mass unemployment and anti-union legislation, appointed Mr Ian McGregor as NCB Chairman at enormous cost ostensibly to make the coal industry more efficient and 'to balance its books' (or even make it 'profitable') but really as an 'axeman' who could successfully close down a sizeable section of the industry and who, if necessary, could defeat the militant miners' leader Arthur Scargill who had been elected to office with an overwhelming 70 per cent of the vote at a pit-head ballot. Mr McGregor had already taken on the unions in the privately-owned US coal industry, and had carried out a substantial reduction in the size of the British Steel Corporation.

An alternative view from the government and its supporters saw the strike essentially as a challenge to democracy. By refusing to hold a national ballot, Mr Scargill had indicated his determination to manipulate the NUM's constitutional machinery and his members in order to mount a political strike intended to unseat the government and bring about an historic victory for the working class. The use of mass picketing and the apparent endorsement of, or at least refusal to repudiate, intimidation and violence, and the union's readiness to flout court orders, for example to call off flying pickets, provided further evidence of the political nature of the strike.

No doubt there is some truth in theories from the political Left and Right. It is likely, however, that both sides fail to emphasize sufficiently the real issues underlying the dispute – the preservation of mining communities and jobs. Clearly those living in pit villages, both miners themselves and their wives and families (the flourishing Women Against Pit Closures Movement offered enormous support to the striking miners), were prepared to suffer both debt and hardship in order to defend their way of life.

Political analyses of the strike and their evaluation are well beyond the scope of this book. However, it is at least necessary in a chapter that offers an up-to-date account of the role of trade unions, collective bargaining, and industrial conflict, to acknowledge that the conduct of the strike has raised many wide issues that may have considerable relevance for other negotiators, for the general pattern of industrial relations in Britain in coming years, and for the wider society. Some of these are formulated below as a series of questions.

- What will be the nature of the 'demonstration effect' of the miners' strike on other trade unions, especially public sector unions, i.e. in what way has the bargaining environment been affected by the dispute?
- Does the decisive shift in the balance of power from union to management in the coal industry limit the union's capacity to fight future pit closures?
- To what extent can the deep divisions which have arisen in mining communities be healed, and what will be the operating implications for the NCB of striking and non-striking miners working together?
- What are the implications for union strength and membership which as a consequence of mass unemployment was already in decline even before the miner's strike began?
- What effects will there be on the unity and strength of the TUC given its failure to mobilize its own member unions to support the miners as Congress had agreed to do?
- What questions are raised about relations between government and the boards of nationalized industries following the dispute?
- Given repeated scenes of open and violent conflict between police and pickets, what are the implications for relations between the police and the community?
- How useful are legislative attempts to control the conduct of industrial relations?

The answers to these and other questions will only be seen as events unfold. What seems clear, however, is that the miners' dispute will be seen as an important landmark in the history of British industrial relations.

8.11 Summary

1. Trade unions are responsible to their members whose views and aspirations they represent to employers and management.
2. The main activity of trade unions is collective bargaining. Collective agreements contain rules which protect employees, but at the same time restrict management freedom to make decisions independently.
3. Trade unions are structured to allow the participation of members in making union policies. However, in July 1984 in the wake of growing concern and debate about trade union power, the Conservative government legislated for greater union democracy.
4. Collective bargaining implies conflicts of interest between employers

and employees. Conflicts may arise over pay, job security, the right to decide issues, technology, and many other factors. Collective bargaining takes place at national, company, and plant level. In the post-war period of full employment plant bargaining has mushroomed and the influence of national bargaining has declined.

5. At plant level, shop stewards negotiate with local managements over innumerable day-to-day issues. The widening scope of plant bargaining means that more and more issues are jointly rather than unilaterally decided by management.

6. Most post-war governments have used incomes policy to control collective bargaining. These have imposed a further set of constraints on personnel policymaking in organizations.

7. A complex mass of employment law places many further constraints on organizations affecting virtually every aspect of personnel policy from recruitment and selection to dismissal.

Exercise

Review your understanding of the following:

independent trade unions
union democracy
collective bargaining
incomes policy
discrimination in employment
unfair dismissal

Further Reading

Whincup, Michael, *Modern Employment Law*, Heinemann.
McCarthy, W. J., (ed.) *Trade Unions* Penguin Books, 1972.
Muir, J. *Industrial Relations, Procedures and Agreements* Gower Publishing Co., 1981.

9

The Ecology of Natural Resources

9.1 Introduction

Business enterprises engage in the production of goods or services for sale in markets. Such production, overwhelmingly the most important business activity, depends essentially upon a sustained and steady stream of resources extracted or harvested from and eventually returned to the biophysical environment. For the business system as a whole, whether considered nationally or globally, the annual flow of inputs of many diverse materials acquired in these ways is truly immense.

The ultimate resource base for the activities of all business enterprises is therefore the natural environment; economic systems are parasitic on ecosystems. Consequently inherent in the extraction, processing, and subsequent transformations of materials into outputs of goods and services by business enterprises, there are complex interactions between these enterprises and the environment, some of which have important ecological or social consequences.

Traditionally business students accustomed to working within the system boundary of the business firm, or of the national economy, have been left largely unaware of these interactions and connections and consequently have glimpsed but a partial and misleading view of the resource acquisition and allocation processes. Such an exclusively business centred view of resource processes yields a rather narrow and fragmentary understanding and provides only limited insights tending to conceal many currently important economic and ecological issues surrounding the continuing availability of natural resources in the late twentieth century.

The use of natural environment as a resource base or waste disposal 'sink' for the residuals of production and consumption may conflict with its other functions – economic, ecological, or aesthetic. The mining of minerals in Snowdonia, for example, may destroy traditional farming patterns; unique mountain ecosystems or wildlife may be irretrievably lost; and millions may be robbed of the loveliness of the forested mountains and less tangibly of the tranquility and stimulus to reflective thought and spiritual catharsis which derive from a 'communion with nature' in such beautiful surroundings.

'Trade-offs' such as these which affect the quality of life of us all largely arise from business decisions concerning the acquisition, use, or disposal of natural resources.

9.2 A Materials Balance Model

The materials balance model* is derived from the first law of thermodynamics from which we know that though matter may be transformed it cannot be destroyed. Applied to the economic system this law of the conservation of matter tell us that the total tonnage of inputs of fossil fuels, minerals, plant products, waste, and other natural resources into production processes are not 'consumed' in any physical sense, but persist albeit in changed forms as residuals which must be either disposed of to the environment or recycled as further inputs to production. Consequently there is a continuous interaction between the economy and the environment as resources are harvested or extracted and eventually disposed of into the atmosphere, water, or land.

In Figure 9.1 the economy is contained in the large rectangle and the environment lies outside it. The 'production' box represents all productive activities in the economic system in which inputs of extracted minerals, metals, fuels, gases, and organic matter (I_A) and recycled inputs (I_R) are transformed into final products (F) and residual wastes (W_P).

The 'final demand' or consumption sector of the economy also generates wastes (W_F), some of which (W_R) are recycled back to production.

Since, in accordance with the law of conservation, all material resources used in economic production and consumption are eventually returned to the environment as wastes, two identities for materials flows between sectors of the economy and the environment are indicated.

For the production sector of the economy we obtain

(1) $I_A + I_R \equiv W_P + F$

For the final demand sector we obtain

(2) $F \equiv W_F + W_R \equiv W_F + W_C + I_R$

Combining (1) and (2) we find that for the economy as a whole

* The discussion of this model draws on Nijkamp, P., *Theory and Application of Environmental Economics*, North Holland Publishing Company, 1977, vol. 1, pp. 5–14

Figure 9.1.   Materials balance model.

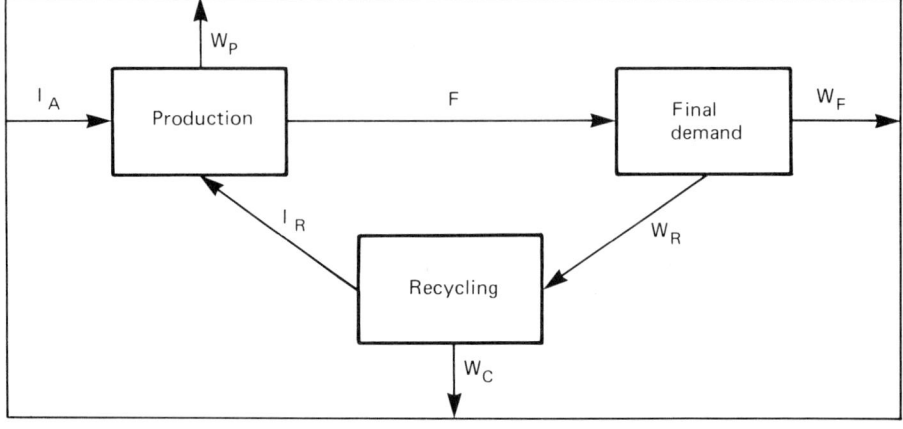

I = inputs; F = final products; W = wastes

(3) $I_A + I_R \equiv W_P + W_F + W_C + I_R$

or

(4) $I_A \equiv W_P + W_F + W_C$

The combined flows of energy and materials from production and consumption are now seen to appear as waste flows. These relationships, however, are static in the sense that the timing of the various flows is ignored. In more dynamic terms, for any given time period waste flows may be less than, equal to, or greater than the resource extraction depending on how much 'embodiment' of materials is taking place in stocks of capital and how much 'sudden death' depreciation is occurring from past flows. ('Capital' here is used to denote long-lived producer goods, housing, and consumer durables whose life is not yet exhausted. 'Sudden death' depreciation occurs when capital is withdrawn from use or abandoned; for example, when a used car is thrown on a scrap heap.) Nevertheless for any period it is reasonable to assume that the two flows will be approximately equal.

A number of important conclusions may be drawn from the materials balance model:

- the model indicates that all economic activities exert *inevitable* claims on the environment both for inputs (the resource base of business activity) and for output (the disposal of residuals);
- since, on a global scale, the immense growth of population, industrialization, and urbanization in the present century has placed growing

pressures on the assimilative capacity of the environment and on finite stocks of many important resources, concern is expressed that in respect of both claims we may be approaching critical limits. In other words the exhaustion of some non-renewable resources may be imminent and pollution may exceed the assimilative capacity of local or global ecosystems. The destruction of many of the world's great coniferous forests by 'acid rain' detailed in Case Study 9.1 is a case in point.

CASE STUDY 9.1

The Rain that Kills

The Black Forest *is* dying.

'If pollution continues at the present rate, most of the fir and spruce trees in the Black Forest will be dead by the 1990s,' says Gerhard Weiser, agriculture and forestry minister for Baden-Wurttemberg. In the past two years, say ministry specialists, the number of healthy firs has dropped alarmingly from 66 per cent to only one per cent. In some areas, 94 per cent of spruce trees are also affected.

What is killing the trees is 'acid rain'. This is produced when the gases emitted by smelters, fossil-fuelled power stations, oil refineries, factories and car exhausts stream into the atmosphere. Sulphur dioxide and nitrogen oxides combine with moisture and oxygen to form sulphuric and nitric acids, which fall to the ground again in acid rain.

Acid rain is a problem throughout the developed world. In Canada and the US, thousands of lakes and rivers are no longer able to support plants and fish. Air pollution from the giant industrial centres of the Great Lakes is the biggest thorn in current Canadian-US relations.

For the Germans, the problem extends well beyond the Black Forest, holding the better part of the ancient woodlands of Central Europe is its poisoned embrace. In Bavaria, the state premier, Franz–Josef Strauss, warned industry last week: 'I cannot wait until the forests are dead before talking action on pollution'. In North Rhine Westphalia, the agriculture and forestry minister, Hans–Otto Baeumer, says: 'Forests which appeared healthy last autumn are virtually bare now. Nature's regenerative powers are at an end here'.

Antidotes are expensive. Earlier this year, the Bonn government compelled new power stations to install gas 'scrubbers' to lower sulphur dioxide emissions from 650 mg per cubic metre of smoke to 400 mg. Nitrogen oxide levels are reduced to 1,800 mg per cubic metre.

The West German power industry says it will cost £1,500 million to install the scrubbers. The first, at an oil-burning power station in West

Berlin, cost £40 million to install and will cost £7.5 million a year to operate. Electricity costs could increase by 20 per cent or more.

(*Source:* Brian Moynahan, 'The Rain that Kills', *The Sunday Times,* 5 June 1983)

- in Figure 9.2 the world is divided into two regions, each having production and consumption sectors, each using materials and energy inputs and each polluting the environment. Looked at from this global perspective the model stresses the interdependence of nations and regions of the world. Both regions interact mutually in the form of flows of products and pollutants indicated by the arrows between A and B. The resource base, economic growth, and environmental quality of any nation are determined by what happens in other nations;
- these interdependencies contain within them possibilities of numerous international environmental frictions and conflicts as atmospheric or water-borne pollution crosses international frontiers or affects a shared environmental medium such as lakes (see Case Study 9.1). Consequently as economic and ecological interdependence continues to grow, the ability of national governments to deal unilaterally with the related problems of materials, energy, and environmental quality will diminish;
- as non-renewable resources are depleted the extraction and use of lower quality ores means that larger quantities of unwanted materials must be processed to retrieve a given quantity of desired material, and clearly implies a tendency for wastes to rise faster than production;

Figure 9.2.   Materials balance model with two regions.

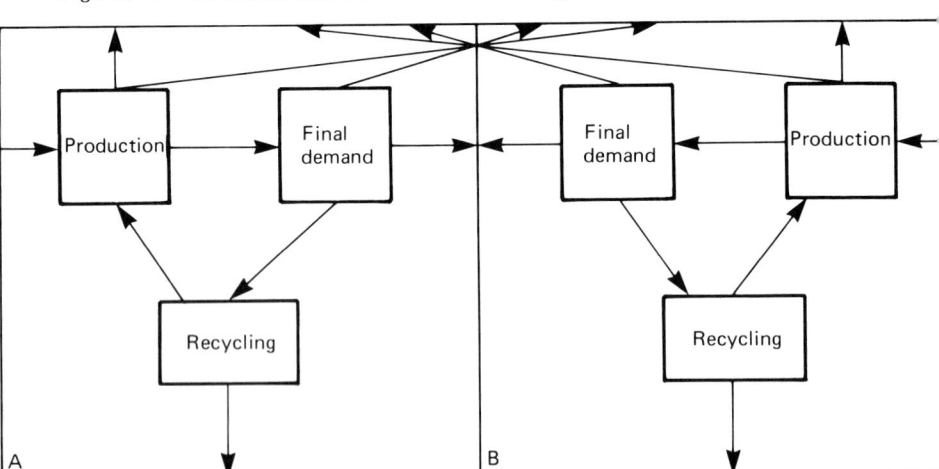

- the model underlines the fact that the aggregate level of materials 'throughput' needed for a given volume of production *decreases* as the efficiency of utilization (i.e. the minimization of waste) *increases*. An important direction for research and development may, therefore, be into the efficiency of materials processes over product life cycles as well as into improved means of waste recovery and re-use;
- lastly, we may identify options for controlling the volume of wastes, including

    (a) residuals treatment by means of recovery and recycling or by means of purifying installations,
    (b) reductions in the rate of production and consumption,
    (c) improvements in technological efficiency, i.e. an increase in usable output per unit of resource input,
    (d) changing the composition of final demand.

9.3 Resources and Reserves

An important distinction is that between resources and reserves. *Reserves* represent the fraction of a commodity that can be recovered from nature at current prices with currently available technology. *Resources* include the total stock of a particular material existing in the earth's crust. Without exception, for geological reasons, resources are substantially greater than reserves, though the ratio varies considerably for different materials. Table 9.1 shows the estimated position for three metals in 1972.

The extent to which in the future resources may become reserves is important in the context of depletion of non-renewable resources. As existing reserves are depleted, production of lower-grade higher-cost ore may take place as increasing scarcity forces up prices. Improvements in recovery methods and the consequent lower costs can similarly make lower grade deposits economic to extract.

Table 9.1. Proven reserves and resources for three metals, 1972.

(1) Resource	(2) Proven Reserves (10^6 tons)	(3) Resource Base (10^6 tons)	Ratio (3)/(2)
Chromium	466	2233	4.8
Lead	144	1854	12.9
Zinc	131	5606	42.8

Source: Adapted from Rajamaran, I., 'Non-renewable Resources: A Review of Long-term Projections', *Futures*, vol. 8, no. 3, 1976, in Lecomber, R., *The Economics of Natural Resources*, Macmillan, 1979, p. 15.

9.4 Renewable Resources

These may be used without depleting their supply. Within this group we may distinguish between flow renewable resources and biologically renewable resources.

FLOW RENEWABLE RESOURCES

Solar, wind or tidal power are important examples of this class of resource, the distinguishing feature of which is that they cannot be depleted, i.e. their use in the present time does not diminish the future available flow.

BIOLOGICALLY RENEWABLE RESOURCES

Fishing grounds, for example, allow of a constant harvest without depletion, provided they are not over-fished. Unlike flow renewable resources depletion is possible and will occur whenever harvested output exceeds the natural rate of replenishment, the latter being governed by ecological factors.

Agricultural land also falls within this group. Throughout history, for example, man has repeatedly overgrazed or overcultivated natural grasslands converting them into man-made deserts.

9.5 Non-Renewable Resources and Exponential Growth

Non-renewable resources – fossil fuels and metals, for example – are necessarily depleted by use. Present use precludes future use. Resource depletion has become an issue because industrial growth has been exponential – a snowballing process requiring continuously increasing quantities of material and energy inputs. The problem is revealed when we think in terms of doubling times, i.e. the time it takes a growing quantity

Table 9.2.   Doubling time of a quantity at various annual rates of growth.

Growth rate (% p.a.)	Doubling time (years)
0.1	700
0.5	140
1.0	70
2.0	35
4.0	18
5.0	14
7.0	10
10.0	7

to double. The relationship between a constant annual rate of growth and the time it takes for a quantity to double is approximately equal to seventy divided by the annual growth rate, as illustrated in Table 9.2.

Because exponential growth is an *accelerating* process, a danger is present whenever growth is constrained by some absolute physical limit. The point is well illustrated by the fable of the lily pond on which there grows a lily plant doubling in size each day. Unchecked the plant will cover the pond in thirty days choking the rest of the pond-life. For most of the thirty-day period it seems small. The owner decides not to cut it back until it covers half the pond, but on the twenty-ninth day, he has only one day to save the pond! Growth on the final day is equivalent to growth for the whole of the preceding twenty-nine day period.

Figure 9.3 showing the typical exponential growth curve assumes population growing within a finite environment at 1.4 per cent per annum giving a doubling time of fifty years and a crisis level of 8 billion people. For a long time the doubling time is no problem, until suddenly population soars to the crisis level in a single doubling time.

Similar reasoning may be applied to the depletion of non-renewables –

Figure 9.3. Exponential growth of population.

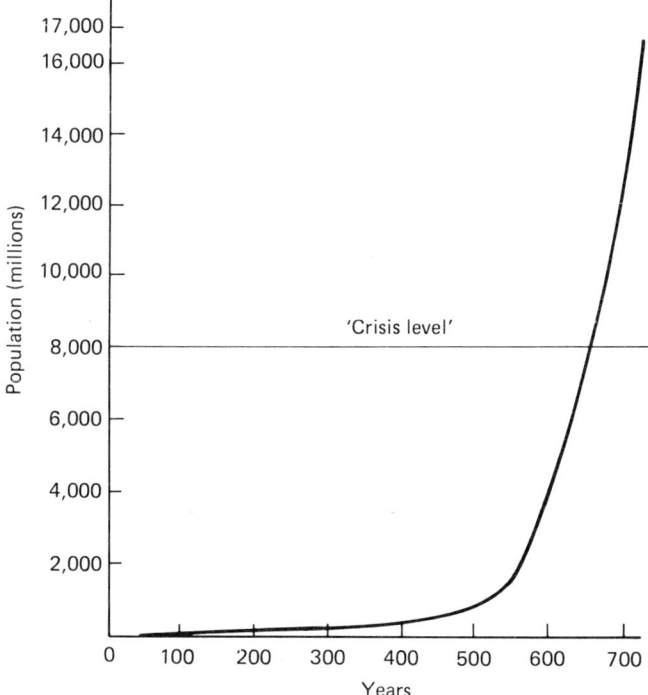

coal, for example. It has been estimated that the 'ultimately recoverable' amount of coal, i.e. all coal thought to be in place within the top kilometre of Earth's crust, would be sufficient to maintain our current rate of coal efficiency use for over 5,000 years. However, if, in the context of the impending exhaustion of oil, demand for coal continues to *expand* at just over 4 per cent per annum, this same 'ultimately recoverable' resource will be exhausted within 135 years.*

9.6 The Depletion of Non-renewable Material Resources

The reasoning about the life expectancy of non-renewable resources based on exponential growth in demand in present in the following extract from a paper delivered to the 1977 Harwell Conference on the Conservation of Materials by Sir Kingsley Dunham, Director of the Institute of Geological Sciences:

> There are present grounds for disquiet about the ability of some ores to meet a long-continued exponential rise in demand; these include silver, lead, zinc, mercury, cadmium, tin, tungsten, antimony, probably also cobalt ... As to petroleum, authorities place its life if exponential demand continues variously between 17 and 100 years; most opinions lie nearer the first mentioned figure.**

The 'pessimists' argue that the existence of undiscovered reserves does not materially affect the conclusion that given exponential growth in use, the lives of many resources are uncomfortably short. In a world of exponentials, because each successive increment lasts less long than its predecessor as demand increases large extensions to reserves make only small differences to resource lives. For example if proven reserves of a mineral R last for 100 years, then at 3 per cent growth per annum a further R lasts for only twenty-three years.

According to Sir Kingsley Dunham

> The possibilities of exploiting much lower concentrates when considered in relation to the exponential rise in demand, lead to the conclusion that the scope is limited unless very cheap energy becomes available.***

In the view of Sir Alan Cottrell, Chief Scientific Adviser to HM Government, the energy demands for mining and concentrating lean ores would be enormous:

---

* Heilbroner, R. L., *Business Civilization in Decline*, Penguin Books, 1979
** Dunham, Sir Kingsley, '*Non-renewable Mineral Resources*', Key-note Paper No. 1 in Proceedings of the Conference on the Conservation of Materials, Harwell, 1974, p. 3
*** ibid, p. 3

Particularly ominous are the really big energy demands for mining and concentrating lean ores. Where this is not necessary – iron and aluminium – the energy of production is only about ten times the ideal thermodynamic which I suppose is not bad (running a motor car is rather similar). But for modern copper, the ratio is more like 70 to 1. Thermodynamically the mining and concentration processes are extremely inefficient, partly because so much energy is wasted in crushing up rock and partly because even when the molecules are in solution, it is extremely difficult to 'get hold' of them – like fishing with a coarse grained net.*

However, the belief that the world will shortly run out of vital resources is strongly challenged by the 'optimists' who, using historical precedent, argue that there is nothing new in the problem of scarcity and that rising prices of depleting non-renewables will trigger the necessary technological developments in a timely way that will provide adequate substitutes and unlock undreamed of reserves of conventional resources and more efficient ways of using scarce resources. Such faith in the operation of the price mechanism and technological solutions is apparent in M. C. O'Dowd's statement of the optimists' case presented in Case Study 9.2.

CASE STUDY 9.2

Why the World Will Not Run Out of Mineral Resources

In discussing the possibility of the exhaustion of the world's resources we must start with the simple distinction between energy and all physical materials. Energy is the only thing which we use up. All materials are merely changed from one form into another and can be changed again. All metals, glass, plastic and paper can be recycled relatively easily with existing technology and to a greater or lesser extent they are recycled. When they are not, this means that the cost of recycling is greater than the cost of producing new materials. If this should cease to be so, recycling would increase accordingly. Recycling and the recovery of waste is a question of cost and price.

Total recycling, however, is not possible. There will always be some losses and except at enormous cost these losses will be significant and in any case even 100 per cent recycling could only support the existing standard of living of the world, not a rising standard of living. Mankind will always have to rely on the recovery of new materials in addition to recycling, and this will always be possible.

The earth is made of minerals. When there are no minerals left there

* Cottrell, Sir Alan, Opening Address to Harwell Conference, op. cit., p. 1

will be no earth. What are we usually talking about when we refer to mineral resources is those readily accessible and highly concentrated deposits of particular minerals which can profitably be recovered at existing prices. In mining parlance only rock which contains minerals which can be profitably recovered is called ore. Everything else is just rock including rock which contains minerals in substantial quantities, but not sufficient to be profitably recovered.

So, what constitutes ore in a particular metal depends on the price of the metal, and this is spectacularly illustrated by the difference in the grades of ore which are worked for different metals. Gold can be mined under favourable circumstances at a grade of 5 grams per ton, that is to say 5 parts per million, and 14 or 15 grams per ton can be mined at great depth. Copper can be mined by open-cast means in a favourable environment (that is one where costs are low) at half of one per cent; for the underground mining about 2 per cent is usually required. At the other end of the scale nobody will look at a deposit of iron ore which contains more than 10 per cent of any material other than iron oxide unless that other material is itself valuable. Enormous quantities of ironstone which are not regarded as even remotely potential economic resources contain as much as 20 per cent iron. All granite and all clay contain substantially more aluminium than the richest copper ores contain of copper.

If follows that we can only talk about available resources of a mineral at a particular price for the mineral and at a particular cost for its recovery. Any change in either of these parameters will change ore into rock or rock into ore, sometimes on a spectacular scale.

Mineral resources are then a question of price and costs. As prices rise or as costs are reduced there are three places to which we can go for new resources. We can go to more inaccessible parts of the earth's surface; we can go to lower grade deposits; or we can go deeper.

(*Source:* M. C. O'Dowd, Manager, Anglo–American Corporation of South Africa Limited, in *The Three Banks Review*, No. 133, March 1982)

Whatever the long-term outlook, there are undoubtedly urgent and growing materials problems with us here and now for many reasons, not least amongst which are those connected with the close relationship between energy and materials consumption to which question we now turn.

9.7 The Energy Transformation System and Energy Requirements for Energy

Most fuels used in industrial society are derived from energy sources embedded in the crust of the earth. *The Energy Transformation System*★

Figure 9.4. The energy transformation system.

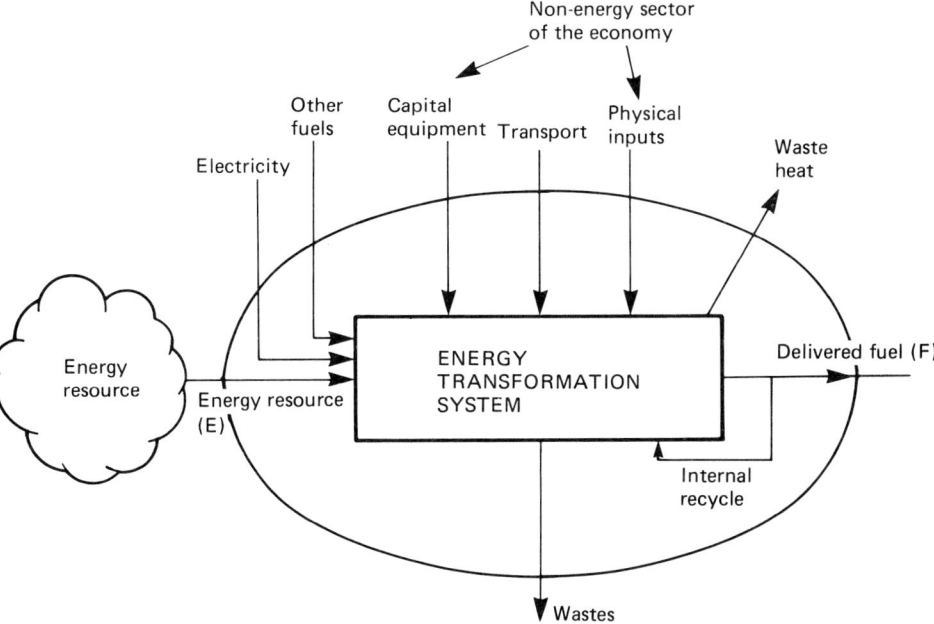

(ETS) is that part of the economic system in which resources in the ground are finally turned into fuels available to industrial or domestic consumers. The many stages of fuel production will vary with different kinds of energy resources. In the case of underground coal, for example, these stages will include exploration, mine construction and development, coal cutting and blasting, haulage to the surface, cleansing and separating procesess, and distribution. Each of these stages will require considerable direct and indirect fuel inputs. The capital equipment (e.g. coal cutting equipment, earth removers, mine installations, etc.) and the material embodied in these will have themselves been produced with the use of fuels – hence there is a further 'recycle' of goods having an implicit energy content from the non-energy sector of the economy to the ETS. Once used the energy ends up as low-grade heat except for the relatively small amount sequestered as products.

Figure 9.4 represents one small part of Britain's ETS – an offshore oilfield. From this we derive a number of useful 'energy accounting' concepts.

In Figure 9.4 the ETS box includes the various stages of producing the fuel – survey, discovery, exploitation, transportation, refining, and so on.

* Slessor, M., *Energy in the Economy*, Macmillan, 1978.

Each step within this sub-ETS will require capital and physical inputs from the non-energy sector of the economy and fuels 'imported' from other sub-ETS. Out of the sub-ETS emerges a flow of fuel, F (in this case oil) based on a primary resource consumption E.

The importance of presenting things in this way is to emphasize that fuel F could not have been derived from resource E without all the other inputs shown in Figure 9.4. Some of the inputs e.g. fuels and materials will need to be supplied into the sub-ETS continuously, and even capital equipment will depreciate and require replacement.

In order to discover the total resource requirement necessary to make F available as a fuel to the non-energy sector we would need to compute the resource requirement value for each input. The total resource requirement to make fuel quantity F available for use will then be the sum of the resource requirements of all the inputs plus the major resource of the sub-ETS i.e. E. We can write this as

(1)   Gross Energy Requirement of the Fuel
      = E + Energy Requirement of other inputs

From this we can derive the *Energy Requirement for Energy* (ERE) as the ratio between the *Gross Energy Requirement* (GER) and the delivered fuel (F), i.e.

(2) $\text{ERE for Fuel F} = \dfrac{\text{GER as in (1)}}{\text{F}}$

'Available' energy sources become more and more inaccessible and expensive as the ERE rises towards unity, and if in addition to the ERE necessary to win a resource from the ground there is further considerable expenditure of energy for dealing with environmental damage associated with extracting increasingly low-grade and physically difficult deposits.

Similar considerations apply to the recovery of materials.

9.8 Conclusion

If the pessimists' arguments are correct then even assuming all the technical and ecological problems could be resolved there may be no long-term 'solutions' to the problem of resource scarcity based on new discoveries of reserves. What, then, can be done about demand? Does part of the answer lie in a much greater research effort directed at discovering new methods of economising in resource use in the fields of product design, manufacture, durability, packaging, marketing, and consumption? To what extent can the life expectancy of resources be increased by better energy and materials management, and by recycling and re-use of materials? These are questions to which we return in later chapters.

CASE STUDY 9.3

Scarce Natural Resources

If present policies were to continue, it is apparent that materials usage in the USA would more than double by the year 2000. The increased level of consumption implies a proportionately heavier burden of pollution, waste, and dissipation of resources. Clearly the US economy must reduce its wasteful use of materials. While the US and State Governments can lead the way and provide a good example, changes in the attitudes of the public as a whole and of those that produce for profit will also be necessary.

The United States has been richly blessed with a wealth of natural resources. For generations we took for granted our seemingly inexhaustible supply of natural resources ... while basking in the glow reflected by our high standard of living.

In the space of less than 200 years, the United States has grown economically from a struggling agricultural colony of Great Britain to an industrial nation that produces more than one-fourth of the world's total gross material product. In the period 1900–1970 while US population increased by 166 per cent, its GNP increased by almost 900 per cent in real terms. A result is that today the US consumes about one-third of the world's raw materials – not including foodstuffs.

(*Source:* D. W. Ballard, *An American View of Materials Conservation*
(Paper No. 2 for U.S. National Commission on Materials Policy,
based on a study by the US Federation of Materials Societies
chaired by D. W. Ballard))

STUDENT ASSIGNMENT 9.1

Scarce Material Resources

1. Re-read previous Case Studies in this chapter. Identify the problems implicit in these extracts.
2. List as a series of *objectives* what you think needs to be achieved in order to resolve the problems.
3. What needs to be done, i.e. what policies can be adopted, in order to achieve the objectives?
4. What are the implications of the problems *and* of the 'solutions' for private business organizations?

9.9 Summary

1. Businesses depend upon an uninterrupted and massive flow of diverse energy and materials inputs obtained from the environment.
2. The use of the environment as a resource base may conflict with its other economic or ecological functions. This necessitates 'trade-offs' between different environment functions.
3. A materials balance model of the economy/environmental interactions is based on the law of conservation of matter, from which we can deduce that all material inputs to production and consumption are eventually returned to the environment as wastes, sometimes with serious ecological and social consequences.
4. All economic activity exerts inevitable claims on the environment for inputs of resources and for the disposal of residuals.
5. There are grounds for concern that in both cases we may be near to critical limits. The exhaustion of some resources is foreseen and pollution may exceed the assimilative capacity of ecosystems.
6. The resources base, economic growth, and environmental quality of any one nation or region are strongly influenced by what happens in other nations or regions.
7. Reserves can be recovered at current prices and with current technology. Resources include the total stock of a material in the earth's crust.
8. The extent to which reserves become resources depends upon the rate of depletion, changes in price, and technological progress in recovery methods and the development of substitutes.
9. Flow renewable resources e.g. solar energy, cannot be depleted. Biologically renewable resources e.g. fishing grounds, can be destroyed whenever harvested output exceeds the ecologically determined rate of replenishment.
10. Exponential growth in population, industrialization, and demand for non-renewables raises questions about the sustainability of continued growth in production and use of many resources.
11. 'Pessimists' argue that so long as exponential growth continues the discovery of new reserves makes little difference to the life expectancy of certain natural resources.
12. 'Optimists' using historical precedent argue that the operation of the price mechanism will stimulate appropriate technology to ensure that resource scarcities will be overcome.
13. Energy requirements for energy and materials may constrain future supplies and increase costs, as well as accelerating the depletion of fossil fuels.
14. Increased energy production and use from conventional sources will

reduce environmental quality, may damage local, regional, or global ecosystems, and may induce artificial climatic change, though the extent of the latter risk is uncertain.

Exercise

Review your understanding of the following:

materials balance model
resources and reserves
flow and biologically renewable resources
exponential growth
energy transformation system
energy requirement for energy

10

Financial Constraints

10.1 Profitability and the Cost of Capital

In a recent analysis of the financing of British industry, the Bank of England* nominated 'the inadequate return on capital assets' after allowing for the depreciation of capital at replacement rather than historic cost as 'the most serious problem in the finance of British business'.

Undoubtedly low and declining levels of profitability in the 1970s and 1980s have been an important factor explaining the poor level of new investment in British manufacturing industry in comparison with its major international competitors during the same period. The extent of the decline in the gross trading profits of British industrial and commercial companies has been dramatic with the real rate of return falling from around 11 per cent in the early 1960s to only 2.5 per cent in 1981 according to a Bank of England estimate.

Thus, when the Wilson Committee reported** in 1980 on the functioning of the British financial system, company profits had been on a downward trend for the best part of two decades. In the wake of the OPEC oil price shocks of 1973 company profits were squeezed even further by accelerating inflation, so much so that in 1974 the real (inflation-adjusted) rate of profit on companies' capital assets fell below the real cost of capital finance, and has remained there since. Though companies experienced a recovery in the real level of their profits from 1974 to 1977 this improvement was soon masked by the effect of the sharply rising interest rates associated with inflation. After 1977 whilst interest rates rose profits again fell. (See Figure 10.1)

The level of trading profits is of course the most important determinant

* *Bank of England Quarterly Bulletin*, September 1980, p. 320
** Cmnd 7837, HMSO, 1980

Figure 10.1. Rate of return and cost of capital.

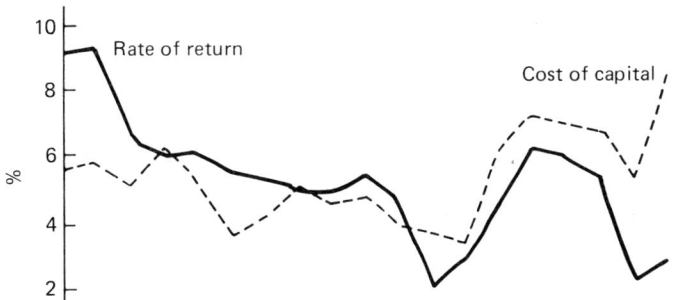

Source: Bank of England Quarterly Bulletin, June 1982.

of the availability of internal funds available for 'ploughing back' into business expansion. Furthermore, as we have seen in Chapter 6, internally generated finance is the most important single source of company funds, financing on average about 70 per cent of corporate investment in fixed assets and stocks in the 1970s.

Shrinking profit levels also have a marked adverse effect on the willingness of industry to borrow long-term in order to undertake new capital investment projects especially by the traditional means of fixed interest debentures, the market for which dried up altogether from the mid-1970s. There are two reasons for this. Firstly, falling profits reduce the amount of indebtedness a company can support, i.e. for any given level of debt, the ratio of interest payments to profits rises leaving less for distribution as dividends and for retention. Secondly, falling profits reduce the adequacy of cash-flow making it difficult for firms to meet rising interest charges.

One effect of inflation and unstable interest rates in the 1970s was thus to divert company borrowing away from the long-term corporate bond market and towards an increasing reliance on bank finance.

Perhaps even more revealing than an isolated look at the effects of declining profits on self-financing is a comparison of internally generated funds with the amounts estimated as needed to maintain the existing scale of business operations. It has been estimated that on average these amounts were covered only 1.4 times in the 1970s compared with 2.1 times in the mid-1960s. What this means is that after paying the costs of simply keeping going at the same level less and less has been internally available for financing business expansion or modernization.

10.2 Capital and Income Gearing

The way in which a company chooses to finance its capital assets gives it a certain capital structure which in turn largely determines the way in which its profits are distributed among the different classes of its security holders. As we saw in Chapter 6 a company with a high ratio of fixed return 'priority capital' (debentures and preference shares) to ordinary share capital is said to have a high capital gearing. Conversely if this ratio is low, the company's capital gearing is low.

Companies with a high capital gearing tend also to have a high income gearing in the sense that 'prior charges' of debt interest and preference dividends claim a large proportion of trading profits.

Although there is no universally applicable definition of 'excessive borrowing' it is clearly the case that some of the practical consequences that stem from high gearing can result in a number of constraints on a company's capacity to raise finance in the future. In order to explain these we must firstly identify some of the potential risks to which investors in a highly geared business are exposed. These include

- Since some of a company's debt will have been borrowed at variable rates of interest, a rise in interest rates will pre-empt an increased proportion of company profits. In 1979, for instance, when interest rates rose sharply the income gearing of British industrial and commercial companies rose to 24 per cent compared with 17 per cent in the preceding year.
- In times of prolonged decline in company profitability the payments to debenture and preference shareholders in a highly geared company may be at greater risk. Legally a company must pay all debt interest. Preference dividends are only payable if profits are available. If, as is commonly the case, a company ranks new borrowing below old, it will be the new debenture holders who bear the brunt of any shortfall in profits. Otherwise all debt-holders will share the risk equally.

  In order to provide a measure of protection for debenture holders against such risks deriving from excessive capital gearing, many companies include a clause in their Articles or Memorandum of Association specifying the maximum permissible ratio of loan capital to share capital. Such clauses are themselves constraints on a company's capacity to finance its needs by borrowing.
- As the recent history of economic recession amply demonstrates it is shareholders' funds that suffer most from falling profits or from any losses incurred, and from interest rate fluctuations. Other things being equal it is shareholders in the more highly geared companies who are most vulnerable precisely because cash flow may be insufficient or only

barely sufficient to meet interest charges, leaving little or nothing for dividend payments.

These consequences of high gearing may constrain a company's capacity to raise finance in several ways including

- when a company with a high income gearing is faced with falling profits and/or rising interest rates less is available for payment of ordinary shareholders' dividends. If dividends are 'unacceptably low' it will be difficult to raise further capital by share issues because potential investors are deterred by the poor performance of the company's existing shares;
- if, in the same circumstances, after paying its prior charges, profits are insufficient to pay adequate dividends, the company may be forced into cutting back on the desired level of retained profits in the belief that shareholders demand income now rather than company saving over time – thus reducing another major potential source of funds;
- if it is seen that shareholders are reluctant to increase their financial commitment to the company, lenders too may be discouraged from risking their funds.

Thus the consequences of high gearing may make it more difficult to generate distributable funds internally and to attract additional share and loan capital.

Before leaving this section the reader is reminded that the purpose of the present discussion is to explain how high capital and income gearing may, in certain circumstances, constrain a company's capacity to raise finance. It should not be interpreted as an attack on high capital and income gearing as such. Company policy on its capital structure will depend on many considerations including changes in corporate taxation, the economic outlook, investment plans, stock relief arrangements, and expected profitability, as well as on the vulnerability it may face with different levels of gearing arising from the legal obligation it has regardless of its circumstances to pay interest compared with its discretion to vary the rate of share dividends. Increasingly in conditions of economic recession a company may have to go on borrowing simply to survive or to finance high interest payments on long-term debt.

10.3 Economic Recession and Monetary Policy

Economic recession has adverse effects on business finance in a number of ways. As production in the economy declines and unemployment rises aggregate demand tends to spiral downwards with an inevitable squeeze on profits resulting. With the onset of recession the fall in profitability can be substantial and rapid. Thus to take a recent instance of this the gross trading profits of British industrial and commercial companies which had already been on a downward trend since the mid-1960s declined even further by about 15 per cent in the third quarter of 1980 compared with the same quarter of the preceding year. In the same periods retained profits fell by nearly one half forcing companies to make drastic cuts in their expenditure.

A closer analysis of this period early in the current recession reveals that companies were forced to react to the associated inhospitable conditions in a variety of ways including

- quite massive cut-backs in stocks – in volume terms amounting to more than £2 billion;
- closures of loss-making operations often with the effect of increasing cash flow as associated working capital was run down;
- the selling off of healthy subsidiaries by highly geared groups.

The cut-back in stocks in order to reduce working capital and so get the level of borrowing down was perhaps accelerated by the government's counter-inflationary monetary policy which culminated in a record level of interest rates at the beginning of 1980 when the Bank of England's Minimum Lending Rate was hoisted to the unprecedented figure of 17 per cent. De-stocking by company A, of course, inevitably results in lower orders from its suppliers Companies B and C, who in turn are forced to cut their stocks and orders to their suppliers. The overall consequence is the well-known downward spiral of demand and an even tighter squeeze on profits. Towards the middle of 1980 the slump in consumer demand was so rapid that it became virtually impossible to continue to shed stocks and companies were forced to reduce output and employment even further. In these circumstances many businesses failed to cover their fixed costs and were forced into heavier 'distress' borrowing in order to survive.

Greater reliance on external finance especially from banks was also forced onto companies as a direct consequence of the halving of retained profits during 1979–80. Paradoxically, the additional demand for bank loans came at precisely the time when the Thatcher government was trying strenuously to restrict them as the main plank of its counter-inflationary monetary policy. Faced with this the government may decide to manipulate interest rates to higher levels resulting in higher business costs and a yet further squeeze on profits.

10.4 The Financing Problems of Smaller Firms

Large well-established public limited companies usually have no difficulty in meeting the Stock Exchange rules and Company Law requirements necessary to raise large amounts of capital on the open market. By comparison small and medium-sized enterprises suffer financial disadvantages which in the absence of government assistance can often act as major constraints on business expansion. Among the many difficulties of raising adequate finance facing small companies are

- private limited companies are legally prevented from inviting the public to subscribe for their shares and are thus denied access to a major source of finance available to large public limited companies;
- small and medium-sized companies may find the costs of 'going public' and raising capital on the open market prohibitive. In general, for example, the Stock Exchange's entry requirement for a would-be public company is for a minimum proposed share capital of £500,000;
- the costs of raising finance on the new issue market are to a large extent independent of the size of the issue so that as a percentage of the cash to be raised costs fall as the amount increases. Hence the smaller the amount required the higher proportionately are the costs of issue, and in many cases too high for small companies to use this market;
- in general internally-generated funds are insufficient to meet the expansionary ambitions of many small companies;
- small, especially newly-formed, firms may also find it difficult to raise long-term loans. Certainly in cases where they are able to borrow long-term they will be required to pay higher interest charges than larger well-established firms where the money is held to be at less risk;
- for all these reasons small firms tend to depend heavily on short-term bank loans, which although normally renewable, may be vulnerable at times of credit squeeze, when high interest rates will also add to the costs of business finance;
- highly-geared small businesses vulnerable to interest rate volatility are likely to be unattractive to potential investors adding to the difficulties of raising equity capital;
- the large institutional investors such as insurance companies and pension funds who supply a high proportion of company finance but who seek security in their investments will tend to prefer to lend to larger more diversified companies and to fight shy of the higher risks of financing the smaller business enterprises about which less information will generally be available.

Several official enquiries have confirmed the existence of financial problems such as these faced by small business firms. As long ago as 1931 the MacMillan Committee on Finance and Industry identified a gap in the capital market for the supply of finance to small and medium-sized firms. However, it was not until after the Second World War in 1945 that any serious attempt was made to close this gap with the establishment of the

Industrial and Commercial Finance Corporation (ICFC) with an initial capital of £15 million subscribed by the clearing banks and the Bank of England and with borrowing powers of £30 million which could be raised solely from the member banks. The ICFC aimed to provide long term or permanent capital in 'small' packages of £5,000–£200,000 (later raised to £300,000).

In the same year a second semi-official specialist institution, the Finance Corporation for Industry (FCI) was set up to supply long-term finance to small firms in the form of mortgaged loan capital. In 1973 the FCI and ICFC were absorbed in Finance For Industry (FFI) whose capital is subscribed by the clearing banks and the Bank of England. FFI provides medium-term loans to industry at fixed and floating rates with its subsidiary ICFC fulfilling its traditional role of supplying funds including equity finance to small firms.

Financial problems highlighted in the 1971 report of the Bolton Committee of Enquiry on Small Firms included the relative inability of small firms to satisfy the requirements of lenders for financial data and assure them of managerial competence. Thus although specialist small-firm financial institutions were now established lack of sufficient financial expertise prevented many small firms from making use of them. Among the recommendations of the Bolton Committee were the establishment of financial advice bureaux to provide firms with information about potential sources of funds; lower rates of corporation tax for small firms to enhance their opportunity to retain earnings; the use of inflation accounting to cut the tax burden on small firms; and in order to reduce administrative and accounting costs exemption for companies with less than a certain annual turnover from Companies Act requirements to disclose their finances.

Since then, successive governments have given increasing recognition to the importance of small firms in the national economy, by introducing a number of tax reliefs including raising the ceilings for the reduced rate of corporation tax and for VAT registration.

Finally, the 1979 report of the Wilson Committee on the Financing of Small Firms recommended a number of measures to improve the financial position of small firms including

- the establishment of a government-underwritten and subsidized loan guarantee scheme;
- an improvement in the supply of equity capital for small companies by (a) the development of an 'over-the-counter' market and (b) the creation of specialist Small Firm Investment Companies through which individual investors would benefit from tax concessions.

The first of these recommendations was implemented with the introduction of the government's Loan Guarantee Scheme in 1981. Much progress towards improving the supply of equity capital for small companies has also been achieved through the development of the now thriving Unlisted Securities Market and the introduction of the Business Expansion Scheme in 1981 and its extension to existing small businesses in 1983. These innovations have already been considered in more detail in Chapter 6.

In recent years further schemes have been introduced to help overcome the financing problems of small business. Currently the range of government measures available is considerable, offering benefits to every form of small business activity.

10.5 Summary

1. In recent years low levels of profitability have reduced the supply of internally generated funds available for business expansion.
2. Declining profit levels dramatically diverted company long-term borrowing away from fixed-interest debentures and towards an increasing reliance on bank finance.
3. High capital gearing ratios may result in a number of constraints on a company's capacity to raise finance in the future.
4. Economic recession has intensified the profit squeeze, forcing companies to de-stock and close down loss-making operations. De-stocking may have been accelerated by government monetary policy resulting in record interest rate levels in 1980. De-stocking results in fewer orders and a downward spiral in demand with an even tighter squeeze on profits.
5. In comparison with big business, small and medium-sized firms have suffered from numerous disadvantages in raising finance. In the recent past many of these have been removed with the introduction of the Loan Guarantee Scheme, the Business Expansion Scheme, the creation of the USM, and a wide range of other government measures designed to help small firms.

STUDENT ASSIGNMENT 10.1

Prestige Carpets PLC

Prestige Carpets PLC needs to raise £250,000 for expansion. Identify and indicate the importance of all the internal and extenal factors the company should take into account in deciding whether to raise the additional funds by borrowing or by share issue. Assume that one of the company's aims is to ensure maximum freedom to raise more finance in the future in order to finance further expected expansions.

(N.B. It may be helpful for the reader to review Chapter 6 before carrying out this assignment.)

Further Reading

Vause, R. and Woodward, N. *Finance for Managers*, Macmillan, 1981

PART IV

RESOURCE UTILIZATION

11

People and Productivity

11.1 Productivity and Economic Performance in the UK

Improvements in the United Kingdom's economic performance and living standards are crucially dependent on productivity improvements. As a major trading nation, Britain's output and employment levels are closely bound up with its international competitiveness, itself the result of the relative productivity performance of this country *vis-à-vis* that of other industrialized trading nations.

The United Kingdom's long history of relatively low productivity *growth* led by 1979 to a situation in which the *level* of value added per man hour in manufacturing was lower than in any other industrial nation. In 1980 manufacturing output per head in Germany and Japan was more than twice as high as in Britain. In the US it was 2.5 times as high.

Throughout the post-war period Britain's productivity growth* has been well below that of all other major industrial countries apart from the US. Since the US is the 'technological leader' and enjoyed a much higher *level* of productivity at the start of the period this means that all the industrialized countries apart from the UK have been steadily catching up with the US. As a 1980 official report put it:

> The evidence suggests that the U.K. has been outstripped not because it has dropped progressively further behind the technological 'leader' the United

---

* Output per unit of labour input. The most appropriate indicator is output per unit of combined resource input. However, labour productivity is much easier to measure and is commonly used. In most circumstances changes in labour productivity are a reasonable indicator of changes in overall productivity except where significant technological changes are taking place.

States, but because equivalent industries in rival economies have taken advantage of a technological gap to grow faster in the process of narrowing it.*

Furthermore, while in several countries the productivity growth trend decelerated in the 1970s, the slow-down in Britain was greater than elsewhere (see Table 11.1).

Table 11.1. Growth of output per head in manufacturing in six industrial countries, 1966–77.

	%
Japan	116
France	70
West Germany	70
Italy	62
Canada	43
United States	27
United Kingdom	27

Britain's poor productivity record is reflected in her falling share of world trade in manufactures and in higher levels of import penetration (Figure 11.1).

The resultant loss of overseas and domestic markets has undoubtedly inhibited the achievement of other goals like full employment and more rapid growth.

11.2 Some Causes of Low Productivity Growth

Among the many important and interrelated reasons for Britain's poor productivity record identified by the NEDC are

- poor industrial relations;
- overmanning;
- disputes disrupting production;
- restrictive labour practices;
- inadequate or inappropriate training;
- diversion of excessive management attention to labour relations.

This list is not exhaustive. This and many other studies confirm that British workers produce less than their Continental, American, and Japanese counterparts because they have less capital equipment available to them.

* *The Tripartite Approach to Industrial Recovery*, National Economic Development Office, 1980

Figure 11.1. Shares in world trade (exports) of manufacturers, 1950–78 (value).

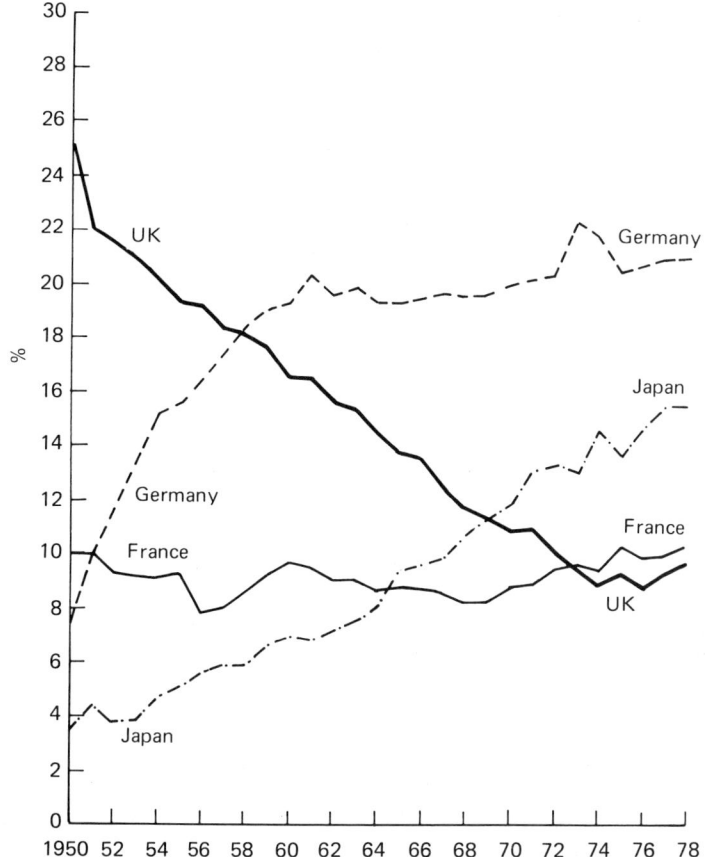

Source: National Institute Economic Review.

The listed factors have resulted in poor productivity performance both directly through the poor utilization of labour time and indirectly by lowering the level of productivity and profitability of a given capital stock and by discouraging investment in new equipment. In emphasizing the complexity of these manpower problems, the NEDC argued that they could only be resolved 'by careful and detailed analysis and work firm by firm and plant by plant'.*

* *Productivity*, Memorandum by the Director General, NEDC, June 1979, para 8(e)

11.3 Productivity Bargaining in the 1960s and 1970s

Improving productivity implies improving the use of *all* resources – plant, buildings, energy, materials, marketing, as well as manpower. Productivity bargaining can provide an important contributory means to this end.

The National Board for Prices and Incomes defined a productivity agreement as 'one in which workers agree to make a change, or a number of changes, in working practice that will lead in itself – leaving out any compensating pay increase – to more economical working; and in return the employer agrees to a higher level of pay or other benefits'.*

The Board distinguished between 'comprehensive' and 'partial' productivity agreements. The former covered a number of related changes in working practices and affect all, or nearly all, the manual workers in an undertaking, whereas the latter normally affect only one practice and often only a single group of workers. Partial agreements had a long history, but comprehensive agreements were a new departure in British collective bargaining.

The first comprehensive productivity deal in Britain emerged in July 1960 when an elaborate set of collective agreements was concluded between the management of the Esso Oil Refinery, Southampton, and the shop stewards of the Transport and General Workers' Union (TGWU), representing the majority of wage earners, and seven other craft unions. Briefly, the company agreed to large (40 per cent) phased pay increases for its workers in return for specified changes in working practices that were preventing a more efficient utilization of labour. These included:

- some relaxation of job demarcations – making labour more flexible;
- withdrawal of craftsmens' mates – and their redeployment on other work;
- increased shift working;
- greater freedom for management in its use of supervision;
- reduction of systematic overtime which had become an important source of inefficiency in labour utilization.

The Fawley agreements heralded a new approach to the solution of urgent problems of industrial relations and manpower utilization. The central principle was that in return for negotiated changes in working practices the employer offered higher earnings and other benefits to employees financed from the savings made by the resultant improvement in resource utilization.

In the late 1960s and again in the mid and late 1970s government incomes policies provoked veritable explosions of productivity bargaining

---

* *Productivity Bargaining*, NBPI Report No. 36, HMSO, 1968

with thousands of deals negotiated. By 1978 most firms had 'self-financing productivity payments' or were planning to introduce them.

Despite these upsurges of productivity bargaining in periods of wage restraint there is little evidence that the *actual* productivity in most firms improved. Indeed in the period 1975–1979 Britain's productivity growth *fell* from about +1.5 per cent to an actual decline of more than −2 per cent.

The reasons behind this lack of association between productivity bargaining and productivity gains are instructive. Undoubtedly productivity bonus payments in many companies were quite simply a means of by-passing wage restraint in order to buy industrial peace. Other criticisms of the productivity bargaining of the 1960s and 1970s help to explain why productivity gains failed to emerge. Among these are:

- it often distorted internal pay structures, and consequently stimulated non-productivity pay claims to restore differentials;
- productivity is either very difficult or impossible to measure in many kinds of work;
- no adequate vetting systems were developed;
- there was a lack of commitment by managements. Professor Bowey's findings* based on a two-year study of the effects of productivity bonus deals in sixty-three organizations indicate that a high proportion of organizations did not even *expect* to achieve positive results. One-third did not anticipate any increase in the volume of ouput; more than 90 per cent expected no resulting decrease in price; more than 70 per cent foresaw no improvements in quality; and most astonishing of all, 43 per cent did not expect their incentive schemes to contribute to improvements in any factors they had identified as success indicators;
- managerial skills in creating a climate of attitudes in which workers would become involved in participative procedures were lacking.

11.4 Negotiating Productivity Improvements

It has been recently argued that some of the factors traditionally thought to hold down productivity are not necessarily the most significant.** For example, productivity is not *necessarily* about reductions in manpower or making people work harder. Rather it is about management's ability to motivate, organize, and equip. Incentive payments obviously help, but the most significant conclusion emerging from recent research emphasizes the

---

* Bowey, A., 'The Effectiveness of Incentive Payment Schemes', *Topics*, no. 9, Employment Relations Resource Centre, March 1983
** Newman, N., '*Pressing for Productivity*', Management Today, March 1982

part that *man-management* (rather than money) has to play in the success of productivity deals.

'The way in which companies manage people is very much linked to their productivity record,' says Richard Worsley of the CBI. 'If you ask companies what resources they put into personnel – e.g. if the personnel director is on the board – you generally find that it's usually low down on their priorities.'* In short, management must have the commitment and the will to improve productivity and the ability to lead and motivate people.

The effective negotiation of productivity agreements is not simple. There appear to be at least five necessary conditions for success:

- Total commitment of top management to an all-out attack on costs.
- The attack on costs and the consequent rewards must be comprehensive (i.e. managers, administrative and clerical staff as well as the shop floor workers must be included).
- A basis for measuring improvements in productivity must be identified. (Commonly the ratio of value added per £ of wages and salaries is accepted as a valid measure.)
- Managements must appreciate the necessity to establish a climate of attitudes in which all employees will be prepared to become involved in identifying and implementing ways and means to improve productivity.
- The development by managements of a more sophisticated approach to negotiations (including a willingness to disclose information and more effective communication).

11.5 Employee Motivation

Employee performance depends on a combination of ability and motivation. If either are low performance will be unsatisfactory. A traditional but still popular view of employee motivation is that most people only go to work in order to earn money. In a work setting the individual is presumed to act as a rational 'economic man' concerned solely to maximize his economic gain, and willing to be regulated and manipulated to this end.

The traditional view is strongly challenged by the so-called 'human relations' school. In the 1920s Elton Mayo and his Harvard colleagues set up a series of studies at the Hawthorne plant of the Western Electric Company which was to last for ten years. The main finding was that work is a *social* as well as an economic experience. The relationships between people at work had a greater effect on work performance than many other factors including incentive payments. The keys to motivation were

---

* ibid., p. 53

Figure 11.2. Maslow's hierarchy of needs.

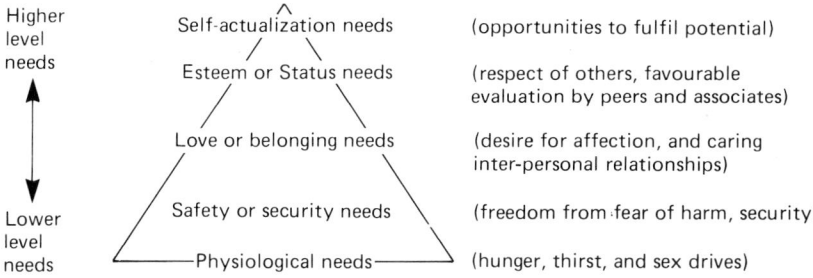

therefore to be found in creating the right social conditions, education, and satisfying inter-personal relationships at work. Workers wanted to feel part of the organizational social system.

According to Abraham Maslow people have a hierarchy of needs ranging from basic physiological needs, e.g. food and drink, to the higher order needs of self-actualization (see Figure 11.2). It is the urge to satisfy these needs that motivates people. As one set of needs is satisfied it ceases to motivate and the next need in the hierarchy becomes the effective motivator. When physiological needs have been satisfied, for example, they no longer effectively motivate; but until they are satisfied other needs are irrelevant. A hungry man is not concerned about self-actualization!

Maslow's ideas are developed in Frederick Herzberg's analysis of employee motivation. Herzberg distinguishes two categories of rewards in an organization, 'hygienes' relating mainly to job dissatisfaction and 'motivators' relating mainly to job satisfaction.

The important *hygienes* are wages and salaries, working conditions, competent supervision, organizational policy and administration, and security. If all hygienes are present at an adequate level this will tend to promote neutral feelings about work. This is because they are expected. The absence or inadequate provision of 'hygienes' will produce feelings of dissatisfaction. Consequently the provision of 'hygienes' such as money rewards cannot motivate: they are capable only of preventing employee dissatisfaction.

According to Herzberg the true *motivators* are not to be found in the circumstances surrounding or conditions attached to a job but in rewards related to the intrinsic nature of the work itself: in achievement, recognition, responsibility, and the prospects of advancement.

It is not difficult to see the strong similarities between Maslow's and Herzberg's theories. Herzberg's 'hygienes' and 'motivators' are comparable respectively with Maslow's lower and higher level needs.

If Herzberg's theory is correct, the supply of effort from workers will not be achieved by money but by creating opportunities for satisfaction of higher order needs in the workplace. By emphasizing job *content* rather than job *context* factors, Herzberg's ideas made a great impact on management practice – an impact which can be seen in the many techniques used to provide such opportunities including management by objectives, worker participation schemes and especially in various forms of job re-design, such as job rotation, job enlargement and job enrichment.

Job enrichment may take a number of forms, which may involve:

- job enlargement – enlarging an employee's responsibilities by adding to his tasks other related tasks allowing the employee the satisfaction of completing a job rather than only part of it, e.g. the assembly of a whole television receiver rather than fitting only one component of it;
- job rotation – allows or programmes employees to change jobs several times during each day. This may reduce fatigue and increase the variety of work thus increasing job satisfaction;
- increased autonomy – allows the employee to be more self-directed and with more freedom to set objectives while at the same time increasing his or her accountability for work performance. This can result in less direct employee supervision;
- introducing more challenging and exacting jobs and providing the necessary training.

There is conflicting empirical evidence regarding the effectiveness of various job enrichment schemes, and no clear reasons have emerged to explain why some have succeeded and others failed. It is clear, however, that motivators and hygienes do not operate similarly for all individuals. There is evidence too that job enrichment is not desired by all work-groups, and that its impact may be more on job satisfaction than job performance.

Studies by J. H. Goldthorpe and others revealed that many workers had 'instrumental' attitudes to work, i.e. work is regarded as the means to earn

STUDENT ASSIGNMEMT 11.1

Student Motivation

What are your own motivations for joining a BEC Higher Diploma course? What do your answers imply for the way the course is designed and administered? What appear to be the most important factors?

CASE STUDY 11.1

The Effectiveness of Incentive Payment Schemes

A team of researchers from the Pay and Reward Centre at Strathclyde University studied sixty-three organizations in Britain which had introduced incentive or bonus payment schemes between 1977 and 1980. Among the major findings of this study were:

1. No two of the payment systems in the study were exactly alike. There were at least eight different ways in which the schemes varied such as the aspect of work which has to be improved to earn extra pay; the size of the group whose performance is to be measured to determine pay; whether the extra pay is fixed or varies; the size of the bonus relative to total pay; the frequency of extra payments; the period of time on which the extra payment is calculated; the conditions which may restrict access to the extra payment and whether the extra pay is shared out equally between all those involved or paid as a percentage of basic pay.

2. Neither the type of payment system itself nor any particular feature of the payment systems were associated with variation in success, i.e. success was not related to the kind of scheme introduced.

3. Variations in social and behavioural factors, and especially variations in the extent of consultation about the scheme prior to its introduction explained much of the variation in success between firms. Those firms where there had been extensive consultation at all levels within the organization, including shop stewards and shopfloor workers, had by far the best results.

4. Detailed case studies provided insight into how extensive consultation contributed to some incentive schemes producing good results, and how the lack of consultation was part of the cause of others failing. Firstly, extensive consultation had taken place in those organizations where the managers were closely involved with workers in day-to-day operations; it signalled a feature of the management style used. Secondly, it provided a mechanism whereby managers learned about problems and issues which needed to be taken into account in the design of the scheme. Only through extensive consultation is it possible to take adequate account of the way in which the scheme will impinge on the people in the organization considering their expectations, attitudes, special interests, inter-relationships, vast experience, interpretations, and reactions. Thirdly, extensive consultation contributed to the employees' interest and understanding of the incentive scheme when it was later introduced.

STUDENT ASSIGNMENT 11.2

Incentive Payments and Motivation

1. What can be inferred about employee motivation in the sixty-three organizations studied?
2. To what extent, if any, are these inferences consistent with theories of motivation outlined in this chapter?

an income with which to achieve satisfactions outside the workplace. These findings suggest that some workers may not seek to satisfy higher level needs and that money, after all, *is* a prime motivator.

A main conclusion of research into motivational theories based on need achievements is that different people seek different rewards from their jobs, and that the same people may seek different rewards at different times. Consequently different motivational strategies will be more effective in some contexts and with some people than others.

11.6 Training

Improvements in the quality of the labour force by means of better education and training can undoubtedly raise productivity and improve the operation of the labour market by making labour more occupationally mobile.

Training implies learning. Above all else, therefore, training specialists are educators whose concern is 'how people learn'. Any training scheme must be solidly grounded in educational theory.

Knowles* has compared the *andragogical*** way in which adults learn with the *pedagogical*** learning of children. Adult learners differ from child learners in several important ways:

- Adults see themselves as self-directed and independent; children are dependent on parents, teachers, and others.
- Because they have not acquired much of it, experience may be of little value to children in the classroom. For adults, experience is an important learning resource. Good training will draw upon and build on trainees' experience.

* Knowles, M., *The Adult Learner: A Neglected Species*, 2nd Ed., Gulf Publishing Company, Houston, 1978
** From the Greek andros = man, and pais = child

- Children postpone the application of much of their learning. If learning is to be meaningful to them, adults need to see immediate application.
- Children's readiness to learn is determined by biological development and social pressures. For adults, readiness is based on the tasks that result from social roles.
- Whereas children's orientation to learning is *subject*-centred, that of adults is *problem*-centred.*

These differences have important implications for the planning and methods of training programmes.

11.7 Training Needs Analysis

A systematic approach to training consists of a number of related stages. Such an approach begins with *needs analysis*, i.e. the identification of training needs within an organization. This is not easy. The starting point will be a review of the organization's objectives and its present position in relation to these. In order to determine the skills and knowledge needed by employees to perform job-related tasks more efficiently, it is necessary to identify the *current* as well as the *desired* abilities of employees. The difference will be reflected in a discrepancy between actual and desired performance standards.

A major source of information on training needs will be the ongoing manpower planning. However, identification of sub-standard work performance does not necessarily indicate training needs, since the cause of the inefficiency may be attributable to perhaps lack of motivation or restrictive practices. In such cases training is obviously not the solution. Needs analysis, therefore, should determine if the problem is a 'training need'. In this context the staff appraisal programme and interview can be helpful in identifying individual needs.

More general training needs are often indicated by external events such as changes in legislation. The Health and Safety at Work Act, 1974, for example, triggered an explosion of training courses.

11.8 Training Objectives and Methodology

Training objectives, based on identified training needs, are usually expressed as a series of post-training behaviours that the employee is expected to display in his work.

Planning the training methodology involves deciding on those training techniques and learning activities which will produce the desired outcom-

---

* Knowles, op. cit.

es indicated by the objectives. The choice of techniques and activities will vary with the employee(s) to be trained. Decisions at this stage will have an important influence on the accomplishment of the objectives.

11.9 Evaluating Training

Post-training evaluation is an essential but difficult step. Effective training should produce beneficial effects on organizational objectives and may be reflected in, for example, increased output per man-hour, reductions in labour turnover and absenteeism, improved product quality and less wastage, all of which could contribute to increased profits. The problem is, however, to make a direct link between training and any of these changes, all of which may occur for a variety of reasons other than training.

Because of this and associated difficulties, training is often evaluated by specialist outside consultants. Internal evaluation is often based on trainee reviews in which employees are asked to indicate the degree of satisfaction with the training. The 'smile-sheets' which emerge from such reviews generally provide very little indication of the success or otherwise of training. Evaluation may be more satisfactory in schemes where measurable, behaviour-linked objectives have been set, but even in these cases the limitation of expressing the objectives in narrow behavioural terms may result in inadequate assessment.

However conducted, evaluation provides feedback for the re-diagnosis of training needs and for the preparation of future training programmes.

STUDENT ASSIGNMENT 11.3

A Training Scheme for B/TEC Higher Diploma and Certificate Students

1. What skills are required by a B/TEC Higher Diploma or Certificate student?
2. Establish the extent to which students in your group possess the relevant skills.
3. From your answers to questions 1 and 2 identify the training needs of B/TEC Higher Diploma/Certificate students.
4. On the basis of the identified training needs derive a set of training objectives for such B/TEC students expressed in terms of post-training behaviours.

5. To what extent should the principles of adult learning theory determine the methods and learning activities on a training programme for B/TEC Higher Diploma or Certificate students?
6. How would you evaluate the effectiveness of such a programme?

11.10 Government Training Schemes

The Industrial Training Act, 1964, established a number of Industrial Training Boards (ITBs) each responsible for training within its own industry. In order to stimulate a more efficient training performance each ITB operated a levy and grant system. Each employer above a certain size was required to pay a levy based on payroll and to receive grant, the value of which was determined by the ITB's assessment of its training performance, with a maximum of 150 per cent of levy. The aims of the 1964 Act were to improve training efficiency and to redistribute training costs more equitably between firms.

The Employment and Training Act, 1973, allowed employers (other than in construction) to opt out of the scheme if they could demonstrate that their training was satisfactory. The Act also set up the Training Services Agency (TSA) to supervise the ITBs' operations and to assume responsibility for the Training Opportunities Programme (TOPs) under which engineering, clerical, and other training places were offered to unemployed persons at colleges, Government Skillcentres, and at employer's establishments.

In 1978 there were twenty-four ITBs covering 63 per cent of British industrial workforce. By 1981, despite Manpower Services Commission (MSC) opposition seventeen of the ITBs had been dismantled.

In December 1981, Secretary of State for Employment Norman Tebbit announced the government's New Training Initiative (NTI) which was to take the form of a comprehensive Youth Training Scheme (YTS) to replace the massively expanded and increasingly discredited Youth Opportunities Programme (YOP)* which had provided work experience and work preparation for unemployed sixteen and seventeen year olds.

---

* Under the YOP, work experience was provided at employers' premises, in community projects, and training workshops. Work preparation was provided in the form of short vocational training courses. At the end of June 1983 immediately prior to its demise, 170,000 young people were receiving training under the YOP scheme. The credibility of the YOP scheme was undermined as it became increasingly evident that employers were appointing YOP trainees rather than full-time employees.

11.11 The Youth Training Scheme

The introduction of the YTS in September 1983 was a response to a long-standing and fundamental training crisis which had undoubtedly been an important reason for Britain's relatively slow productivity growth since 1945. In post-war Britain only about one half of sixteen year-olds have received systematic education or training compared with more than 80 per cent in France and 90 per cent in West Germany. The problem of youth training was made more urgent by the onset of economic recession and by a rapid rate of technological change in the late 1970s and 1980s, both of which have contributed to a huge increase in the level and duration of unemployment, especially of the sixteen to twenty year-old age group.

The intention was to give every sixteen year-old school leaver not in full-time education who wants a place on the YTS a foundation year of good quality training and a bridge between school and work. The training concentrates on increasing the adaptability of young people by providing them with non-job-specific skills which will enable them to progress to specific skills training either through an apprenticeship system open to entry at any age and based on standards of competence rather than time served, or through an expanded system of adult training and retraining.

Computer literacy is an important component of the training and increasingly new technology has been introduced into YTS projects giving the 460,000 young people who entered the scheme in 1983 'hands on' experience of computers as part of their year's preparation for the world of work. Specially established Information Technology Centres also play an important part in the YTS.

YTS programmes include both on-the-job and off-the-job training. On-the-job training, whether employer based or on community projects, is supported and reinforced by learning at Colleges of Further Education or training centres. Employers acting as agents for the MSC get a block grant for each trainee to provide a year of integrated work experience and training.

At the time of its inception great hopes were entertained for the YTS. In the words of Employment Minister Peter Morrison 'No longer will our teenagers be regarded as a lost generation. They will be a newly-found generation having skills of great value to an employer. These skills will be equal to or superior to their counterparts in Germany, the United States, or Japan'.* At the same time grave doubts about YTS effectiveness were being expressed. An editorial in the August 1983 issue of an eminent training journal** commented that the YTS 'looks all the world like a

* Department of Employment Press Release, September 1983
** *Industrial and Commercial Training*, vol. 15, no. 8, August 1983, p. 235

death or glory exercise. We have got to the stage where the numbers-game is all-important'.

In April 1985 Employment Secretary, Tom King, claiming the 'great success' of the scheme, confirmed the Government's intention to build on this by extending the YTS training period to two years from April 1986.

Whether or not the YTS has succeeded is difficult to assess. After nearly two years of operation it is estimated that slightly less than a half – 48 per cent – of trainees found employment. On the other hand, it is very worrying that 38 per cent of trainees went straight back to the dole queue.

Measuring success in terms of percentages of trainees subsequently finding work ignores a number of important questions – what kind of job; how long do people stay in it; what career (if any) does it lead to?

Perhaps of even more concern is the fact that the *pattern* or social structure of youth unemployment seems to have been untouched by the scheme. Writing in *The Guardian* (5 July 1985) the director of Youthaid, the pressure group on youth training, claimed that: 'one of the main disappointments of the scheme . . . is that it does not seem to have broken any of the traditional barriers to work. If you go into YTS with one 'O' level, you are twice as likely to get a job, than if you have nothing. Young women get women's jobs, young blacks are much less likely to get jobs than young whites'.

11.12 Summary

1. Among the many factors accounting for Britain's relatively poor productivity performance are a number relating to inefficient labour utilization and poor industrial relations.
2. Comprehensive productivity bargaining involving changes in working practices and arrangements in exchange for higher pay from the resultant savings offer an important means to improved productivity.
3. Productivity bargaining mushroomed in periods of government incomes policies in the 1960s and 1970s, but actual productivity gains were disappointing.
4. For productivity negotiations to be effective they must be comprehensive in coverage of employees, and entered into in a climate of attitudes, induced by managements, in which all employees will become involved in identifying and implementing ways of improving productivity. An essential precondition for success is the commitment of top management to an all-out attack on costs.
5. The efficiency of labour depends upon ability and motivation.
6. No single theory of employee motivation contains the whole truth, though each may contribute something to an understanding.

7. Research into needs-achievement theories suggests that different people seek different job rewards.
8. The importance attached to money rewards varies significantly between different workgroups.
9. Different motivational policies will be more effective in some work settings than others, and with some workgroups and individual employees than others.
10. Motivation depends both on the attributes and needs of the person, and on characteristics of the setting, such as monetary rewards, work and social conditions, and administration.
11. Ability can be improved by appropriate training. Training always implies learning; therefore training schemes should be firmly grounded in educational theory.
12. The ways in which adults and children learn differ in important respects. For example, adults tend to be self-directed, independent, and experienced, wishing to see immediate application of their learning in problem solving.
13. A systematic approach to planning training involves a number of related stages – needs analysis, setting objectives, deciding upon methodology, and post-training evaluation.
14. The government's involvement in industrial training is evidenced by the work of the MSC, the ITBs, and the TSA.
15. In September 1983 the government's comprehensive Youth Training Scheme was introduced, offering unemployed young people college- and workplace-based training for flexibility and in computer skills.

Exercise

Review your understanding of the following:

    productivity
    productivity bargaining
    Maslow's hierarchy of needs
    Herzberg's 'hygienes' and 'motivators'
    job enrichment
    andragogical learning theory
    training needs analysis
    the Youth Training Scheme

Further reading

Pratt, K. J. and Bennett, S. G., *Personnel Management*, Cassell, 1982.

12

The Efficient Use of
Energy and Materials

12.1 Introduction

In the manufacturing sector, materials and energy are required for manufacturing, packaging, and distributing goods as well as for lighting, heating, and ventilating factories, warehouses, and offices. A moment's reflection reveals that service industries are also dependent upon energy and materials for lighting, heating, delivery, and often for performance of the service.

12.2 The Efficient Use of Energy in Industry

In the early 1980s it was estimated that Britain's energy bill amounted to over £20,000 billion per annum or well over £2 million per hour. Industry alone accounted for some 40 per cent of this massive total; industry together with commerce and agriculture accounted for 50 per cent. Throughout the 1970s continually rising fuel prices had a direct and damaging impact on business costs and profits. An official view is that energy prices will more than double in real terms by the end of the century.

We are increasingly aware that the conventional fossil fuels have finite, and in evolutionary terms, quite short remaining lives, and that in the near future oil and gas (which currently account for more than 60 per cent of primary energy use in developed countries) are likely to become scarcer and more expensive. We are equally conscious that supplies of energy and materials are subject to political as well as to potential geological limits, and that important environmental and therefore social and political questions of public acceptability surround both the use of fossil fuels and the development of nuclear power. Whatever alternative sources may be developed in the future it seems, at least for several decades ahead, that the days of cheap and plentiful energy are most unlikely to return.

For the business community the combination of depleting resources and rising costs demands a higher priority for energy conservation and management. In marked contrast to our international trading competitors such as France, Germany, and Japan, Britain is relatively self-sufficient in energy. Paradoxically this makes energy conservation even more imperative in Britain because our competitors have a greater incentive to re-think and adapt their plant, processes, and products to use less energy. If Britain does not do the same, bearing in mind the forecast doubling of energy prices by the year 2000, we may find ourselves uncompetitive in world markets.

12.3 Energy and Materials

As we saw in Chapter 9 the supplies of raw materials, components, machinery, and buildings are all themselves vitally dependent on the use of energy. As non-renewable metals and minerals are used up growing energy requirements are needed in order to explore, develop, extract, purify, process, and transport the less accessible and more difficult deposits. The conservation of materials is thus inseparable from the conservation of fuels – the one promotes the other. Consequently, if industry is to conserve energy effectively and remain competitive in world markets then 'right from the design of the product, the direct energy used in its manufacture and the considerable indirect energy used in the materials it is made from, will have to be minimized and energy policies will need to be adopted to facilitate this process'.*

12.4 Energy Policy in the Business Enterprise

Over the past decade or so, energy management has emerged as a recognized activity in its own right. From the standpoint of the business firm an ongoing energy policy will be reflected in the containment of energy costs and thus will make an increasing contribution to cost control, competitiveness, and improved profitability. In the public sector, cost control is equally vital to ensure the efficient use of scarce resources and to obtain value for taxpayers' money. A long-term energy plan for the enterprise will relate the energy factor to future business objectives.

An essential pre-condition for the success of an energy policy is a strong and expressed commitment to energy conservation on the part of the Chief

---

* National Economic Development Council, *Industrial Implications of Energy Policy*, 1978

Executive or his equivalent. Ideally, a specific member of the Board will take on personal responsibility for energy conservation and put into effect what Hancock* calls a 'first strike' energy-conserving programme to lay the foundations for a more comprehensive energy policy.

It will be important to measure the success of the policy at constant (i.e. inflation-adjusted) prices per unit of output or service supplied using the starting date of the policy as the base line.

At the end of say two years (long enough to allow measurement of performance) it may be necessary to re-adjust the policy in the light of experience and changing conditions within the firm and externally. It is crucial to set carefully calculated realistic performance targets based wherever possible on consultation and agreement with all interested parties and expressed in terms of a percentage reduction of energy cost per unit of output or service to be saved.

A further component of policy concerns the incorporation of an energy statement in all proposals for capital investment. Since payback periods often extend ten years or more into the future it is vital that full account is taken of energy use in the operation of new buildings and machinery if the rising cost and increasing scarcity of energy are not to render plant uneconomic before the end of its operational life.

In order to monitor the policy and provide basic data upon which decisions can be taken, an energy audit system will be formulated and applied. The energy audits will record all forms of energy consumption within the organization and provide information on its costs and uses for production, space heating, lighting, refrigerating, ventilation, cleaning, and so on.

If the policy is to be effective in its primary objectives of saving energy and reducing costs it will be important to create an 'energy awareness' and the commitment of all employees to its success. This in turn calls for clear communication of the policy and the targets, motivation, and training for the total workforce, together with dissemination of regular feedback on progress made towards the achievement of targets.

Responsibility for the overall policy will rest with senior management who already carry sectional responsibility for cost effectiveness and for control of the relevant areas of the workforce, machinery, and equipment, and who are therefore in the best position to ensure success.

For the policy to succeed it needs to be seen to be effective. Consequently, progress should be carefully monitored by senior management who will ensure that a reporting system indicates the success of the various departments and sections of the organization as well as those areas where further efforts are necessary to improve energy conservation. Progress

---

* Hancock, C., 'Facing up to Energy in the Future', *Management Today*, July 1981

reports should be sent directly to the top manager within the organization, e.g. the chief executive in a company.

Finally, the benefits of the policy should be clearly identified in terms of financial savings of the target level of x per cent of the total annual energy bill for the organization. These savings may then be expressed as a direct financial contribution to profitability allowing for energy inflation over the period of the policy.

Hancock has outlined the essential features of a 'first strike programme', the objective of which would be to remove the larger causes of energy wastage. Such a programme consists of two components:

- a technical energy survey;
- an initial energy audit.

The technical survey will aim to identify points in the enterprise's energy distribution system where avoidable losses or unjustifiable uses occur. It may reveal, for example, unnecessary openings in buildings through which heat is lost; inadequate or absent insulation; excessive steam or air pressure; unnecessarily bright lighting; or continuous and unnecessary idling of motors. A 10 per cent reduction in energy use is commonly achieved as a result of such an energy survey.

The first stage of the initial energy audit will be to measure and cost all types of energy purchased by the enterprise in the previous year. The results expressed in common units will be analysed in order to show whether the organization has bought the most cost-effective energy for its purpose. On the basis of this information it will be possible to draw up an energy balance sheet showing for each type of energy used the actual or estimated consumption by department. These consumption figures can be related to production, building space, outside temperatures, number of employees, or whatever other factors the enterprise considers to be relevant. Finally, for each major energy 'consumer' within the enterprise it will be possible to identify a number of alternative ways of conserving energy either by changes in customary ways of doing things or by investment in new or modified plant and equipment.

The information yielded by the initial energy audit will provide the basis for some preliminary policy decisions including, for example

- the setting of energy savings targets related to objective criteria such as output;
- decisions concerning the purchased energy mix;
- the drafting of a preliminary energy budget based on interim consumption norms derived from historical month-by-month records of output, climate, and so on.

12.5 The Role of the Energy Manager

Many larger organizations now appoint specialist energy managers. This is an important step, emphasizing the priority which the enterprise attaches to energy conservation. In smaller organizations it is equally advisable to designate a specific member of the management team as energy manager, even if he or she is only able to devote part of his or her time to this function along with a range of other duties.

The role of the energy manager is highly integrated with every aspect and function of the business from product research and design to processing and marketing. Like other functional managers, the energy manager is an essential part of the wealth-creating team whose concern is with ensuring the future competitiveness and profitability of the enterprise, and it is on his contribution to these goals that he will be judged.

In a paper prepared for a recent Department of Energy sponsored National Energy Managers Course, Henshaw listed the main qualities required of a successful energy manager. Important among these are:

- the ability to communicate well with a capacity to listen as well as talk – this includes the ability to use appropriate language and analogies to all levels from director to shopfloor employee;
- the ability to be a good administrator, able to generate, analyse, and manipulate essential information on energy issues without which there is no framework within which to manage, take decisions, or justify expenditure;
- the ability to prepare clear, lucid, interesting, and concise reports;
- a preparedness to consider and examine all possibilities, however unlikely these may initially appear;
- an approach which is enthusiastic, articulate, persuasive, and which rests on sure knowledge of the facts;
- a willingness to accept that the advice and knowledge he or she proffers will sometimes be disregarded in decision-making, but that this does not necessarily indicate failure on the part of the energy manager;
- a good understanding of people.

The reader will readily recognize that these are just those abilities which are required of the good and effective manager whatever his particular specialism within the management team.

Having mentioned the qualities required of an effective energy manager, we now outline his objectives and responsibilities in the enterprise which will usually include:

- reporting directly to the Board or the Chief or Senior Exectuive;
- developing and maintaining a cost-effective energy audit system which

on a regular basis will supply and analyse information on energy purchases, costs, stocks, consumption, and so on. The energy manager will be the focal point for records of energy use and the person directly responsible for their analysis. He or she will require access to financial and other data, and it may be necessary for metering or other monitoring equipment to be installed in certain cases;

- relating energy consumption to unit of output of product or service and deriving agreed attainable departmental targets in consultation with relevant heads of sections or departments;

- preparation of an energy budget on the basis of analyses derived from the energy audit system. This should be regarded as important a policy objective as the financial budget. The budget will establish consumption norms for each consumer in the organization, who will be held accountable for his energy record as he is for output, quality, cost control, and so on;

- setting up an Energy Action Group consisting of other managers selected for their skills, responsibilities, and levels of authority to assist in the co-ordinating of the efforts of all energy users in the enterprise. It is through members of this group that the energy manager will have that essential and direct communication with the general workforce. In large organizations (e.g. NHS or public corporations) it may be sensible to have more than one action group covering different locations or activities. The energy manager's role here will be to cross-fertilize between the groups;

- maintaining an up-to-date technical library of energy-saving products and systems, services, and techniques in order to provide management with information, recommendations, and technical advice on these matters;

- to liaise with external groups in his own industry and with research organizations, professional bodies, government organizations, local energy managers' groups and so on. The Regional Energy Conservation Officer of the Department of Trade and Industry will advise on government measures and grants to promote energy conservation;

- to examine, appraise, and advise upon any political, legislative, and regulatory measures relating to energy to assess their possible impact on the organization's activities and products;

- to monitor changing developments at global and national level which affect energy availability and costs and to advise senior management on their possible effects on the enterprise. This involves attempting to read the future with all its uncertainties, and is an enormously difficult if not impossible task. Nevertheless, no one but the energy manager should be closer to the energy scene to interpret the evolving energy situation. Failure to predict the future effects of shortage, sudden price escalation, and conversion costs may have disastrous effects on profitability or the capacity to achieve other organizational objectives;

- to advise on all new capital investment projects if plant and equipment are not rapidly to become uneconomic due to rising energy costs;
- in conjunction with the action group to initiate and prepare practical and easily understood energy codes of practice setting out simple rules or guidelines relating to methods of using energy within the enterprise;
- to increase and sustain an energy awareness at every level within the enterprise. This is a most important aspect of the energy manager's job which often means changing deep-seated attitudes and practices. The creation of energy awareness will require persuading, educating, and motivating the entire workforce. The aim is to make energy conservation an integral part of the routine practices in the organization by making everyone aware of the need to conserve. This calls for effective communication of what is proposed, why it is proposed, how they can help, and for regular feedback of information on the progress made towards the achievement of targets. Considerable diplomacy will be needed – no one likes to be told they are using energy inefficiently. Well organized and planned training sessions involving two-way discussion of problems can also be helpful.

Many smaller firms will not have the resources or staff to appoint energy managers, even on a part-time basis. This most certainly should not be taken to mean that nothing can be done about energy conservation. Energy conservation has been described as the substitution of intelligence and prudence for purchased fuel. It has amply demonstrated that good housekeeping (such as switching off unnecessary lighting or heating; closing windows and doors; and maintaining machinery and equipment regularly) aided by the use of checklists can achieve significant energy savings for relatively little expenditure of time and money.

12.6 Information Technology and Energy Conservation

Small variations in heating of a building can have a significant impact on the final fuel bill. For instance, maintaining a building's temperature just 1°C above the required level can result in a 10 per cent increase in heating costs. A twenty-minute error in heating start time adds 4 per cent to heating costs.

A number of microprocessor-based energy control systems are currently available, designed to provide the accuracy which will prevent such waste. Applied to the control of building heating, ventilation, and lighting, these systems can cut fuel bills by up to 30 per cent and at the same time improve working conditions. A typical system consists of one or more microprocessor-based control units which can work independently or be linked to a central supervisory unit. This, and the modular design, makes it possible to provide systems cost-effectively regardless of the size of buildings.

Big improvements have been made on traditional controls which regulated only one variable to a pre-set level. The more integrated approach changes the plant conditions in order to meet the building's needs while using minimum energy by taking into account all the variables affecting its environment. The result is an energy control system that matches itself to the particular building. As no two buildings are identical, this is an essential requirement if energy savings are to be maximized. Control of heating is based on a self-adapting modelling technique used to predict the required heating performance. The system can be used to control lighting (e.g. automatic turn-off at the end of the working day, turning off unneeded lights when daylight is adequate, and adjusting illumination levels); heating or cooling (automatic control of start/stop times, adjustment to air temperature or of outside air used to reduce the

Figure 12.1. Increasing energy prices and falling electronic costs.

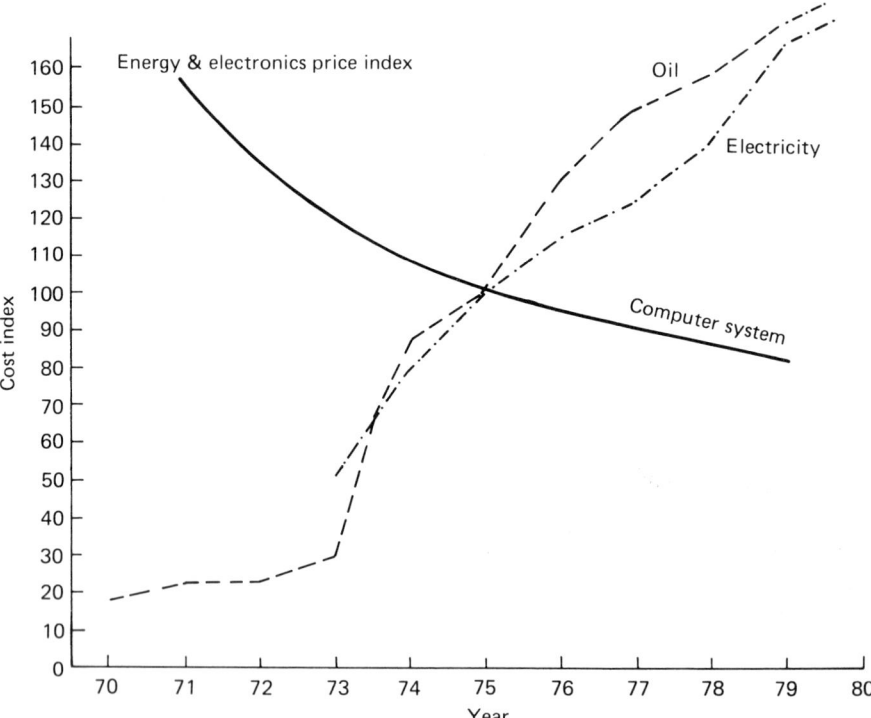

Source: Industrial Management and Data Systems, February/March, 1981.

amount of heating or cooling required); limiting maximum peak demand use (when electricity charges are higher) by load-shedding where this is possible.

All control units are self-adaptive, i.e. they learn the actual characteristics of the building. Thus, as the equipment actually matches itself to the building to provide the best possible results the problems of inaccurate set-up are largely avoided. Self-diagnostic routines which check the operation of the control units and the validity of the data arising from their sensors leads to quick and appropriate action to remedy waste detected from faults in the system.

The supervisory computer is a simple device which allows its user to find out simply what is happening and what has happened in the building, and to change what will happen. It is used to progress all working information to each control unit – temperature, working hours, holidays, shutdowns, etc. This information is set up for each day of the week. The supervisory computer also provides current information on any sensor in the building and keeps a daily log of all major variables. Such a system also aids preventative maintenance by storing a suitable schedule and information as to when any item has reached its maintenance target. Figure 12.1 shows that advanced automated control of energy use has been made economically viable by a combination of increasing energy prices and falling electronic costs.

12.7 The Wider Context of Conservation

Looked at from a wider social perspective the many benefits of using energy and materials more efficiently include:

- a less rapid use of non-renewable fossil fuels and minerals reduces dependence on overseas supplies which for political reasons may be subject to sudden disruption or price increase;
- the environmental damage associated with the production and use of energy and the mining of fuels and metals is extensive, consequently the less energy and materials used per unit of output the more is environmental quality preserved;
- a less wasteful use of energy and materials helps to preserve resources for future generations;
- from a macro-economic viewpoint, sustained energy and materials conservation can play a crucial part in keeping down the level of unit costs in industry, thereby helping Britain's international competitiveness, trading performance, and balance of payments;
- a wasteful use of resources is a luxury that not only can we no longer afford but one which is morally offensive in a world in which millions live in extreme poverty.

STUDENT ASSIGNMENT 12.1

Energy Conservation in Woodlands Furniture PLC

You have just been appointed as trainee manager with Woodlands Furniture PLC, a manufacturer of high class furniture. You are asked to investigate the potential for energy conservation within the enterprise. How would you proceed?

Remember the importance of:

1. Reporting and good communications.
2. Creating an energy awareness.
3. The use of an energy survey and energy audit.
4. The need for energy conservation to be cost-effective.
5. The availability of advice and funding.

Present your findings as a short report to the Chief Executive.

STUDENT ASSIGNMENT 12.2

Outline the initial steps you would take to promote greater energy conservation in your home, your college department, or your place of employment.

12.8 Waste Management Policy Through the Product Life Cycle

A comprehensive waste management policy would therefore involve not only an ongoing and effective system of energy management, but 'a coherent system of measures concerning the design, manufacture and use of products as well as reclamation and disposal of wastes and aiming at the most efficient and economic reduction of the nuisances and costs generated by waste'.* The opportunities for saving materials and energy are

* *OECD and The Environment*, OECD, Paris, 1979

probably as great as those aimed at increasing supplies. A manufacturing company's demand for these resources is affected by decisions taken throughout the product life cycle and specifically its demand for non-renewables will be affected by:

- the design features of its products and their packaging. It is at this stage that the kinds and quantities of materials to be used are specified;
- the durability (i.e. useful lives) of its products, and related to this the extent to which the products can be re-used or their constituents recycled when the goods themselves can no longer be used;
- the manner in which its products are used by customers, which depends to some extent on design features and marketing style. Educating the customer on the effects of different modes of consumption, e.g. a dashboard dial indicating m.p.g. at different vehicle speeds, can also help;
- the energy requirements for manufacturing and distributing products and for the materials on which those activities depend;
- the choice of processing and fabrication methods determines how much waste is generated;
- the energy requirements in use;
- the research programmes through which the knowledge is developed which may lead to more efficient materials processing and methods.

Decisions taken at the design stage in particular will have crucial effects on the subsequent use of materials and energy. Product design is strongly influenced, and perhaps almost totally determined in some cases, by the nature of the 'product concept', i.e. the group of needs or desires the product is intended to satisfy. Product concepts are embodied in society's cultural values which they themselves help to shape. These values, embracing such things as fashion, modernity, ostentation, prestige, and status, may be influenced strongly by advertising and other media presentations.

Because product concepts affect the size, extent of useful life, range of accessories needed, and energy requirements in use of products, they can have a major impact on business resource consumption. And because cultural values tend to change only slowly they place limits on the speed, direction, and risks involved in changing the product concepts which so strongly condition product designs. Yet it is precisely by changing product concepts or introducing new ones that finite resources can be conserved or conversely used up more rapidly.

If, for example, large size of a house or a car or a lawn mower or whatever was no longer seen as a prestige symbol, or if newness was demoted down the scale of social values and as a desirable product attribute, designers could begin to attach more importance to designing products for durability, easy repair, preventative maintenance, recyclability of materials, and so on.

Specific design actions promoting materials and energy conservation might include some of the following:*

- simplification – the elimination of the needless features of a product, e.g. foregoing elaborate changes in style of automobiles intended to increase sales by what has been called 'cosmetic obsolescence', i.e. the social obsolescence of otherwise useful items that are no longer 'trendy';
- miniaturization – designing smaller products where size is not of critical functional importance;
- materials selection – the careful matching of the characteristics of the materials used with the functional requirements of the products avoids over-design of products and packaging. Corrosion and excessive wear can be minimized by good materials selection;
- design for greater useful product life;
- design of products for easy recovery and recycling.

CASE STUDY 12.1

Extending the Product Life

Certainly the supply of materials can be extended and the accompanying burden on the US environment eased by improving the durability or useful life of our products. This approach has been offset to a large degree over the past few decades by 'cosmetic obsolescence' practices stimulated by media advertising and product designs that defied preventative maintenance, easy repair and economical recycling of the basic materials. The solution for these faulty past practices lies with the product designer and his employer who must adopt a 'conservation ethic'. It is going to take the combined efforts of the US government, national academics, academia and the professional technical societies to indoctrinate the engineering and management professions with an effective concept of maximizing materials effectiveness.

(*Source:* Ballard, D. W. *An American View of Problems of Materials Conservation*, National Commission on Materials Policy, 1974)

* Ballard, D. W., *An American View of Problems of Materials Conservation*, National Commission on Materials Policy, 1974

STUDENT ASSIGNMENT 12.3

Product Durability

Consider and report on the following questions:

1. To what extent does the private enterprise have a social responsibility to design products that will last longer?
2. To what extent does designing products with a view to extending their useful life conflict with (a) traditional business goals of sales and profitability? (b) product concepts and cultural values?
3. To what extent is private enterprise likely to adopt a policy of greater product durability?
4. Has government a part to play in encouraging conservation through the manufacture of longer-lasting products? If so, what kinds of measures should government introduce?
5. Consider the implications for

   (a) exporting
   (b) employment
   (c) profits
   (d) growth

12.9 Using Materials More Efficiently

In a world of finite resources the wasteful use of energy and materials is increasingly regarded as anti-social by large sections of public opinion. Waste adds to environmental pollution; waste is the planned obsolescence of many products; waste is the ubiquitous piles of ugly litter. Consumer associations, conservation and environmental groups, and even political parties campaign ever more vigorously to stop the destruction of resources and ecology.

The socially responsible business firm will willingly respond to public demand for improved efficiency in the use of materials. But this will not be easy since it implies abandoning conventional rationality which lauds an increase in sales revenue brought about by built-in obsolescence or cosmetic obsolescence; the promotion of sales through elaborate and ostentatious packaging; and the striving to expand continuously the range of consumer wants.

12.10 Summary

1. Present and future supplies of energy and materials are subject to diverse geological and political constraints. These are likely to continue to have direct impacts on business costs and profits.
2. A combination of depleting resources and rising costs demands a higher priority for energy conservation and management in business firms.
3. Since growing energy requirements are necessary to extract, process, and transport industrial raw materials, the conservation of materials is inseparable from the conservation of fuels.
4. In recent years energy management has emerged as a recognized activity in its own right. An essential requirement for a successful energy policy is strong commitment from top management.
5. A 'first strike' programme to eliminate the larger causes of energy wastage consists of a technical energy survey and an initial energy audit. The former aims to identify avoidable losses and unjustifiable uses of energy within the organization. The latter measures and costs all energy usage in common units and relates the results to production, building space, outside temperatures, or number of employees.
6. The initial energy audit provides the basis for energy savings targets, decisions for the purchased energy mix and the preliminary energy budget.
7. The role of an energy manager is highly integrated with every aspect and function of the business. He or she will be required to develop a cost-effective energy audit system, prepare an energy budget, establish an energy action group, advise on technical, market, and political matters, and create and sustain energy awareness throughout the organization.
8. Microprocessor-based energy control systems can cut fuel bills by up to 30 per cent.
9. The more efficient use of energy and materials produces benefits not only for the individual enterprise but also for the wider society.
10. A comprehensive waste management policy involves measures relating to the design, manufacture, packaging, and use of products as well as efficient reclamation, re-use, or disposal of wastes.
11. Product concepts are embodied in society's cultural values which they help to shape. Product concepts affect the size, extent of useful life, and energy requirements in the use of products, and consequently have a major impact on business resource consumption.
12. Materials and energy conservation can be promoted by the simplification and miniaturization of products, by careful materials selection, and by design for greater durability and easy recovery and recycle.

Exercise

Review your understanding of the following:

business energy policy
energy audit
the role of the energy manager
the wider context of conservation
waste management through the product life cycle

Further Reading

International Energy Agency, *Energy Management Guide*, OECD, 1980.
International Energy Agency, *Energy Management: An Effective Approach to Strengthen Energy Conservation*, OECD, 1980.
Payne, G. A., *The Energy Managers' Handbook*, IPC, 1977.

PART V

FORECASTING, CONTROLLING, AND MEASURING RESOURCES

13

Manpower Planning and Staff Appraisal

13.1 Manpower Planning

The Department of Employment has described manpower planning as 'a strategy for the acquisition, utilization, improvement and retention of an enterprise's human resources'. Its basic tasks are to identify and measure potential future imbalances between labour demand and supply and to devise appropriate manpower policies to offset or minimize such imbalances. Manpower planning is also expected to contribute to greater efficiency in the utilization of labour. It may therefore have the following main objectives:

- to ensure that the organization has adequate (but not more than adequate) *numbers* of people with the right training and experience available to meet the present and future demand for the organization's good or service and to achieve whatever organizational objectives have been set;
- to contribute to the provision of secure and stable employment for individual employees;
- to improve the efficiency with which manpower is utilized;
- to contribute to the control of manpower costs.

Given these objectives, it is apparent that manpower planning is an integral component of the wider activity of corporate planning and should be linked to the overall objectives of the organization. Manpower plans both depend upon and affect other key areas of planning such as finance, marketing, sales, production, and technological innovation. It is therefore a multi-disciplinary process, the success of which depends upon the co-operation and expertise of management and staff having various functional responsibilities within the organization, as well as upon the

Figure 13.1.   The manpower planning process.

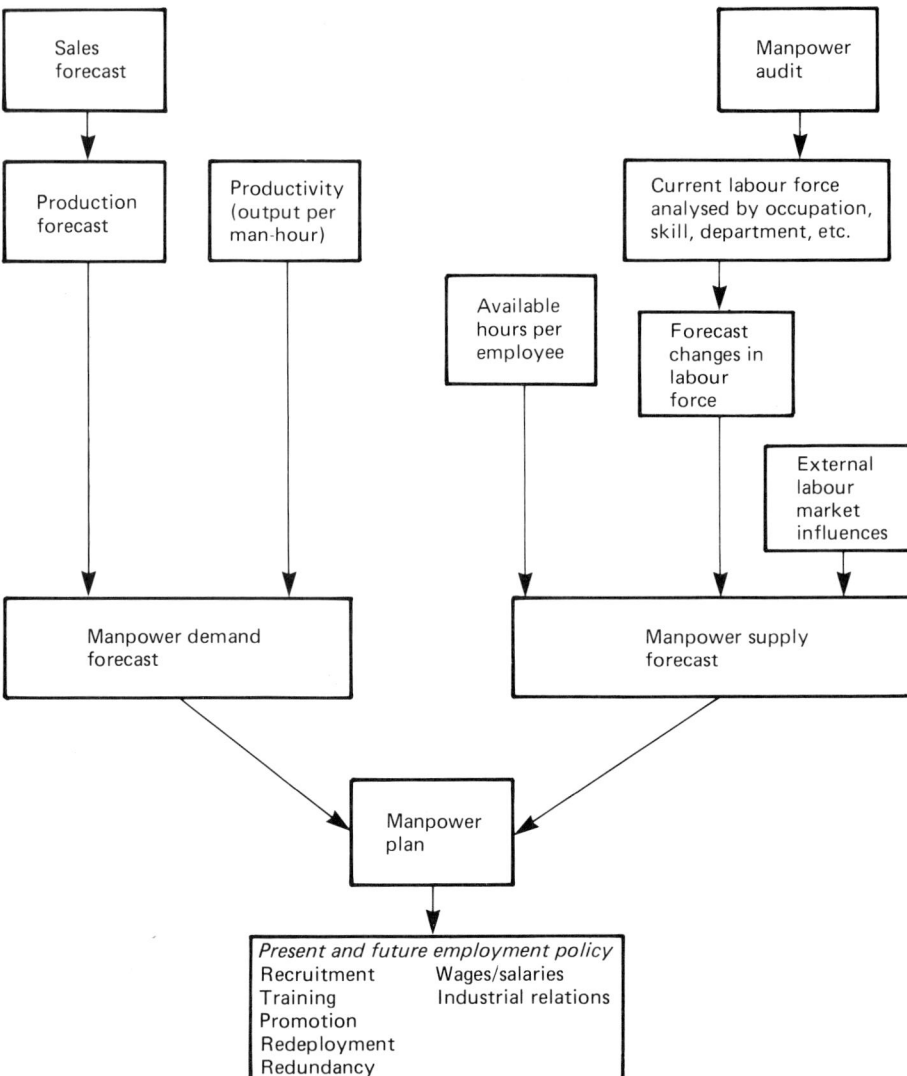

contribution of the personnel specialists who may have overall responsibility.

The manpower planning process entails:

- an audit of existing manpower resources. This has value in highlighting problems requiring immediate attention as well as providing a basis for forecasting future supply;

- a forecast of future manpower requirements which will derive from production and sales or demand forecasts together with influences such as changes in technology and in organizational structure;
- a manpower supply forecast taking account of trends within the organization such as labour turnover, promotion, retirement, and redeployment;
- an attempt to determine and predict manpower costs. This involves co-operation with the accountant and with other departments.

If the plan is to contribute to effective decision-making which is its main purpose a continuous flow of information will be required both from within and from outside the organization in order to forecast future demand and supplies of skilled labour, including managerial and administrative staff. (Figure 13.1 summarizes the manpower planning process.)

13.2 The Manpower Demand Forecast

The manpower demand forecast relies heavily on information from the marketing department in the form of sales forecasts. The attempt to relate forecast production levels and required manpower may be based on *ratio-trend analysis*. For example if in a Mail Order company, the ratio of packers to orders is 1 : 200, then an extra packer would be required for every increase of 200 in the number of orders. Productivity improvements would of course increase the ratio of orders to packers, and some estimate of the potential for this would also be necessary. A similar kind of analysis can be based on the ratio of one category of employee to another, e.g. if in a manufacturing enterprise the ratio of supervisors to operatives is 1 : 20 then for every additional 20 operatives needed, one extra supervisor must be recruited.

In large and complex organizations, computerized econometric models may be constructed on the basis of statistical data analysed to show measured relationships between all the many variables which are likely to affect the organization's manpower demand (e.g. sales, technological innovation, etc.). Such models will be based on management assumptions and judgements about the future. Thus although econometric models can reduce uncertainty the predictions thrown up by the model will only be as good as the judgements built in to it. Mathematical manipulation, however sophisticated, does not avoid the need for managerial judgement.

13.3 The Manpower Supply Forecast

In order to forecast changes in labour supply information will be required not only about the current labour force, but also about labour turnover and retirement trends, redeployment, training, and so on. The supply of man-hours will vary with changes in the level of overtime working, shift patterns, absenteeism, accidents and sickness. Changes in the external local labour markets will indicate changes in the availability of different skills and movements in comparative earnings of different categories of employee. Again in those large organizations using computerized mathematical models supply variables such as those mentioned above can be incorporated alongside the demand variables to provide a comprehensive picture of the future manpower situation subject always to the important qualifications already mentioned.

The basis of any plan is information. In the particular case of planning, nothing less than a comprehensive manpower information system, parallel to the financial information system provided by the accountant, is required. Since gathering relevant information is often costly, the extent to which it will be available will depend upon management's judgement of the balance between the costs of data collection and the benefits of effective manpower planning. Much of the information needed will already be available if accurate personnel records and statistics are maintained, in which case the costs will mainly arise in the analysis of the data.

It will be apparent to the reader that manpower planning is a comprehensive, continuous and often complex activity. Adjustments to the plan are constantly made in the light of feedback from within the organization and changes in the environment. Given the many uncertainties about the future, manpower planning tends to operate within fairly short-term time horizons i.e. of five years or less. However, since different categories of employee require differing lengths of training, if the plan is to produce the necessary corrective to any imbalance between supply and demand, the period of the manpower forecast will tend to be determined by the 'lead times' for training the relevant kinds of labour.

In an age of rapid technological change, changes in the capital labour ratio are inevitable and the product range and sales of an organization may be subject to unexpected change. The uncertain pace of technological innovation and the rate at which employees need to be retrained, redeployed, recruited or made redundant cannot be precisely determined in advance. Among many other uncertainties are those concerning the rate of economic growth, changes in incomes and consumers' tastes and preferences.

For many categories of non-manufacturing labour forecasting is even more complex. Consider, for example, forecasting the supply and demand for doctors for a number of years ahead.* The demand for doctors

* Example from Hunter, L. C. and Robertson, D. J., *Economics of Wages and Labour*, Macmillan, 1969

depends on (a) the size and structure of the population, (b) the ratio of doctors to population regarded by society as socially desirable, (c) the organization, financing and management of the NHS, (d) the incidence of illness and the kinds of illness, and (e) the emigration of doctors from developing nations to the UK. Since changes in all these variables cannot be forecast with any degree of certainty, how can we forecast any future 'shortage' of doctors?

For all these reasons manpower forecasting is invariably subject to a large degree of uncertainty and imprecision. Nevertheless the primary value of manpower planning to organizations is as a means of reducing uncertainty. Imprecise as it may be it can enable organizations to improve the quality of their employment policies. As a NEDO report has pointed out

> Manpower planning enabled them [companies surveyed] to foresee changes and identify trends in the labour force earlier than would have been possible and meant that employment policies could be adapted in good time so as to avoid major problems.*

CASE STUDY 13.1

Medical Manpower Planning

There are any number of people who will point out the terrible waste of resources in setting up a manpower information system. The reality is, however, that unless we know how manpower is being used, the other management information systems are of very little use in planning resources for services.

The implication, of course, is that better management information and quality of service are in some way mutually exclusive when in reality they are entirely complementary. You need only ask the managing director of B.L. what he regards as the most important influence on the quantity and quality of cars he produces to understand the importance of the manpower resource in his organization. And if you were to suggest to him that he should plan his production and development without knowing how many people he was employing or how many hours they were working he would regard you with disbelief. If you were to suggest to him that he should attempt to run his business on the basis of statistical returns which were more than a year old he would probably laugh.

* *Case Studies in Company Manpower Planning*, a summary of a joint MSC/NEDO Report, NEDC, 1978

Yet, this is what the Health Service has been doing for years. Manpower returns with which to compare performance with other authorities in the NHS are produced on a yearly basis and are usually at least a year out of date. Such information is adequate for regional or national planning purposes because it indicates trends, but it is of very limited use for day-to-day control. And to a certain extent this is what is wrong with information gathering in the NHS; information is produced for the wrong purposes, and resources for purchasing new technology tend to be concentrated in the wrong areas. We have concentrated on providing information for planning in the past when we were not aware of how existing resources were being used.

In the report the Group dealt with the very important and yet largely uncharted area of linking manpower, financial, and activity information to provide in a true sense a management information system. There was not enough time in our deliberations to give this subject proper attention but pilot districts were to look at the practicality of using a combination of finance codes and payscale codes to derive the occupation descriptions currently identified within the national list of occupation codes.

I understand that a considerable degree of success has been achieved already in this work and that technically it is possible to use these methods to produce the occupation descriptions. This being so, it should be possible to identify manpower utilisation with the expenditure in a particular location, provided the financial coding system is structured accordingly. The 'missing link', therefore, appears to have been discovered but I have no doubt further development work will be required before the NHS is convinced.

Having established the manpower being used in a particular location and the cost of using it, it only remains to link this information with output and it is in this area we start to run into problems. First of all, how do you define output or, as it is more commonly referred to in the NHS, workload? Is there one measure of workload in a hospital? Or is the measure itself a combination of interacting factors which come in different mixes and proportions depending upon the unit? I am not able to do justice to this subject, nor could I within the confines of this article. There is no doubt, however, that this link between manpower and expenditure on the one hand, and activity on the other must be found, otherwise we will never be able to measure reliably the performance of a unit or district over time or, indeed, one unit with another. And if we cannot do that, can we reasonably claim to be managing and planning the Heath Service? Ask the man from B.L!

(*Source*: Young, I. 'Observations on the implications of Korner Working Group on Manpower', *Health Services Manpower Review*, vol. 9, No. 2, August 1983, pp. 10–12)

STUDENT ASSIGNMENT 13.1

Manpower Planning in the National Health Service

In the context of a vigorous debate about the proper level of public expenditure on the NHS, the government argues that greater efficiency in the use of resources within the service can result in improved patient care.

1. In what ways do you think that effective manpower planning can contribute to a higher standard of medical care? How can standards of care be measured?
2. Broadly speaking, what kinds of information would be needed to make the necessary manpower forecasts?
3. In general terms, how could such information be obtained?
4. How precise would the manpower forecasts be?
5. If there is a degree of imprecision, does this invalidate the manpower planning exercise?

13.4 Staff Appraisal

Simply stated, staff appraisal involves the measurement of human performance in work roles with the objectives of evaluating the performance and/or the potential of existing employees of an organization. In recent years there has been an increased use of staff appraisal systems by private and public employers, and concurrently a growth in the number and sophistication of appraisal methods. This is perhaps surprising, given that most authorities agree that appraisal results are somewhat vague and unreliable, and that the development and implementation of an appraisal system may be costly and fraught with risk. To understand its increasing popularity we examine appraisal in some detail paying particular attention to its objectives, its potential benefits and its links with virtually every other aspect of personnel management.

The two broad objectives of appraisal are

- to provide management information;
- to foster employee growth and development and through this to improve employee motivation.

Perhaps the best way to evaluate the first objective is to imagine a large company with no appraisal system. In such an enterprise manpower decisions such as promotions, salary changes, staff transfers, dismissals and so on are still made. But the information upon which such decisions are based comes from 'the grapevine' i.e. the informal sometimes uncon-scious (!) and often unreliable appraisal of subordinates which managers and supervisors carry out as part of their day-to-day contact. The question is, 'How can management operate the enterprise and make decisions when information on one of their most costly resources is so highly question-able?'.

Obviously decisions in general are better decisions the more accurate is the information upon which they are based. Staff appraisal provides such information to management in order to improve the quality of manpower decisions. The information though not perfectly accurate will be of a better standard and less subjective than that gained from the 'grapevine'.

The second general objective of staff appraisal – to achieve higher levels of employee motivation – is perhaps less certain in its outcome.

More specifically staff appraisal offers the following potential benefits to employing organizations:

- the provision of an objective basis for pay awards;
- the improvement of individual efficiency in work roles;
- the provision of information for manpower planning and corporate planning by revealing skill supplies and shortages;
- the provision of data for recruitment policy;
- the identification of weaknesses calling for additional training;
- the identification of employees whose abilities are being under-utilized, leading to promotions or redeployment;
- the provision of feedback on the effectiveness of recruitment and training programmes;
- greater accuracy in the measurement of job performance can improve job effectiveness thus helping employee growth and development through fulfilment of their potential;
- an increase in motivation deriving from employees' awareness of regular observation/measurement by managers.

Staff appraisal systems take many forms, the choice among which depends upon the objectives an organization wishes to achieve through appraisal, as well as other factors such as the nature of its technology and industrial relations policies. No single appraisal method will be suitable to all organizations. The description which follows necessarily therefore provides only a generalized and simplified account of staff appraisal.

In any kind of scheme there are essentially three stages:

- preparation of a report on each employee to be appraised;
- an interview with each employee based on his or her report;
- appropriate action determined by the outcomes of the first two stages.

The report is based on a standardized form on which various job characteristics derived from job analyses are listed. Associated with each of these appears a linear scale, say one to five, upon which the appraiser records his assessment.

The interview can be regarded as a mutual learning situation affording opportunities to build employee morale and confidence and for offering appropriate assistance such as further training where this is necessary. There is no doubt that open, honest, and constructive discussion can help to build up mutual trust and commitment between management and other employees.

After the interview it is important that any proposed and agreed follow-up action is implemented quickly. Such action could, for example, take the form of training, regrading, salary increase, promotion or transfer. In rare cases it may even consist of some kind of disciplinary measures.

The simple three-stage outline of staff appraisal conceals many of the complexities and difficulties which can arise in practice. Important among these are:

- Who is to carry out the appraisal? In principle this could be the supervisor or immediate superior of the employee, groups of supervisors, senior management, the employee him or herself, and/or sources outside the organization (e.g. clients). In one well publicized case the U.S. Armed Forces introduced a system of appraisal by subordinates which, needless to say, did not always prove to be very popular!

  Commonly, the appraiser is the immediate supervisor who has day-to-day contact with the employee and experience of his or her work and who is thought to be best equipped for this task. This practice, however, holds a serious role conflict for the supervisor. On the one hand, the supervisor is being asked by his/her superior for accurate information on individual employee performance (and inevitably this implies on the *differences* between individuals). On the other hand, the whole basis of good supervision is the maintenance of trusting relationships with employees. If rewards are associated with the different assessments this makes the supervisor's task of maintaining trust even more difficult. This problem is summed up graphically in Figure 13.2.

- For reasons hinted at above, there may be resistance to appraisal procedures by both appraiser and/or employee. Supervisors may fear the disruption of good relationships with employees or may in any case dislike 'playing God'. Employees may show nervous or even hostile reactions and seek ways of circumventing the process if they feel threatened by the appraisal. The outcome may then be distorted as the staff to be appraised produce defensive or stereotyped responses or even

Figure 13.2.   Role conflict in staff appraisal.

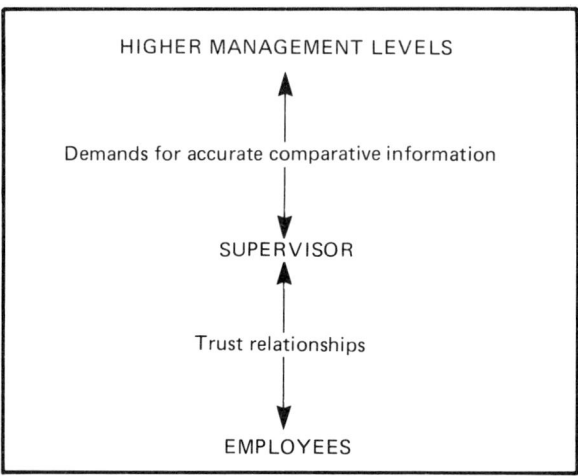

as a group decide to 'buck the system' by working to rule or performing well just before the appraisal and then relaxing.

- However sophisticated is the design of the appraisal scheme, the problem of subjectivity is likely to manifest itself in some form or other. Pratt and Bennett★ mention four common manifestations of subjectivity in staff appraisal:

  (a) the 'halo' effect and stereotyping – a particular behaviour shown by the employee leads the appraiser to bias favourably or unfavourably other factors in performance;

  (b) constant error – since some appraisers tend to use only the upper end of the rating scale and some only the lower end it is difficult to compare assessments by different appraisers;

  (c) central tendency – this arises when (as is common) raters tend to exclude the higher and lower ends of the appraisal scale, grouping all employees as 'average'. Though this may be accurate it is more likely to be an indicator of the appraiser's unwillingness to judge his or her subordinates;

  (d) recency – behaviour immediately preceding the appraisal may unreasonably colour the assessment.

These are formidable problems which emphasize the importance of careful design of the appraisal system.

As we have already pointed out there is no single universally applicable

★ Pratt, K. J. and Bennet, S. G., *Personnel Management*, Cassell, 1982 appraisal scheme which can meet the needs of all organizations. Nevertheless some features of appraisal may have more general applicability. These include:

- Senior management must be firmly committed to appraisal;
- The trust and commitment of employees is more likely to be won, if employees are involved from the planning stage, where appropriate, through their trade union representatives;
- Appraisal is more likely to be acceptable if it applies to all grades of staff irrespective of their status;
- Appraiser training can help to develop awareness of, and skills for dealing with subjectivity, as well as knowledge of the techniques and practice of staff appraisal;
- The appraisal should be based on an analysis of job requirements as reflected in performance standards. Graphically:

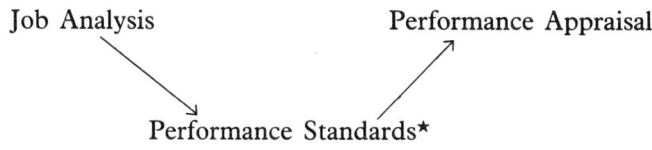

Job Analysis   Performance Appraisal

Performance Standards*

- The performance standards should be communicated to and understood by those who are to be appraised;
- The performance characteristics should be behaviourally based, so that ratings can be determined by objective observable evidence;
- Abstract personality traits (e.g. loyalty or honesty) should be avoided unless they can be defined in terms of observable behaviour;
- An 'appeals' procedure which allows those who disagree with their assessment to state their case;
- When follow-up action has been promised, implementation should be speedy, or an explanation of delay given.

STUDENT ASSIGNMENT 13.2

Student Appraisal

You are asked to design and implement an appraisal scheme for the group of students to which you belong. In designing such a scheme consider the following questions:

* Rowland, K. M. and Ferris, G. R., *Personnel Management*, Allyn and Bacon, Inc., 1982, p. 211

(a) What should be the objectives of such an appraisal?
(b) Who should carry out the appraisal, i.e. rate the various 'job characteristics?
(c) Who should interview the student on the basis of his or her report?
(d) What performance-related characteristics should be rated?

1. Submit a written answer in the form of:
   (a) A standardized appraisal form.
   (b) A short report on the design and implementation of the scheme.
2. If you can come to an agreement arrange to implement the appraisal scheme in consultation with your tutor(s).

Submit:
(a) A short analysis of the results of the appraisal.
(b) A brief statement of the following action to be taken.

13.5 Summary

1. Manpower planning is 'a strategy for the acquisition, utilization, improvement and retention of . . . human resources'.
2. The manpower plan is an integral component of the corporate plan.
3. The process of manpower planning entails an audit of existing manpower, forecasts of future manpower requirements and supplies, and an attempt to predict future manpower costs.
4. The basis of effective manpower planning is information. In some cases a comprehensive manpower information system (analogous to the accounting information system) will be set up.
5. In larger, more complex organizations, computerized econometric models are used to analyse the many variables likely to affect future manpower demand and supply in order to produce the necessary forecasts.
6. Staff appraisal involves the measurement of employee work performance and potential in order (a) to evaluate such performance and potential, and (b) to improve employee motivation.
7. In the absence of a formal appraisal system manpower decisions relating to promotion, transfers, upgradings, and so on are made on the basis of 'grapevine' information.
8. There are many forms of staff appraisal, all of which aim to provide information which will improve the quality of manpower decisions and contribute to a more effective use of human resources.
9. Staff appraisal involves a rated assessment of job-related tasks derived from job analyses; an interview; and appropriate follow-up action.
10. The decision about who is to carry out appraisals is difficult and can

have important consequences for trust relationships between line managers and workers.

11. An appraisal system appropriate to the particular organization needs to be carefully designed, if human relations and related difficulties are to be avoided.

12. Among the preconditions for successful staff appraisal are a firm commitment from the top; employee and union involvement in planning and designing; appraiser training; the use of measurable behaviourally-based performance standards and communication of these to employees; an appeals procedure for those who disagree with their assessment; and, finally, speedy implementation of follow-up action.

Exercise

Review your understanding of the following:

the objectives of manpower planning
ratio-trend analysis
econometric models
variables affecting future labour demand
variables affecting future labour supply
the objectives of staff appraisal
the problem of subjectivity
performance standards

Further Reading

Case Studies in Manpower Planning, MSC/NEDO Report, NEDO, 1978.
Pratt, K. J. and Bennett, S. G., *Personnel Management*, Cassell, 1982.
Institute of Personnel Management, *Manpower Planning*, 1982.

14

Accounting as a Management Tool

14.1 The Annual Accounts

The Companies Acts require companies to keep adequate financial records. Though there is no statutory requirement as to the precise form in which a company should show financial information in its annual accounts it is required to produce a profit and loss account (or income and expenditure account), together with a balance sheet, and to present these to the Registrar of Companies and to shareholders and others with a long-term interest in the company, at least twenty-one days before the annual general meeting.

The first stage in the preparation of a set of business accounts is to put together the profit and loss account. This summarizes the various transactions over the accounting year ending on the date of the balance sheet. The completed profit and loss account is a statement of sales revenue, costs, expenses, and profit (or loss) generated over the year. It shows the income received by the company and how that income has been used.

The sales revenue or turnover figure shown in the profit and loss account is derived from sales invoices prepared on the despatch of goods, and not from the payment of these which is usually not received until some time later. The difference between the value of invoices and revenue actually received will show up on the balance sheet in the figure for debtors. Similarly the cost figures relate only to what is consumed during the accounting year and not necessarily to amounts paid out in that period. Thus, if raw materials are purchased for £50,000 in the year, but only £30,000 worth are used in production, the profit and loss account is only charged with the latter figure. The remaining £20,000 represents an increase in stocks and will be shown as such on the balance sheet. If these and similar adjustments are not made, the annual accounts will fail to show an accurate view of the state of the business.

The trading account and appropriation account may be looked at as part of the profit and loss account. In the trading account direct costs of production (e.g. direct labour and materials costs) are deducted from sales revenue to show a figure for gross profit, i.e. profit before indirect or overhead costs have been deducted. The appropriation account shows how net profit (profit after all expenses are deducted) is distributed, e.g. as dividends and additions to reserves.

The essential structure of a company's profit and loss account is shown in Table 14.1. For comparison purposes it is usual to set out figures for the previous year alongside those for the current year.

The balance sheet is a statement of an enterprise's total assets and total liabilities on a certain date usually at the year end. Thus it shows what the business owns (its assets) and what it owes (its liabilities). The use of a double-entry book-keeping system means that total assets will always equal total liabilities.

Table 14.1.   Structure of a profit and loss account.

		1985		(1984)
LMN PLC				
Profit and Loss Account				
Sales revenue		1000		(800)
less direct cost of sales:				
Direct labour	300		250	
Direct materials	200	500	150	(400)
Gross trading profit		500		(400)
less overhead expenses for				
Selling and distribution	75		40	
Administration	100		120	
Finance	75	250	40	(200)
Net profit before taxation		250		(200)
less taxation		50		(40)
Profit available after taxation		200		(160)
Appropriated as follows:				
Reserves	50			(40)
Dividends	150	200		(120)
Earnings per share[1]		25p		(22p)

Note [1] Earnings per share, calculated by dividing available profit by the number of ordinary shares in issue, is an important indicator of company performance for the ordinary shareholder.

Assets are classified into (a) current assets such as debtors, stocks, work-in-progress, and other self-liquidating assets which are converted into cash during the normal course of business; and (b) fixed assets – plant, machinery, and land, for example, which tend to remain unchanged in the business over longer periods.

Liabilities include all monies owed by the company to outsiders and to the owners of the business. They may be either current, such as creditors or bank overdrafts, or long-term liabilities such as shareholders' capital or mortgage loans.

The balance sheet in displaying total assets and liabilities essentially shows a still picture of a business at a particular moment in time. Traditionally balance sheets were presented with a left-hand side showing

Table 14.2.   Balance sheet – tabular presentation.

HJK PLC
Balance Sheet at 31.12.85.

(1)	Current assets			
	Cash at bank		1,000	
	Debtors		18,000	
	Stock and work-in-progress		11,000	30,000
	Less			
(2)	Current liabilities			
	Trade creditors		14,000	
	Taxation		2,000	
	Dividend		2,000	
	Bank overdraft		2,000	20,000
(3)	Net current assets			10,000
(4)	Fixed assets			
	Freehold premises		14,000	
	Machinery and equipment	8,000		
	less depreciation	2,000	6,000	20,000
(5)	Total net assets			£30,000
	Financed by			
	Term liabilities			
	Mortgage loan			10,000
	Shareholders' funds			
	Ordinary shares		15,000	
	Profit and loss account		5,000	20,000
				£30,000

liabilities and a right-hand side showing assets whose totals were equal. Today a tabular presentation as shown in Table 14.2 is more usual.

14.2 Ratio Analysis

Providing that the figures are an accurate reflection of the true position of the business, financial ratios derived from annual accounts can be used to highlight the causes of business problems. Ratio analysis may be particularly helpful in assessing the profitability and financial stability of an enterprise.

Ratios to assess profitability are derived from both the balance sheet and the profit and loss account. The key ratio here is:

$$\frac{\text{Net profit before tax}}{\text{Capital employed}}$$

Capital employed is equivalent to total assets less current liabilities. This ratio provides the foundation for a closer look at the many factors that can influence the return on capital. What represents a good return will, of course, vary with different types of business.

The return on capital is influenced by both profit and asset turnover. To analyse the influence we need two further ratios – the ratio of profit on sales and the ratio of sales to capital employed. Since net profit is found by deducting direct and indirect costs of sales from revenue the profit on sales ratio (the profit margin) can be stated as

$$\frac{\text{Sales less cost of sales and expenses}}{\text{Sales}}$$

This shows the net income resulting from sales and is usually expressed as a percentage. If the ratio falls over time further analysis of the cost structure will be worthwhile. In particular explorations of the following ratios are likely to be helpful

- $\dfrac{\text{Cost of sales}}{\text{Sales}}$

- $\dfrac{\text{Selling and distribution expenses}}{\text{Sales}}$

- $\dfrac{\text{Administrative expenses}}{\text{Sales}}$

- $\dfrac{\text{Financial expenses}}{\text{Sales}}$

Figure 14.1.   Pyramid of ratios.

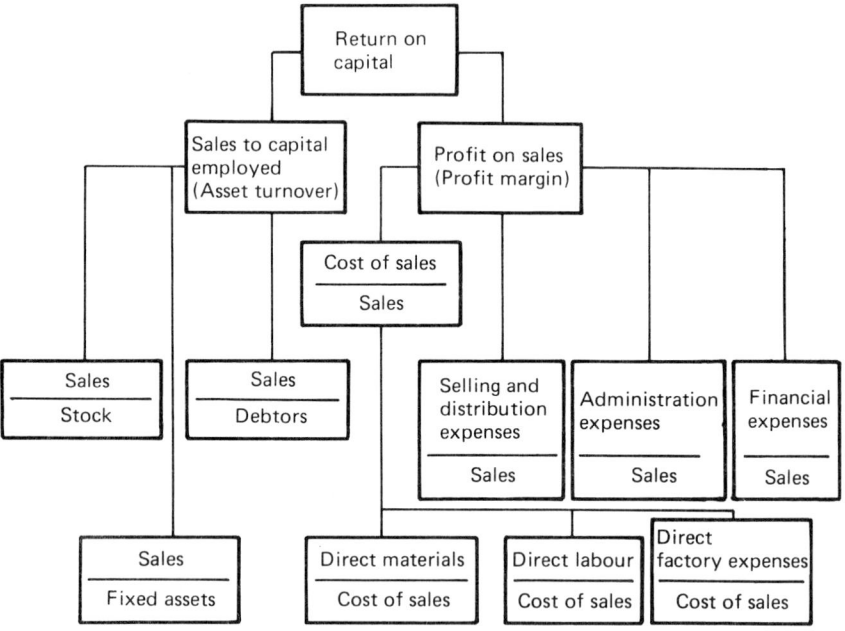

Source: Understanding Your Annual Accounts, Barclays Bank, August 1983.

The first of these is of particular importance as it contains all direct production costs, the components of which can be monitored by investigating the ratios of direct materials to cost of sales; direct labour to cost of sales; and direct production expenses to cost of sales. Any differences from year to year may then be explored and appropriate action taken. The structure of ratios is shown in pyramid form in Figure 14.1.

The sales to capital employed ratio shows the frequency with which assets have been converted into sales during the year. The effective use of assets can be checked by ratios which look at the following subsidiary ratios which indicate whether the rate of asset turnover is improving:

$$\frac{\text{Sales}}{\text{Fixed assets}} \qquad \frac{\text{Sales}}{\text{Stock}} \qquad \frac{\text{Sales}}{\text{Debtors}}$$

The first shows whether an increasing sales value is being obtained from fixed assets. Great care is required in calculating the second and third as balance sheet figures are for one day only. Average levels of stock and debtors during the year should be used. These ratios might indicate whether stock levels are too high or whether a tighter control on outstanding debt is needed.

A second broad purpose of ratio analysis is to provide information on liquidity and financial stability. Relevant information is derived from the balance sheet. Two ratios can help to assess the cash position of a business in relation to its current obligations. Firstly, a ratio of current assets which can be realized fairly quickly (e.g. cash, debtors) and those liabilities which have to be met in the near future indicate how flexible the business can be in meeting its liabilities. This ratio can be stated as

$$\frac{\text{Current assets less stock and work-in-progress}}{\text{Current liabilities}}$$

It is closely allied to a second ratio

$$\frac{\text{Current assets}}{\text{Current liabilities}}$$

which also indicates how the business is placed to meet its obligations when they fall due.

Finally, as we have seen in other chapters, an important guide to financial stability is provided by capital gearing ratios such as

$$\frac{\text{Shareholders' funds}}{\text{Other liabilities}}$$

STUDENT ASSIGNMENT 14.1

Analysing the Annual Accounts

You are given the following data* for WX PLC at 31 December 1985:

	£'000
Ordinary shares issued	100
Reserves	150
Sales Revenue	1100
Creditors	160
Direct cost of sales	700
Freehold factory	140
Long-term loan	250
Stock	300

* Assets and liabilities are valued at 31 December 1985. Other items relate to trading for year ended 31 December 1985

Debtors	250
Overhead expenses	400
Machinery	100
Short-term borrowing	180
Cash at bank	20

1. Present this information in the form of a balance sheet and profit and loss account for WX PLC.
2. Calculate gross profit and net profit. (For the purpose of this assignment taxation is ignored.)
3. Calculate the following ratios:

   (a) Profit on capital employed;
   (b) Profit on sales;
   (c) Sales on capital employed;
   (d) Current assets on current liabilities

4. Of what value are these ratios to WX PLC? How is their usefulness increased when they are compared with

   (a) The ratios of previous years?
   (b) The ratios of other companies in the same industry?

14.3 Sources and Application of Funds Statement

A second way in which annual accounts can be used for control is through the preparation of 'sources and application of funds statements'. These statements compare the balance sheets of successive years in a way which highlights the relationship between assets, liabilities, and capital, and their impact on company liquidity. This comparison, e.g. of a company's balance sheets for two successive years, will show how the figures (adjusted for inflation) have changed during the intervening year. Each change will represent either a **source** or an **application** of funds.

Funds are provided from two sources, (a) an increase in a liability, or (b) a decrease in an asset. For example extra borrowing or a reduction in stock levels are sources. Funds can be applied in two ways, (a) to reduce liabilities, or (b) to increase assets. Thus a reduction in creditors or the purchase of a computer are both applications of funds.

If a statement of sources and applications is prepared for a period of several years it is possible to see where funds have been generated and how they have been used. Financial performance can be assessed more easily than if the balance sheet for each of the years were studied. Analyses of this kind enable a company to see, for example, the extent to which its long-term assets have been financed out of long-term funds and whether a surplus has been left to provide working capital. Sources and application of funds statements may highlight less obvious trends and indicate where action is needed. This may also be used in corporate planning.

14.4 Budgets and Budgetary Control

A budget may be defined as 'a quantitative expression of a plan of action prepared in advance of the period to which it relates'.* This definition emphasizes that the processes of planning and budgeting are tightly interwoven. In practice the two processes may be indistinguishable. A second definition again stresses the inter-connection between planning and budgeting: 'A budget is a specified quantified plan over a period of time for units of the organization against which performance may subsequently be assessed'.** In this version, however, two further aspects of budgeting are highlighted – the co-ordination of the activities of different parts of the organization, and control over the performance of the organization. Between them the two definitions identify the three key integrated functions of budgeting

- planning
- co-ordination
- control

Our concern here is with the third of these – the process of budgetary control. However, since this cannot be isolated from planning and co-ordination we now consider each of these in turn.

An organization's plan provides the means by which it is hoped that its objectives can be realized. It will be formulated taking into account many factors including the availability and cost of human, material, and financial resources, current investment projects, market opportunities, and so on.

A precondition for effective planning and related budgeting is the existence of overall objectives clearly defined in measurable terms. This is by no means simple even in private enterprise for which economic theory assumes an overall objective of profit-maximization. For example, even if such an assumption were broadly correct how can this goal be interpreted if no time scale is specified. It may be possible to make large profits in the current year, but only at the expense of future profits – or vice versa.

Behavioural theories of organizations and their objectives emphasize the diverse social and psychological goals pursued by senior managers who tend to control large areas of decision-making. Such objectives are not easy to define and in any case must be reconciled (usually by negotiation) with

* Asch, D. C., *Cost Accounting and Budgeting*, Macdonald and Evans, 1983, p. 133
** Vause, R. and Woodward, N., *Finance for Managers*, Macmillan, 1981, p. 168

the objectives of other interest groups within the enterprise such as those of shareholders and employees. In large organizations objectives may be constantly shifting as the balance of power between these groups changes and as external pressures from government, local authorities, suppliers, customers, or other pressure groups make themselves felt.

Budgets are usually prepared both for individual departments, for the business as a whole, and for different aspects of the firm's operations such as sales, cash, income and capital budgets. All the departmental or functional budgets are brought together in the master budget – in the private sector a profit and loss budget.

Balancing the departmental budget, i.e. ensuring that expenditure does not exceed the appropriated amount, is an important responsibility of the departmental head who, through his or her budget, is allocated certain resources and given a specific job to perform within the framework of overall business objectives. A well-prepared departmental budget encourages departmental managers to make careful analyses of all existing operations for which they hold responsibility.

Budgetary control is an important management tool that helps not only to give precision to plans and to set standards of performance, but also helps to co-ordinate the diverse activities of the enterprise into a unified whole.

Budgetary control has been defined as 'the establishment of budgets relating the responsibilities of managers and requirements of a policy, and the continuous comparison of actual with budgeted results either to secure by individual action the objective of that policy or to provide a basis for its revision'.*

The essence of budgetary control is the use of a set of budgets to help fix management responsibilities in such a way as to allow continuous comparisons of actual with planned results to be made and for variations between the two to be reported upon, analysed, and acted upon quickly. A well-prepared annual budget showing details on a monthly basis provides a yardstick which can be used to monitor business performance throughout the year.

A number of features are inherent in an effective system of budgetary control, including

- budgets realistically based on past performance help to fix managerial responsibility and induce financial discipline by providing detailed operational plans for each department or aspect of the business. These plans will specify resources available, how they are to be used, and the expected result of their deployment;

* Asch, D. C., *Cost Accounting and Budgeting*, Macdonald and Evans, 1983, p. 133.

- budgets specify the position that the company through its policies *plans* to attain, rather than a forecast of a future position. If planning is one of the keys to business success, budgeting requires businesses to prepare a series of detailed plans capable of responding to changing circumstances as they arise outside the enterprise;
- the budgetary control system helps senior executives to delegate responsibility for departments or sections of the business to individual managers. Delegation without loss of control is possible because progress can be monitored by the budget and because problems can be identified and rectified before they get out of hand;
- control is effected by measuring the results of an activity and by the continuous comparison of these actual results with those planned in the budget. Where there are significant variations, these can be analysed and the necessary corrective action can be taken.

The budget documents are invariably cast in money terms showing estimated income and expenditures for a given future time period, derived from the careful analysis of past records and trends in the performance of all aspects of the business operation. The preparation of the budgets involves making different basic assumptions about the future and these should be made explicit in the budget. Ideally preparation will involve the participation with all concerned at all levels within the organization. This ensures that plans are disseminated and understood by those with responsibility for carrying them out.

In some cases management will see the budgetary/planning process as a means of enhancing motivation. Targets may be set within the budget framework with this end in view. In such cases, however, it is important that budgets are not used as a punitive control device when targets are not achieved which may merely succeed in incurring the resentment and lack of co-operation from the staff. If budgets are to be used for control purposes the plan must be based on realistic levels of achievement that represent at the same time desirable improvements and realistic goals. This once again emphasises the need for participation by all involved.

The following outline describes the sequence of events that might be followed by a small manufacturing company in the preparation of their budgets.*

- The Managing Director holds a preliminary budget meeting with his sales manager, works manager, and accountant to discuss the major policy questions which have to be resolved:

---

* This outline is adapted from *Improving Your Financial Control* prepared by Barclays Bank Business Advisory Service.

(a) Financial targets, e.g. percentage return on sales, percentage return on capital?
(b) Price changes to be introduced – how much and when?
(c) Wage increases expected – how much and when?
(d) Changes in materials costs expected – what assumption about inflation should be made?
(e) New products and markets – approximate evaluation of new sales potential.
(f) Stocks of finished goods – how much is to be carried?

- The results of the above and of any other policy matters resolved are summarized briefly to become the policy framework for the budget.
- The sales manager now prepares his budget taking into account
  (a) the participation of his staff in arriving at estimates;
  (b) is the budget to be based on individual products, product groups or other classification?
  (c) is it more useful to prepare the budget in quantity or sales value terms, or both?
  (d) the strength of competition, the general economic climate and conditions for the industry;
  (e) any special marketing plans, new products or markets, expected sales volume, pricing policy, seasonal variations, and productive capacity.
- The managing director, sales manager, works manager, and accountant review the sales budget and after any necessary modifications the managing director approves it.
- The works manager then prepares his production plans taking into account the sales forecast, production capacity, working days in each month, shutdown periods, stockholding requirements, and other relevant factors. The production plans are likely to be broad approximations, month by month, expressed in money terms at sales prices, i.e. the result indicates when during the year the budgeted sales are to be produced. On this basis the works manager prepares his direct cost budgets for materials purchased (taking into account when materials are needed and any cost increases expected) and for labour (taking into account numbers needed and wage increases anticipated).
- Each manager then prepares his or her own departmental overhead budget (containing figures for items such as heat, power, rent, maintenance, insurance, etc.) taking into account expected cost increases and any cost reduction projects planned.
- From the above the accountant assembles the profit and loss budget, taking into account changes in taxation, depreciation, interest charges and so on. Each section of the budget should have a summary worksheet together with whatever supporting schedules are appropri-

ate. The overall summary of all sections becomes the profit and loss budget.

- The managing director reviews the profit and loss budget, compares it with financial targets and decides whether further changes are required. If necessary some budgets are re-worked.
- The managing director holds a final budget meeting which adopts the budget as the company's financial plan for the coming year.

Today the preparation of budgets is often a computerized operation involving a growing number of sophisticated accounting forecasting and modelling techniques. Computerization enables management to investigate a large number of budget plans based on alternative sets of assumptions, to choose between them, and thus to improve the level of satisfaction which their chosen model gives.

14.5 Standard Costing and Variance Analysis

A central problem facing all organizations is how to achieve the best output of goods or service from a given set of resource inputs. In order to execute their primary function of ensuring the efficient use of resources, decision-making managers need relevant information. The purpose of the costing system is to provide management with the detailed cost information which will enable them both to assess the economic implications of decisions about resource use and to control the ongoing business operations.

For control purposes cost information is most useful when it can be set against standards that in some sense reflect an efficient use of the organization's resources. For this reason most manufacturing firms use a system of standard costing which involves setting standards for each process of production or unit of operations.

Standard costing is closely akin to budgetary control and is used in conjunction with the latter to effect greater control of business operations. The difference is in scope rather than purpose. Thus, whereas budgets are concerned with functions, departments, and the enterprise as a whole, standard costing tends to be applied to 'units' of activity, i.e. particular products, components, or processes.

Costs can be either 'variable' or 'fixed' – those which vary with the level of production and those which do not. Variable costs are directly related to producing the goods or service a company intends to sell. These are the **direct** costs of purchasing raw materials and/or components needed for production and of paying wages to employees directly engaged in producing the product.

Other expenditures – the costs of capital, rents, general management, and of administration, for example, are not directly linked to the volume of production. These are the **indirect** costs of the product, also known as fixed costs or overheads. Costing involves the detailed analysis of all fixed and variable costs incurred and the allocation of these to particular jobs, processes, and products.

Standard costing involves making predetermined estimates of what costs should be under normal operating efficiency and comparing these with actual costs as they arise. Such comparisons can quickly identify and control any problems that may arise.

Variance analysis is the process of in-depth analyses of the causes of variances, i.e. differences between actual and standard costs, into their component elements. It should be noted here that the variances observed do not themselves provide answers to questions, but rather show the questions that should be asked. As with budgeting, a standard costing system enables each responsible manager to see the impact of his area on the success of the organization.

Setting realistic standards, which are at the same time challenging and attainable with maximum effort, requires much development work and the generation of a large volume of information deriving from standardized methods of work study and measurement and taking into account numerous factors including production techniques, materials requirements, plant layout, and estimates of future changes in wage and material costs. In some firms standards may be set for the purpose of employee motivaton as well as for control, in which case they may be linked with an incentive payment scheme.

In setting standards the cost accountant will need to work closely with those who are concerned in the relevant functions – the purchasing and production managers for materials standards and the personnel officer for labour standards, for example.

The following simplified examples show how standard costing and variance analysis assist in the control of resources.

For a forthcoming period the cost accountant in close consultation with other managers has established a standard of 500 kilograms of materials at £3 per kilogram for a given planned volume of output. In arriving at this standard, account has been taken of standard quantities required (including an allowance for inevitable losses in production), trends in materials prices, availability of discounts, and so on. Thus

Standard cost of materials = £1,500 (£3 × 500 kilograms)

The actual materials cost of the given volume of production turns out 600 kilograms at £3.50 per kilogram = £2,100, resulting in an overall adverse variance of £600. Analysis reveals two sources of the variance – a **price** variance (the actual quantity of materials used x the price difference =

£300); and a **usage** variance (the standard price x the usage difference = £300).

This indicates that both the purchasing and production sides need investigating to establish the causes of the variances and the extent to which they are avoidable. If the market price of materials has risen, there may be little the company can do, short of major long-run actions such as product redesign or the development of substitutes. Alternatively, questions of purchasing policy and technique may be raised.

In the case of direct labour a similar procedure is followed. On the basis of work measurement and analysis a standard time and rate of earnings are set. Any variance between standard and actual costs may be attributable to an **earnings** variance and/or a **time** (or efficiency) variance. Investigations of each component of the overall variance may suggest, for example, that the pay system is inappropriate, or that supervision is too lax, or that productivity negotiations are required. Alternatively, any adverse time variance may be attributable to inefficient machinery pointing to a need for more regular maintenances.

STUDENT ASSIGNMENT 14.2

Variance Analysis

CD Ltd, a single product manufacturer, has compiled the following standard costs:

Materials required to produce 1 unit	6 kilograms
Price per kilogram	£4.50
Hours required to produce 1 unit	5
Wages per hour	£2.00

Actual production and costs for month ending 31st March 1985 were as follows:

Units produced	120
Materials used	780 kilograms
Cost of materials used	£3,900
Hours worked	660
Wages paid	£1,386

1. Calculate and analyse the materials and labour variances.
2. Outline the steps you would take to deal with the materials and labour variances.

14.6 Contribution Accounting

Contribution accounting based on value-added enables effective decisions to be made concerning the best alternative use of a firm's resources. 'Contribution' here refers to the difference between the revenue generated by an activity and the direct costs of that activity. It represents, therefore, the contribution that the activity makes to overhead costs and profit.

Added-value is the money value of the output of an activity less the purchased resource inputs to the activity, e.g. raw materials, components, fuel, and services. Added-value is therefore the increase in the money value to these bought-out resources resulting from the application of human skills and knowledge to create a finished good or a service of greater value.

The relationship between added-value and contribution is seen in Figure 14.2.

This kind of analysis is useful for many purposes within an organization including analyses of the way in which total revenue is distributed between

Figure 14.2.   Contribution

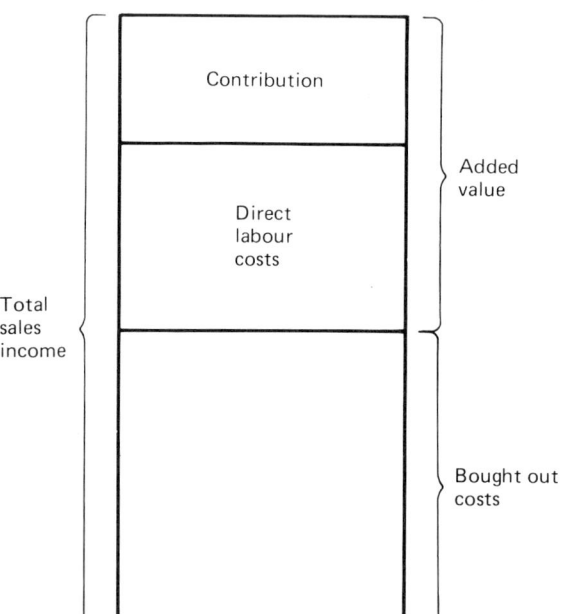

Source: Bentley, T., 'Added value and contribution', *Management Accounting*, March 1981.

employees, managers, owners, and other interest groups; pricing policy; 'make or buy' decisions; and production mixes.

As a basis for control contribution accounting offers the following possibilities:

- it enables a number of ratios to be calculated which can be used to measure the success of control;
- it ensures that costs are only charged to the activity where they are measured;
- it enables standard costs to be more easily prepared and operated;
- managers can be given specific targets in terms of contribution.

The most important ratio is that of contribution to value added. By calculating the fraction of value-added left after the skills that created that value-added have been paid for, it is possible to measure the level of productivity. In this context productivity is a measure of value created as a percentage of effort expended, i.e. the contribution ratio (see Case Study 14.1).

CASE STUDY 14.1

Contribution Accounting and Value Added

In two competing companies producing the same product known as a 'fluke', the approach taken is different. The Flickswitch Co has concentrated in the automation of the production line and buys the majority of its components. Each fluke sells for £3 and this is divided as shown below:

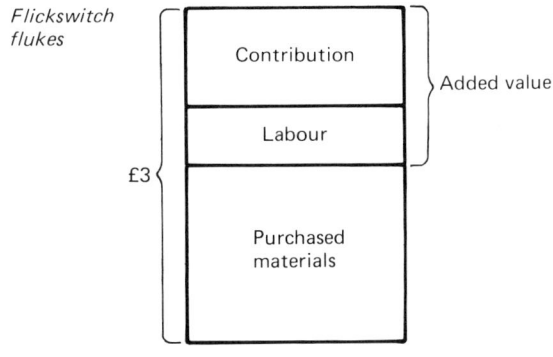

The Handwork Co has always produced the fluke from the raw materials and has developed considerable skill in this form of production. The company employs twice as many people as Flickswitch. It sells flukes for £3, which is made up as shown below:

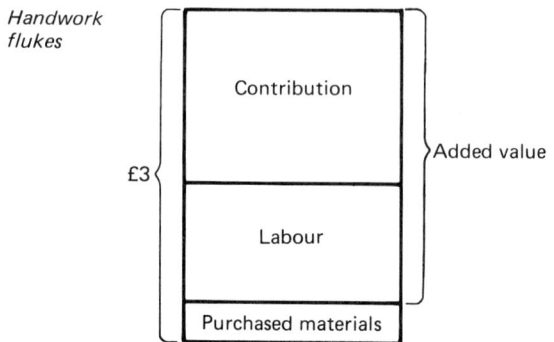

It would appear from this that the contribution per fluke is greater for Handwork than Flickswitch. Though this is true, it probably has to be in order to support the higher service and control costs caused by employing twice as many people.

Looking at the contribution ratios

Flickswitch $\dfrac{\text{Contribution}}{\text{Added value}} = \dfrac{1.00}{1.50} = 0.66$

Handwork $\dfrac{\text{Contribution}}{\text{Added value}} = \dfrac{1.50}{2.50} = 0.60$

It is clear that Flickswitch is more productive.

(*Source:* Bentley, Trevor, 'Added Value and Contribution', *Management Accounting*, March 1981, p. 21)

14.7 Investment Appraisal

A detailed review of the techniques of investment appraisal is beyond the scope of this book, though it is beneficial to consider briefly the major factors involved.

Discounted cash flow (DCF) is a well-known and widely used technique for evaluating proposed investment projects in the private sector where profitability is the primary consideration in the decision. DCF involves a three-part calculation – estimating a revenue stream, estimating a costs stream, and 'discounting' both to make them comparable in terms of present values. If the present value of the revenue stream over the lifetime of the investment exceeds that of the costs stream, the net present value of the project is positive, i.e. the present value of the net earnings of the project is expected to yield a positive return.

The discounting process requires some explanation and justification. Discounting can best be understood as the reverse of calculating a future value of a sum of money using compound interest. For example, if £100 is invested at 10 per cent per annum compound interest, for five years, we can calculate that the £100 will be worth £110 next year and £121 (i.e. £110 × 10%) the following year and so on. The shorter way of calculating these future values is to use the formula

$$\text{Final Value} = \text{Sum invested} \times (1 + r)^n$$

where 'r' denotes the rate of interest and 'n' the number of years for which the sum is invested. Thus £100 × $(1 + 0.1)^5$ = £161. This also tells us that if the interest rate is 10 per cent, £161 in five years' time is worth £100 now.

The formula for calculating the present value of a sum of money to be received in the future is

$$PV = \frac{\text{Final Value}}{(1 + r)^n}$$

The rationale for discounting future cash flows in order to convert them to their present values is derived from the fact that the money invested in any investment project could have been used in alternative ways, for example it could have been lent out at interest, used to buy equities, or to pay higher dividends to shareholders. The most valuable alternative use to which the funds could have been put establishes the minimum acceptable rate of return on the investment project and hence the rate of discount to be used on the appraisal. For example, if the company places a low value on alternative uses of the funds, the discount rate will reflect this and more investments will be acceptable than when higher values are placed on the alternatives. Since the discount rate is the cut-off rate for judging the acceptability of investment projects its calculation is of great importance. The basis of calculation may be the cost of capital, i.e. a weighted average of the cost of loans and equity capital at current rates of interest; or what is regarded by the company as an 'acceptable' rate of return; or an estimate of the rate a shareholder could get on the Stock Exchange by investing the funds otherwise to be used for the investment.

If, applying the formula, the net present value is positive, the actual rate of return must be greater than the discount rate indicating that the investment is likely to yield more than could be earned by using funds in their next best alternative use. If the net present value is negative the funds could earn more in an alternative way.

If several alternative investment projects are under consideration, those with a negative NPV at the chosen rate of discount will be rejected. Those projects which show a positive NPV can be ranked using the ratio relating the size of the return to the amount of capital outlay:

$$\text{Acceptability index} = \frac{\text{NPV}}{\text{Capital outlay}}$$

14.8 Cost Benefit Analysis

Cost benefit analysis attempts to solve the problem of making a rational choice between alternative courses of action. It involves enumerating and evaluating *all* the costs and benefits of each of the alternatives, and formulating and applying criteria of choice between them.

It is especially appropriate to use cost benefit analysis on a range of problems that have three distinguishing characteristics:

- there is a choice to be made between alternative courses of action, e.g. between investment projects; disinvestments; and resource reallocations;
- time and space enter into the picture in a significant way, so that it is important to take a *long* view – looking at possible impacts in the further as well as the nearer future, and a *wide* view – allowing for diverse side effects on many persons, communities, industries, or regions;
- there are significant divergencies between the private and total costs and benefits of an activity, e.g. where there are injuries to society resulting from corporate action giving rise to social costs.

Given these characteristics it is apparent that cost benefit analysis is closely associated with decision-making in the public sector in which huge investments (or disinvestments) in nationalized industries and social services have important effects both in space and time.

Cost benefit analysis can also be a useful technique for socially responsible private enterprises. An example or two will enable the reader to see its relevance.

Assuming a need for additional electricity generating capacity, should the CEGB invest in a coal-fired or a nuclear power station? Should a third London airport be located at site A, B or C? Should a new motorway be built along route X, Y or Z? Should government spend £x million on improved hospital casualty facilities or spend the same amount on better motorway safety measures?

The essential steps in cost benefit analysis are as follows:

- identify and value the future stream of all the expected benefits of a project under consideration in money terms;
- using an appropriate discount rate, estimate the present value of the future stream of benefits (= B);
- identify and value the present money cost of the immediate investment (= K) and using the same discount rate identify and compute the present value of all future operating and maintenance costs (including social costs) over the expected lifetime of the project (= 0);
- if the ratio $\dfrac{B}{K + 0}$ is greater than one benefits are greater than costs and vice versa;
- if alternatives are being considered, those yielding the highest excess of B over (K + 0) are chosen.

The calculation of all present and future private and social costs and benefits involved in each alternative and the expression of these in terms of present value enables rational choice to be made between the alternatives.

However, applying this technique to particular cases raises many problems to which there are no easy solutions. Among the difficulties are:

- on what bases are intangible costs and benefits to be valued? For example, how could the aesthetic, spiritual, and ecological losses involved in building a power station in, say, Snowdonia, be compared with similar kinds of losses involved in building it elsewhere? How can a money value be placed on the separation of primitive people from their land?
- the choice of discount rate has a crucial effect on the evaluation but what is the appropriate rate at which future streams of costs and benefits can be converted to their present values?
- how should the important questions of uncertainties be dealt with especially when comparing streams of costs and benefits which extend far into the future?
- on what basis can benefits be weighted? This inevitably involves the use of value judgements. Different value judgements produce different outcomes from the analyses. Should a distinction be made between benefits that contribute positively to happiness and those that merely remove misery created through man's actions?
- with what degree of accuracy is it possible to estimate the life of the project? How can the possibility of a 'sudden day of reckoning' when benefits disappear totally or costs soar infinitely be incorporated in the analysis?
- the information needed to estimate future costs and benefits may be unavailable or too expensive to obtain.

These are formidable practical problems of great practical significance. Furthermore, since costs and benefits may be experienced by different groups in society both raise important distributional questions. For all these reasons cost benefit analysis does not make decisions 'objective' or 'scientific'.

Nevertheless, by attempting to enumerate and evaluate the wider costs and benefits and by disturbing cosy notions of 'efficiency' based solely on narrow profitability criteria, and by forcing into the open valuation issues that would be concealed in a purely financial appraisal, it can help decision makers to arrive at better choices from a 'public interest' viewpoint. At the end of the day political, social, and moral choices must still be made whenever there are conflicting objectives. If these are not made explicit they are concealed in the relative values of objectives and in the weights allocated to different costs and benefits, all of which have an influence on the outcome.

This discussion of cost benefit analysis is only a brief introduction to the complex field of non-market decision-making.

14.9 Summary

1. Financial ratios derived from the annual balance sheet and profit and loss account can help to assess the profitability and financial stability of a business.
2. A budget is a quantitative expression of a plan of action over a specified period of time for units of an organization against which performance may subsequently be assessed. The three key functions of budgeting are planning, co-ordination, and control.
3. Budgetary control is a management tool that helps not only to give precision to plans and set standards of performance, but also helps to fix responsibility and co-ordinate activities.
4. Effective budgetary control involves producing realistic budgets specifying the position the business plans to attain; the delegation of responsibility to departmental managers; the comparison of actual with budgeted results; and the investigation of any significant differences.
5. Standard costing is applied to particular products, components, processes, or other 'units' of activity. It involves setting estimates of what costs should be under normal operating conditions and comparing these standards with actual costs as they arise.
6. Variance analysis involves detailed in-depth analyses of differences between standard and actual costs in order to establish the causes of such variances so that appropriate corrective action can be taken.
7. Contribution accounting based on value-added provides a sound basis

for analysis and control. The ratio of contribution to value-added is a useful measure of productivity.

8. Discounted cash flow is a technique for evaluating investment projects. It involves estimating future flows of revenues and costs and discounting these to their present values. If the net present value is positive a project will be expected to yield a positive return indicating that more can be earned than would be possible using the funds in alternative ways.

9. Cost benefit analysis is an appropriate technique of appraisal when projects have impacts extending long into the future and wide in terms of their effects on people, communities, and regions, and when significant social costs or benefits have to be taken into account.

10. Cost benefit analysis involves the complex tasks of identifying and evaluating *all* expected future costs and benefits associated with a project, and expressing these in terms of present value. Among the difficulties inherent in such analyses are the valuation of intangible effects, the choice of discount rate, dealing with uncertainties, the weighting of benefits, forecasting the life of the project.

11. At bottom, cost benefit analysis is based on a series of value judgements, which if not made explicit, are concealed in the relative values of objectives and the weighting of benefits and costs.

Exercise

Review your understanding of the following:

    balance sheet
    profit and loss account
    ratio analysis
    sources and application of funds statement
    budgets
    budgetary control
    standard costing
    variance analysis
    contribution accounting
    discounted cash flow
    cost benefit analysis

Further Reading

Asch, David C., *Cost Accounting and Budgeting*, Macdonald and Evans, 1983.

Gowland, D. H., *Modern Economic Analysis*, Butterworth, 1979.

McEntegart, R. C., *Costing and Budgetary Control*, Polytech Publishers, 1980.

Bentley, T., 'Added Value and Contribution', *Management Accounting*, March 1981.

PART VI

RESPONDING TO CHANGE

15

The Introduction of
Microprocessor Technology

15.1 The Nature and Scope of the New Technology

The 'microprocessor revolution' essentially consists of the use of micro-electronic integrated circuits which can cram enormous data-processing power on to tiny devices (silicon chips) with the result that miniscule computers can efficiently and inexpensively store and process vast amounts of information. There is no doubt that 'information technology' represents the most potentially pervasive single technology since the Industrial Revolution, with immense potential scope for automating the production and distribution of goods and services.

The forms which the new technology takes are many and varied. We focus here on just two of these, industrial robots and word processors.

An industrial robot is a machine which moves, manipulates, joins, or processes components in the same way as a human hand or arm. A robot contains three basic elements:

- the mechanical structure (including the artificial wrist and gripper);
- the power unit (hydraulic, pneumatic, or increasingly electrical);
- the control system (increasingly mini-computer or microprocessor).

The essential characteristic of these hybrids of mechanical, electrical, and computing engineering is that they can be programmed to perform certain tasks.

Currently robots tend to be used mainly though not exclusively in the automobile, and in metal-working and forming industries to carry out the fairly straightforward tasks of spot welding, paint-spraying, die-casting, and machine loading. The Mini Metro, for example, is automatically welded by robots, which is estimated to allow British Leyland to produce an additional 342,000 cars a year with 70 per cent fewer workers*.

---

* Example taken from Donaldson, P., *IOX Economics*, Penguin Books, 1982, p. 147

Word processors represent the most significant use of microelectric equipment in the office and are expected to form the core of the 'electronic office' of the future. There are many kinds of word processors ranging in complexity from electronic typewriters with a storage facility to large computerized text handling machinery costing tens of thousands of pounds. All word processors perform five basic functions, i.e. the entry, storage, retrieval, editing, and printing of text. The productivity gains which can be realized from the introduction of word processors can be in excess of 100 per cent. For example, an industrial research establishment reported in a measurement experiment designed to evaluate word processors of different kinds, an overall increase in output of 127 per cent on one particular type of equipment.*

The application and potential uses of the new technology are so varied that every field of industry and commerce will be affected by it. The new technology can be used in:

- creating new products such as word processors, electronic mail, TV games, toys, video cassette recorders, miniaturized calculators, and, in the field of capital goods, numerically controlled machine tools which allow them to be rapidly switched to other jobs thereby giving greater flexibility in production;
- modifying existing products adding sophistication as in programmed cameras, or reducing costs, such as domestic appliances and cash registers. For example, an automatic sewing machine uses a single microprocessor to control the sequence and pattern of stitches, replacing 350 gears and other components. Cars, washing machines, cookers, and other appliances are being changed by microelectronic adaptations;
- controlling industrial manufacturing processes, materials handling, and transport. Computer-aided manufacture systems tend to be introduced by companies with complex stock and work-scheduling problems. Such systems have resulted in lower stock-holdings, more rapid rates of stock turnover, less wastage of stock, and better delivery of final products**;
- increasing the versatility of design processes enabling alternatives to be systematically and rapidly explored and tested. Computer-aided design enables draughtsmen to work on a visual display unit (VDU) allowing errors to be corrected or alternatives tried out with relative ease and simplicity;
- processing, storing and analysing data automatically sensed and re-

* Department of Employment, *The Manpower Implications of Microelectronic Technology*, HMSO, 1979
** *ibid*

corded with facility to increase or decrease the distance between input and output and monitor it at any intermediate stage.

15.2 Advantages of the New Technology

A 1979 Report by R. G. Sell of the Work Research Unit* revealed the following perceived advantages from adopting the new technology:

- better machine control and consistency, allowing greater precision;
- better and quicker information about the state of a process leading to less work in progress;
- improved machine programming allowing greater product versatility;
- reduced labour costs;
- faster response time in dealing with errors, including typescript;
- more thorough testing of a wider range of options possible in design;
- communication of information in marketing, buying, and process control is more direct, accessible, and rapid.

It is now generally agreed that the future for British manufacturing industry significantly depends on the extent to which, and the pace at which, it introduces microelectronic technology. The new technology is seen as a significant way of raising productivity, improving product competitiveness, and halting the contraction of Britain's industrial base. Despite the widespread recognition of the importance of the new technology and its derivatives, Britain has a relatively slow rate of adaptation in this field. Japanese industry, in particular, makes much greater use of the new technology.

An important constraint on a more rapid diffusion of new technology in British industry is the evident difficulty experienced by many organizations in managing its introduction, especially the numerous human and industrial relations aspects.

15.3 Trade Union Concerns

In general union policies have not been hostile to the introduction of new microprocessor technology. Many unions accept its inevitability and their concern is with the terms on which it is introduced. The General Secretary of the T.U.C. sums up the position thus:

> The new technology has been described as the second industrial revolution. We have to make sure that unlike the first, the second revolution that is now upon

---

* Work Research Unit, *Managing New Technology*, 1979

us will not trample underfoot the interests of those directly affected. It is not just a question of accepting the new technology or fighting it. The issue is how we maximize the benefits and minimize the costs.*

15.4 New Technology Agreements

Technological change throws up many issues of great concern to organized labour. A fundamental aim of the unions is to ensure that such change is by agreement. Consequently in organizations having well developed bargaining arrangements unions will try to ensure that technological innovation having major effects on the workforce is not unilaterally imposed by management prerogative. In practice this means that

- full agreement on the range of negotiating issues is a precondition for technological change;
- there will be full employee consultation from the initial planning for technological change and at every phase of implementation;
- a new technology agreement will be negotiated dealing with questions such as employment security, hours of work, manning levels, working conditions, pay, training, health and safety, and so on.

New technology agreements may be 'substantive' one-off agreements relating to specific technological change, or more usefully where consultation and bargaining arrangements are less well developed, procedure agreements that will establish the arrangements whereby the two parties can jointly consider and negotiate every aspect of any major technological change now and in the future.

15.5 Employee Involvement and Joint Consultation

Not all employers will introduce new technology by negotiating agreements with trade unions. Such an approach may be impracticable in organizations in which the workforce is either non-unionized or insufficiently organized to bargain effectively. Whatever degree of unionization exists in a particular firm, there is much research evidence indicating that employee commitment and involvement through joint consultation is central to the effective introduction of new technology.

An example of this is a 1983 NEDO Report** on the experience of technological innovation in the electronics industry itself, which suggests that the management of technological change is most effectively handled 'when all available talents in the workforce are harnessed and utilized,

---

* TUC Report, *Employment and Technology*, 1983
** *The Introduction of New Technology*, NEDO, 1983

when consultation enhances real choice'. The report goes on to say that 'Companies should therefore engage in widely based consultation (including the workforce most directly affected and their representatives) at the earliest practicable stage'.

15.6 Disclosure of Information

A prerequisite for either efficient consultation or for negotiation of a new technology agreement is the provision to the workforce and their representatives of *all* the relevant information on which key decisions are to be based.

Although the Employment Protection Act, 1975 obliges employers to disclose to recognized independent trade unions any information without which they could be materially impeded in collective bargaining there is no legal compulsion on organizations to provide all the industrial and commercial information to employees in all circumstances. Nevertheless there is impressive evidence to show that organizations that *do* inform and consult their employees and their representatives gain significant improvements in industrial relations. It follows that providing better flows of information to employees and their union representatives is an important means of winning employee acceptance of, commitment to, and involvement in, change.

Negotiations will require detailed information on the ways in which existing work patterns will be affected, on the alternatives for using the present staff especially in regard to training, grading, pay systems, manning levels, hours, redundancy pay, and potential health effects. Whether or not it is the intention to complete a new technology agreement, disclosure of information should be linked with regular consultation.

A Department of Employment Study Group on Microelectronics* found that many innovative companies stressed that labour-cost saving was not the primary motive for introducing new technology. In the case of one major development in the field of computer-aided manufacture the Study Group was told that the primary objectives were less work-in-progress, better delivery dates, and lower-cost stock control. Other companies emphasized benefits such as lower energy use, better plant utilization, and reduced plant downtime as non-labour-cost benefits arising from innovations. Detailed quantification of non-labour-cost savings arising from innovations would clearly be useful in defining the area of negotiation between management and unions.

* Department of Employment, *The Manpower Implications of Microelectronic Technology*, HMSO, 1979

15.7 Bargaining Machinery and Issues

If bargaining for change is to be effective, representation of the whole workforce will be necessary. This implies the development, if it does not already exist of *joint* union machinery, i.e. of multi-union negotiating bodies representing all or a very large percentage of employees.

If, in this way, traditional union demarcation lines are not allowed to become an obstacle to progress, the unions can approach the negotiations having established clear and specific objectives derived from their general aims of maintaining and improving employment and living standards for their members. These objectives will relate to every issue raised by the introduction of new technology including

- security of employment;
- training and retraining;
- pay;
- hours of work;
- health and safety;
- job content and grading;
- the use of new technology to monitor individual work standards.

15.8 New Technology Agreements and Job Security

The co-operation of the workforce will be strongly linked to their view of what action is planned to secure jobs. It is important, too, to stress that because the potential scope of the new technology is so vast, very real anxieties are felt by the unions about the future of employment. Unlike technological 'revolutions' of the past, there will, the unions believe, be no 'displacement effect' this time (i.e. service industries, equally affected by the new technology will be unable to absorb workers displaced from primary production and manufacturing) and jobs will be lost permanently.

There appear to be some grounds for union fears. Even in the growth industry of information technology itself (computers, office machinery, telecommunications) over 25,000 jobs were lost in the decade 1970–1980. In the computer sector alone employment declined from 51,000 in 1970 to 44,000 by 1980. In the same period output rose from £240 million to £1.8 billion. In telecommunications employment fell from 87,000 in 1970 to 68,000 in 1980 while output rose from £250 million in 1970 to £900 million in 1980.

Consequently trade unions see it as vital both to press for legislation and to negotiate agreements with employers in order to protect the job security of their members. Particular concern has been expressed about groups such as women*, young people, and ethnic minorities whose bargaining position is often relatively weak and who already suffer disproportionately from unemployment. For these reasons unions wish to control the *pace* of change to allow the social impact to be minimized and spread more fairly.

At the level of the organization or workplace unions will seek greater job security and wherever possible the expansion of job opportunities and to this end may demand full involvement in production and manpower planning. In particular negotiators will press for a 'no redundancy' clause in the new technology agreement. This may involve a joint union/management exploration of the potential for new markets for existing products and of product diversification.

The experience of companies who have entered into no redundancy agreements has been to reduce the fear of, and resistance to, new technology. This is a strong argument in favour of such agreements wherever these are feasible. However, if such agreements are not to lead to over-manning in the future, management will almost certainly seek acceptance of greater manpower flexibility by the unions. Such flexibility, essential if the full benefits of new technology are to be reaped, involves a firm commitment to training.

The TUCs advice to negotiators suggests several ways of avoiding redundancies even when job losses are accepted as an unavoidable consequence of the new technology. In such cases unions may seek

- to limit recruitment in order to achieve the reduction of the workforce over a period of time. If there is to be no ambiguity or vagueness about this commitment, precision will be sought in the wording of this provision, e.g. 'No external recruitment in particular [named] occupations should occur for which there are vacancies until certain grades of existing employees have been given an opportunity to fill them after training where appropriate';
- arrangements to redeploy workers in alternative employment at other plants or departments within the organization. Negotiators may seek guarantees that every worker affected by work reorganization should (a) be offered alternative employment and (b) be given first priority for vacancies he/she is qualified to fill.

So far, major redundancies have often been avoided by redeployment. However, as organizations find it more difficult to expand or as natural wastage *declines*, redeployment will become more difficult.

---

* In a 1980 survey by the Equal Opportunities Commission, *Information Technology in the Office: the impact on Women's Jobs*, it was predicted that by 1985 21,000 typing and secretarial jobs (about 2 per cent of the present secretarial workforce) were expected to be displaced by the introduction of word processing technology and that the maximum displacement of 170,000 or 17 per cent could be expected by 1990. (*Incomes Data Services Study 252*, 1981.)

- resettlement allowances to cover travel expenses, removal and house sale costs, and so on;
- agreement on appropriate courses of retraining;
- the elimination of overtime in those occupations directly threatened by the possibility of redundancy;
- a review of sub-contract work;
- the introduction of temporary short-time working complemented by adequate guaranteed work arrangements.

15.9 Legal Implications of Redundancies

In situations where redundancies are unavoidable, certain legal provisions (mainly in the Employment Protection (Consolidation) Act, 1978) must be taken into account by the employing organization. With the exception of workers aged under eighteen, or over the statutory retirement age all redundant employees who have completed 104 weeks service with their current employer are entitled to redundancy pay, the amount of which is determined by length of service and age at redundancy. The lump sum redundancy payment compensation is limited to the last twenty years of service and is based on a national weekly wage (determined from time to time by the Secretary of State for Employment) as follows:

- for each year of employment at age forty-one or over but under sixty-five/sixty for women – one-and-a-half week's pay;
- for each year of employment at age twenty-two or over but under forty-four – one week's pay;
- for each year of employment at age eighteen or over but under twenty-two – half week's pay.

The employer can recover a portion (at present 41 per cent) of such statutory compensation from the Redundancy Fund maintained by the Secretary of State for Employment. Any payment in excess of the statutory figure must, however, be met by the employer.

The Employment Protection (Consolidation) Act, 1978, also provides for statutory consultation by the employer with his workforce if there is an independent recognized trade union and with the Secretary of State for Employment. If 100 or more workers are to be dismissed at one establishment within ninety days, the employer must consult the trade union(s) at least ninety days before the dismissals start. If ten or more workers are to be dismissed at one establishment within thirty days, the employer must consult the union(s) at least thirty days before the redundancies take effect. In these situations, the law requires the employer to disclose in writing to the union(s)

- the reasons for the redundancies;
- the numbers and descriptions of workers to be made redundant;
- the total number of workers in the occupations affected;
- the proposed method of selecting who should be dismissed;
- the proposed method of carrying out the redundancies.

In practice unions are likely to aim for maximum advance warning and to obtain longer periods of notice than those laid down by law.

In all cases (whether an independent trade union is recognized or not) the employer is required to give advance notice to the Department of Employment in accordance with a timetable laid down by the Secretary of State. Currently this requires that if ten or more are to be made redundant within thirty days, at least sixty days' notice must be given. If more than 100 are to be made redundant over a period of ninety days, at least ninety days' notice must be given.

An employer is legally obliged to allow affected employees with at least two years' service 'reasonable' time off to seek alternative employment or retraining.

15.10 Unions and Redundancies

In cases where they accept that redundancies are unavoidable, trade unions will in practice attempt to negotiate higher standards than the minimum laid down by statute. Indeed their agreement to participate in procedures whereby the size of the workforce can be reduced by dismissals will often be dependent on the 'quid pro quo' of higher redundancy payments.

In such cases, too, the union may press for the establishment of a joint union management committee to implement and supervise the redundancy process. Of particular importance will be the selection process. Unions will wish to emphasize

- voluntary redundancy i.e. the company asks for 'volunteers' who are offered compensation above the statutory level. If there are more volunteers than required, final selection would be by the joint committee;
- early retirement, with the full occupational pension entitlement and a substantial lump-sum compensation.

If the required reduction in the workforce cannot be achieved in these two ways, unions will aim for joint agreement on the selection procedure. A commonly used, and equitable basis is 'last in, first out' (LIFO), but often this has to be modified to take account of special circumstances in the organization.

Whatever method of selection is agreed upon, the unions' concern will be to maximize the benefits for those who are to be dismissed. More specifically they may seek

- redundancy payments above the statutory minimum;
- time off with no loss of earnings to seek alternative employment or training. (Unions may wish to negotiate what is 'reasonable');
- unemployment benefit paid by the organization for redundant workers who are unable to find other jobs e.g. the difference between state unemployment benefit and two-thirds of average earnings for twenty-six weeks;
- no loss of occupational pension (e.g. the agreement may provide for transfer of pension rights, or 'freezing');
- resettlement allowances in cases where workers are redeployed elsewhere within the organization to cover, for example, travelling expenses, removal and house purchase/sale costs, etc.;
- where plant closure is involved, retention bonuses to be paid to workers who stay on to assist with the plant run-down.

15.11 A Shorter Working Week?

The TUC have argued that the introduction of new technology provides great scope for reducing the length of the working week. A decisive reduction in the number of working hours per week could assist in limiting unemployment effects and provide greater leisure time. The essence of the TUC argument is that new technology will enable reduced hours to be associated with greater increases in hourly productivity thus holding down costs and at the same time creating extra jobs. This would both enable existing employees to share in the benefits of the new technology in the form of increased leisure, while maintaining and improving their earnings, and help to create additional jobs for the unemployed. For these reasons many unions seek to link technological change with reductions in the working week, the working year, and, indeed, the working lifetime.

If the desired effects are to be realized, any attempts to bargain for reductions in normal working hours clearly need to be associated with the reduction or elimination of systematic overtime. This should be a bargaining priority. Indeed it is common, as one union national officer has recently pointed out, to find excessive overtime being worked by those who retain their jobs, whilst large numbers of their colleagues employed in the same organization are being made redundant*. In this officer's opinion it is unlikely that the situation is remediable through collective bargaining and legislation is needed to restrict permissible overtime by law.

* Webb, T., 'Union Tactics for the High-Tech age', *Resource Management*, May 1983

15.12 Health and Safety Implications

Another area of major concern relates to health and safety. This is particularly so in offices and other places where many of the new computerized systems involve working with computer display screens or visual display units (VDUs). Eyesight screening and rest pauses have become standard features of many collective agreements covering many office and other workers for whom computerization has meant VDU-based work tasks.

It now seems that much of the early concern about the health effects of VDUs has no medical basis. Nevertheless the Health and Safety Executive has felt it necessary to provide official guidance on the subject. This guidance supports many of the principles enshrined in collective agreements including the need for frequent breaks away from the VDU. The HSE guidance concludes, however, that the 'majority of symptoms described by VDU operators are a reflection of bodily fatigue'.

Opinions continue to differ about the extent to which VDUs pose health hazards. Union concern persists and negotiators will continue to press for the safeguards they consider necessary to protect the health and safety of their members when negotiating new technology agreements.

15.13 Pay Structures and Grading

New technology brings changes in the nature of individual jobs and consequently changes in skill requirements. Herein lie a number of problems:

- disruption of existing pay structures;
- 'de-skilling' of some jobs;
- danger of a polarization of the labour force into a minority of highly-paid workers with much job satisfaction and a majority now 'de-skilled' who get low levels of pay and satisfaction from their work. (Skill shortages* can exacerbate this problem when companies offer 'market supplements' over and above agreed pay levels in order to attract skilled workers from elsewhere.)

It is important to recognize that the introduction of new technologies can have contradictory impacts on different sections of the workforce which may result in rivalry or conflict between employees. In such cases consultations and negotiations will require sensitive handling by both sides and prior anticipation of how the introduction of microelectronic technology is likely to affect the nature of skill, for example, by transforming traditional engineering jobs into computer based ones.

---

* In 1980, for example, NEDO reported a shortfall of 16,000 computer programmers and 7,000 professional electronics engineers

Union negotiators will wish to ensure that present pay levels are maintained and improved and that any additional skills required by operatives are taken into account in assessing their pay grades. The blurring of distinctions between manual/white collar; staff/hourly paid; skilled/semi-skilled/unskilled provides the opportunity to bargain for improved conditions of service for all employees and to move towards a single status workforce. At least one successful company management has itself initiated policy in this direction as a contribution to the smooth adoption of new technology. Bonar and Flotex Limited, a manufacturer of high quality carpets, simply abolished differences between staff and shopfloor conditions of employment.* There is no clocking in and everyone is paid monthly; all pension and sickness benefits are the same and all 'perks' are known to everybody.

15.14 Control over Work

Advanced computer-based information systems can be used to measure and monitor individual work performances very closely. Indeed for some manufacturers (e.g. of word processors) built-in supervision (which, incidentally, threatens the jobs of many supervisors) is a major selling point. The detailed performance information which the new systems can yield can conceivably be used by managements to reorganize or speed up work and/or to reduce employment.

According to one researcher** 'the precise direction of innovation by the companies that introduce the new technology often has little to do with improved efficiency or better production . . . microelectronic applications to production machinery usually comes in the form of control devices . . . new technology is essentially bound up with control over the pace of production and the quality of output'.

Workers have a deep-rooted mistrust of any form of 'spy in the machine' who measures and records work performance, absence from the machine, and so on. In one Danish retail store cashiers went on strike until such surveillance programmes were obliterated from the computerized cash registers and in a Leeds firm VDU operators subverted the policing mechanism in their word processors by pushing the space button so that they were recorded as working whilst having a chat and a cup of tea!

Unions are very concerned about the use of new technology in work surveillance and in the storage and retrieval of all forms of personal data***. Thus negotiators will seek (a) to gain written assurances that no

* Wyles, C., 'New Technology: First Set Your House in Order', *Works Management*, April 1982
** Wilkinson, Dr B., 'Battling IT Out on the Factory Floor', *New Scientist*, 9 December 1982
*** The Data Protection Act 1983, designed to protect individuals with regard to personal data, includes personal data on employees

information acquired by computer-based systems shall be used for individual or collective work performance measurement and (b) to establish procedures covering the storage and use of personal data of any kind.

15.15 Managing Change

The way in which technological innovation is managed depends to a great extent on the degree to which an enterprise is financially and commercially viable and on its past record of managing employee relations. These are no simple solutions for any organization, and the generalized guidelines offered below are not and could not be universally applicable.

Nevertheless, there is little doubt that the change will be easier for those companies who have through enlightened and open personnel management over a period of time gained the trust and confidence of their employees. In many organizations winning the trust and commitment of all those who will be affected by the changes will be a prerequisite for successful innovation. This may imply that a commitment to 'management prerogative' must give way to a more participative approach in which the systematic effects of a proposed technological innovation are explored and the plan for its implementation developed by *all* those in the organization who are likely to be affected. This might imply a system of planning groups at various levels with employee representatives for various groups of workers involved in each of these.

The Work Research Unit* has found that a 'participative strategy' for the management of change has a number of advantages:

- it affords opportunity to learn in the organization, to live with new technology, and how to cope with change as part of the way the company normally functions;
- it involves people as participants rather than recipients of change;
- it results in better quality outcomes both for the company from a commercial viewpoint and for individuals;
- the process of 'selling' the new technology, of getting acquainted with it and its effects is not a separate issue but an integral aspect of the change;
- it helps to identify those matters about which negotiation between management and employee representatives is needed and agreement must be reached either before or after implementation has provided some experience.

A participative strategy implies openness and trust between management and unions and employees. This can only be achieved over a

* Work Research Unit, *Managing New Technology*, 1979, pp. 6–7

considerable time period as the attitudes of the interested parties evolve and an awareness of the value of a participative approach becomes accepted. Furthermore it is probably the case that much of industry in the United Kingdom (unlike in some other competitor countries) still operates on the basis of major decisions being made in the boardroom and formally passed down to the workers through the trade union representatives.

Finally, in some cases a company may be forced by market realities to act quickly, whereas unions will wish to slow the pace of change to spread its impact. In such situations there will be an obvious tension between the needs of the company and those of employees.

Whatever strategy is selected it will be important that a strong management team is developed and given authority to get on with the job of bringing in the new technology. This implies full support for the team from the top levels of management, regular management training in human relations and technology and management development policies to encourage professionalism and team work.

If the size of the workforce is to be reduced it is important to develop equitable and agreed policies for retraining, career counselling, early retirement, resettlement, a satisfactory redundancy package, and so on, and to include the cost of these in the initial appraisal of the new technology.

15.16 Some Lessons from Experience

A survey* carried out in 1983 by the MSC's Employment Relations Resource Centre (ERRC) in conjunction with the Engineering Employers' London Association revealed that about 90 per cent of the respondent companies had made provision for training managers in technical system appreciation, but only 28 per cent of these companies had extended training to any consideration of how the new technology might impact on the organization and its employees. Some 85 per cent of the companies were involved in negotiation or consultation about new technology, but in only 15 per cent had employees and/or union representatives received any form of training other than training beyond technical familiarization. Most companies apparently saw no value in assisting their union representatives to negotiate and consult about the impact of new technology, despite the availability of TUC courses on the subject.

Other findings of the survey include

- management understanding of employee and trade union responses to new technology is often low;

---

* 'Advanced Technology, The Employee Relations Impact', *Topics* No. 13 Employment Relations Resource Centre, November 1983

- personnel specialists rarely have an integral role in the exploration of the feasibility of a technical change, the planning process, installation and commissioning of equipment;
- the management responsibility for implementing change often lacks definition, i.e. it is often unclear as to who is responsible or what is the span of responsibility of, say, the technical expert;
- engineers often plan the implementation of the new technology using computer-based systems. However, such programmes rarely include detailed planning on employee relations aspects of the change;
- there is little evidence of planning in relation to issues for negotiation or consultation;
- technical specialists who discuss details of the new technology with shop stewards are often ill-equipped to do so. There is confusion as to whether they are negotiating or informing. Such specialists are rarely given any guidance or training to equip them in handling such discussions;
- insufficient attention and reward is given to groups of employees who are not immediately affected by technical change. This again is indicative of a lack of planning and a failure to consider the overall effect on the organization and its employees.

On the basis of their findings the ERRC researchers argue strongly for the involvement of personnel and employee relations specialists at the earliest stage of any technological innovation. Too frequently the human aspects are left until the technical change has been designed, sanctioned, and contracts placed.

In stressing the need to gain employee commitment to change, the researchers argue that

> ... the most robust basis from which to effect technological change is that of audit and analysis of existing employee relations structures and practices. The organisation's capacity to accept change can then be assessed and strategies developed to maximise the benefit of the technology*.

A WRU study** of companies in different industries in which significant technical changes had been undertaken found that in regard to the *process* of change:

- the *training* of employees for new tasks had been too little and too late;
- there was insufficient *communication* with employees about the changes;
- the process was attempted too quickly.

---

* Advanced Technology, The Employee Relations Impact, *Topics* No. 13, Employment Relations Resource Centre, November 1983
** Work Research Unit, *Managing New Technology*, 1979, pp. 12–13

On the *content* of changes it was found that:

- initial investment decisions were based on inadequate data and over-optimistic forecasts of savings;
- there was little attempt to establish teams to manage the changes which were just expected to happen;
- focus tended to be largely on technical aspects leaving problems of work organization to be dealt with at a later stage, after irreversible decisions about technically 'best' solutions had been taken.

STUDENT ASSIGNMENT 15.1

The Introduction of New Technology at XYZ Ltd

XYZ Ltd is a British manufacturer of plant and machinery for the food processing industry. Since about 70 per cent of its production is normally exported, XYZ is highly sensitive to competition from its more innovative foreign rivals.

Since the onset of world recession in 1979 the company has found itself in an increasingly difficult position. Sales revenue and profits have both declined substantially and rapidly. Much of this decline has been attributable to a dramatic fall in export sales.

Faced with this situation the board of XYZ fear that if the company is to have any chance of avoiding insolvency it must move quickly into the field of electronic control systems in order to survive.

As a first step in this direction XYZ have engaged a firm of consultants to advise on the feasibility of various microprocessor applications. When the shop stewards representing XYZ manual workers (who belong to one of two craft unions or the general union recognized by XYZ) hear rumours of the company's proposals they object vigorously and demand an immediate meeting with management about the issue.

Substantive and procedural negotiations have taken place at workplace and company level for many years and historically the company has tended to adopt a 'fire-fighting' approach to its relations with employees and their unions i.e. dealing with trouble as it arose on a piecemeal basis. XYZ has never developed a long-term, coherent, and consistent industrial relations policy.

Following the shop steward protest, XYZ management sense that getting the thing accepted' by the workforce is likely to be the greatest obstacle to innovation of the new technology. Management immediately call in a firm of management consultants to advise them on how to proceed. Meanwhile the joint shop stewards' committee has demanded immediate consultations preparatory to the negotiation of a 'new technology agreement'.

Tasks

1. As a research officer of the general workers' union (GWU) representing about 65 per cent of XYZ's manual workers, advise the joint shop stewards' committee (JSSC) on the preparation of their case. Specify objectives, supporting arguments and the specific kinds of information required.
2. As a management consultant advise XYZ on how best to deal with its unions about the introduction of the new technology.
3. Assume that you have now reached the negotiating position where it is accepted by the unions that redundancy is inevitable. As research officer of the GWU advise the JSSC how *now* to proceed.
4. As research officer of the GWU advise the JSSC on the law relating to redundancy and in particular advise them of the company's obligations concerning consultations with trade unions over any proposed redundancies and whether an employee who felt he had been unfairly selected for redundancy had any remedy.

15.17 Summary

1. The applications of the new microelectronic technology are so varied that every sector of employment is likely to be affected by it.
2. There are significant potential benefits to be gained by those organizations who successfully introduce the new technology.
3. A major constraint upon the more rapid diffusion of new technology in British industry is the problem of handling the human and employee relations aspects of change.
4. Trade unions, whilst not in general opposed to technological innovation have many concerns and reservations about the terms on which it is introduced.
5. The effective negotiation of new technology agreements requires a full disclosure of information to employees and their union representatives at every stage of the project. Disclosure of information is equally important where employers attempt to bring in new technology on the basis of joint consultation.
6. In order to minimize the effects of technological innovation on employment, unions will often try to negotiate a 'no redundancy' agreement. Where reductions in the workforce appear to be inevitable limitations on recruitment, redeployment, retraining, and the limitation of overtime may help to prevent redundancies. If redundancies are unavoidable unions will seek 'voluntary redundancies' and attempt to improve on the statutory payments and conditions due to redundant workers.
7. In addition to job security, other industrial relations issues such as

training and retraining, pay, grading, hours, health and safety, and job content and control are raised by the introduction of new technology.

8. The trust and commitment of employees is an essential pre-condition for successful innovation.

9. For many organizations the adoption of a 'participative strategy' will be advantageous when managing change. Personnel and employee relations specialists as well as engineers and technical managers should have an integral role at the earliest stage of any proposed technological innovation.

Exercise

Review your understanding of the following:

new technology agreements
disclosure of information
the law on redundancies
union concerns about new technology
participative management

Further Reading

The Manpower Implications of Microprocessor Technology, Department of Employment, HMSO, 1979.

How to Introduce New Technology – A Practical Guide for Managers, Institute of Personnel Management, 1983.

Haining, B. and Goodridge, M. 'Advanced Technology: The Employee Relations Impact', *Topics*, 13, Employee Relations Resource Centre, Cambridge, November 1983.

16

Resources in the Future

16.1 Introduction

It is fashionable to refer to a number of related economic, social and political changes as the crisis of the 1980s. Although different writers offer different explanations and emphasize different aspects of the crisis, most are agreed that the economic recession which has afflicted all industrialized countries since 1979 is quite different from the regular cyclical downturns in economic activity which have characterized the post-war period. Latham-Koenig*, for example, argues that the word 'crisis' may be inappropriate since it connotes a temporary situation which with the application of suitable remedies will quickly return to normal. According to this view it is most unlikely that we will be able to return to the growth rates and employment levels of the 1960s or 1970s even if sustained economic recovery emerges in the 1980s. The western economies may indeed be undergoing a 'giganic mutation'** or a 'crisis of society' affecting not only economic affairs, but involving a fundamental questioning of social and economic structures, cultural norms, and values.

Among many factors underlying the 'crisis' are:

- unprecedented growth in Third World economies which since the mid-1960s has disrupted growth in industrialized countries. Attracted by higher returns an increasing flow of foreign investment has diminished investment in the industrialized world and contributed to a changing power balance in the world economy;***

* Latham-Koenig, A. L. 'Changing Values in Post-Industrial Society and Implications for Management', *European Management Journal*, vol. 2, no. 1, Summer 1983
** Rocard, M., former French Minister of Planning, 'Les Enjeux de la Décienne, 1980 – Discours D'Installation de la Commission Nationale de Plannification'
*** For a fuller account see Beenstock, M. and Willcox, P. *The Causes of Slower Growth in the World Economy*, LBS Forecasting Unit, April 1980

- an aspect of the changing power balance is that western firms will experience increasingly severe competition from firms in newly-industrialized countries (NICs) not only in the goods markets but for the acquisition of increasingly scarce natural resources. Already the pressure in the US and Western Europe for protectionist measures owes much to the growth of imports of clothing, leather goods, footwear, textiles, and electrical machinery from the NICs since the 1960s;
- the growing interdependence of the international economic and political system embracing many critical related issues including population, income distribution, energy, food, arms control, technology, and financial transfers;
- the mounting global threat to the ecological bases of production and quality of life arising from the destruction of renewable resources, the depletion of non-renewables, and the degradation of the physical and social environment by pollution★;
- the huge rise in unemployment which is both a cause and a consequence of the 'crisis';
- less tangible changes in values and attitudes. Heilbroner★★, for example, refers to the 'erosion of the spirit' of capitalism and a 'hollowness' at the centre of business civilization from which the pursuit of material goods diverts our attention for a time but that in the end insistently asserts itself. This 'hollowness' is attributable to 'the relentless effort to persuade people by a ceaseless flow of half-truths and careful deceptions to change their lifeways'; to 'mindless commercialization of life . . . that is sapping business civilization from within'; and to the disregard by business for the value of work.

Whether or not the 'crisis' amounts to a 'gigantic mutation', perhaps to some form of post-industrial society, what is clear is that, because both societies and firms are dynamic organisms which must adapt to, interact with, and counter-influence their environment, the nature of business activity, goals, and policies is changing and will continue to change quite rapidly.

Whilst there is not room here for extensive discussions of these momentous issues the remainder of this chapter takes a closer, though inevitably partial look at one or two important trends and their possible

---

★ See for example *The Environment: Challenges for the '80s*, OECD, Paris, 1981; *The Global 2000 Report to the President on Global Resources, Environment and Population*, U.S. Government Printing Office, Washington, 1980; *North-South: A Programme for Survival* (The Brandt Report), Pan Books, London, 1980

★★ Heilbroner, R. L., *Business Civilization in Decline*, **Penguin** Books, 1977. See also Chapter 8 in Kempner, T., *et. al.*, *Business and Society*, **Penguin** Books, 1976

impact on business organizations and their resources. We focus specifically on some aspects of the following:

- economic and ecological interdependence;
- the destruction of renewable natural resources;
- raw materials in the future;
- unemployment;
- the growing demands for employee and societal participation in business decision-making;
- the business firm in the future.

16.2 Economic and Ecological Interdependence

In April 1981 the Environment Committee of the Organization for Economic Co-operation and Development (OECD) held a special session on 'The OECD and Policies for the 1980s to Address Long-term Environmental Issues'. At the request of, and with the support of, member governments (i.e. governments of the western industrialized nations) the Committee sought expert advice on a range of questions including 'What are the most critical of the long-term issues on resources and the environment?' and 'To what extent do these issues derive from the activities of OECD member countries?'.

The Committee's* report echoed the theme of the Brandt Report that 'the world is now a fragile and interlocking system whether for its people, its ecology, or its resources'.** The report, appropriately entitled *Economic and Ecological Interdependence*, contained eleven papers, two of which were concerned with fundamental resource issues:

- the maintenance of biological diversity;
- the loss of cropland and soil depletion.

From the development of these and other papers one overriding theme emerged: the interrelationship between resources and environment issues on the one hand, and sustainable economic development on the other.

16.3 Agricultural Land

Most of the land in the world that is best suited for crop production is already being farmed. This amounts to only about 11 per cent of the world's land area (excluding Antarctica) that presents no serious limits to agriculture. The rest is either desert, or permanently frozen, or consists of unsuitable (e.g. toxic or mineral-deficient) soils (see Figure 16.1).

* *Economic and Ecological Interdependence*, OECD, Paris, 1982
** *North-South: A Programme for Survival* (The Brandt Report), Pan Books, London, 1980

Figure 16.1.   Breakdown of earth's surface.

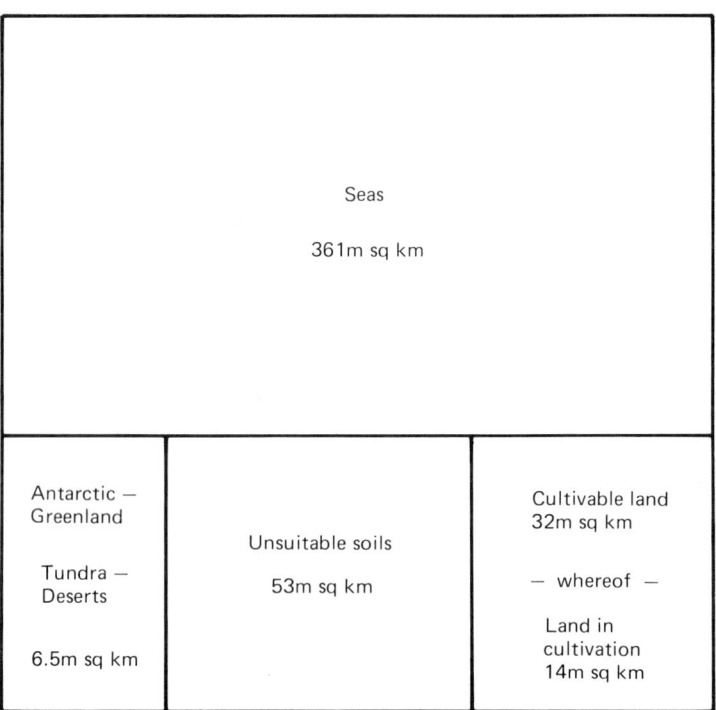

Seas

361m sq km

Antarctic — Greenland	Unsuitable soils	Cultivable land 32m sq km
Tundra — Deserts	53m sq km	— whereof —
6.5m sq km		Land in cultivation 14m sq km

Even using the most optimistic set of technological assumptions, it appears that the 14 million square kilometres of cultivated land could not be much more than doubled. In the industrialized countries considerable prime quality cropland has been permanently converted into urban industrial areas, recreation facilities, motorway and other transportation infrastructure, and reservoirs. According to the OECD at least 5,000 square kilometres of cultivable land in western industrialized countries are lost annually to urban sprawl.

In developing nations the rate of loss of cropland is increasing partly because of conversion to non-agricultural uses, but more significantly because of soil degradation which has accelerated sharply in most developing countries. In such countries it is often the very poor of the rural areas – about one-third of the world's population – locked often into a desperate struggle for survival who, in their efforts to satisfy their needs for food and fuel, disrupt their own life support systems. Thus deforestation and over-farming accelerate the destruction of soils and genetic resources which constitute the future basis of agriculture.

The 1982 OECD report* returns us starkly to the world of exponentials:

> If the current rates of conversion of agricultural land to non-agricultural uses continues in OECD countries and if the current rates of land degradation continue in developing countries, within 20 years more than one third of the world's arable land could be lost or destroyed.

16.4 Biological Diversity

Biological diversity embraces genetic diversity (the variability in a given species) and ecological diversity (the number of species in a community). The OECD report* explains the issue as follows:

> The genetic base of many of the world's crops and livestock has narrowed, making them more vulnerable to pests and diseases and to changes in soils and climate. At the same time, the world's genetic resources essential for reducing that vulnerability, as well as for producing a great range of pharmaceutical and industrial products, have been depleted, and this trend continues. Some 25,000 plant species and more than 1,000 vertebrate species are threatened with extinction and as much as 10 per cent or more of all species on earth could be extinguished over the next two decades. Extinction of species on such a scale is without precedent in human history.

The most serious threat to species is the destruction of habitats such as forests and wetlands. In many developing countries tropical rain forests, which contain about one-third of all species in the world, are being exploited at an unsustainable rate without regard for their ecological value. The loss of vast areas of rain forests as a result of clearance for timber, plantations, ranching, and agriculture, as well as for fuel, involves not only an enormous destruction of species and genetic materials but also may threaten local, regional, and perhaps even global ecological stability.

A number of economic and social consequences of the destruction of forests include:

- the dependence of medicines and other pharmaceutical products on natural drugs obtained from plant and animal species for their main active ingredients;
- the dependence of bio-medical research upon a continuous supply of wild-caught animals, e.g. African chimpanzees now on the endangered species list;
- the supply of timber, pulpwood, fuelwood, fodder, fruit, fibres, pharmaceuticals, resins, gums, waxes, and oils from tropical rain forests, useful to developed and developing countries alike, upon which many developing countries are heavily dependent for export earnings;

---

* *Economic and Ecological Interdependence*, OECD, Paris, 1982

- the dependence of agriculture in the industrialized countries for future productivity increases and decreased pest and disease vulnerability on genetic resources from tropical countries.

16.5 Raw Materials in the Future

Some non-renewable resources such as iron, aluminium, and magnesium are so abundant in the earth's crust that the limiting factors on their production are much more likely to be (a) the energy requirements for extraction and purification, and (b) their political concentration, rather than their physical exhaustion.

Historically, technological development and substitution have been important variables in the raw materials sector and many assume that they will continue to combat materials and energy scarcities in the future. In their study of the US economy from 1870 to 1960, for example, Barnett and Morse* concluded that production techniques had improved to such an extent during the period that anticipated tendencies towards rising costs associated with increasing materials scarcities had been successfully eliminated (and even reversed).

However, many studies emphasize a further important constraint on future resource extraction, use, and disposal, namely the environmental side-effects. Even the optimistic study of Barnett and Morse predicts that these side-effects will eventually prevent technological progress from containing or reducing materials costs as it has hitherto.

In a report on *Resources, Society and the Future*** prepared for the Swedish Secretariat for Future Studies, Bertelman and others emphasize pollution and other environmental effects as a 'very important constraint' on man's future supplies of raw materials. It is, they argue, unrealistic to assume that society and individuals will passively ignore pollution until its effects on production, health, and longevity become disastrous.

In a commentary on technological progress reflected by improved production techniques, the development of substitutes, and environmental engineering, Bertelman and his colleagues pose three important questions:

- will technological solutions be found?
- what sort of technology will be developed (and how acceptable will this be to the community)?

* Barnett, H. J. and Morse, C., *Scarcity and Growth*, Resources for the Future, Baltimore, 1963
** Bertelman, T. and others, *Resources, Society and the Future*, Secretariat for Further Studies, Stockholm, 1980

- what costs will technological progress impose (i.e. both economic costs and costs in terms of greater social, political, and ecological risks)?

The reader is invited to consider these important questions in the light of technologies currently being deployed. Case Study 9.2 is a case in point.

STUDENT ASSIGNMENT 16.1

The Raw Materials Content of Consumer Goods

In a Bill placed before the Swedish Riksdag (Parliament) in 1976 it was proposed that companies should be placed under an obligation to declare their consumptions of energy and raw materials in the production of consumer goods.

Had the Bill become law the energy and material content of products would have to be declared to consumers in the same sort of way as the ingredients of manufactured foodstuffs are displayed at present, thus giving consumers a better idea of the natural resources they are actually consuming.

The Bill followed much public advocacy in Sweden and analyses of the energy and materials content of many products had already been carried out by environmental and public interest groups in order to focus criticism and debate on what they regarded as the wasteful product policies of business enterprises.

Under the proposed law companies would also have been required to compile and publish product specifications showing among other things raw material consumption during the service life of the product including the possibilities for recycling.

The grounds for the proposed legislation were: 'Our natural resources are finite and we must economise on energy . . . . Solidarity with the peoples of the world therefore demands of this highly industrialised country that we should shoulder our responsibility and carry out a long-term transformation of our pattern of living'.

Assuming similar proposals to these have recently been enacted and are now legal obligations on companies in Britain, address the following:

1. Analyse the implications of the new laws for the product design and marketing policy of *either* (a) Home Entertainments PLC, a manufacturer of music centres, video recorders, televisions, etc., *or* (b) Speedwell PLC, a manufacturer of motorcycles.
2. What advantages and what problems do you envisage in complying with the new legislation from the point of view of

   (a) the business enterprise
   (b) society at large?

3. In your opinion should business firms take into account matters of public interest, irrespective of legal obligations and irrespective of their effects on profits?
4. To what extent do you think the new law would cause companies to modify traditional goals?
5. Assuming that the firms mentioned at 1 above compete with foreign firms for export markets, do you foresee any special problems arising for these firms?
6. In what other ways could companies be induced to use resources less wastefully?
7. Give your opinion of the argument that laws such as these are necessary as an expression of '. . . solidarity with the peoples of the world'.
8. What other aspects of contemporary business activity are, or may become, matters of public concern and pressure which may lead to legislative controls?

16.6 Unemployment

In the short space of a few years the level of unemployment in the OECD countries will have risen by almost 50 per cent, from 24 million at the start of 1981 to 35 million by 1985. World economic recession and many other forces continue to push unemployment to higher and higher levels. One of these forces, the increasing competition from newly-industrialized countries, has already been mentioned. Others include demographic change which will continue to add to the OECD's labour force at an annual rate of 1 per cent into the foreseeable future; the contraction of manufacturing in most industrialized countries, and the failure of services to provide new jobs for workers displaced from manufacturing; problems of structural change associated with the microprocessor revolution; and finally, a relative fall in product innovation coinciding with rapid improvements in manufacturing processes due to electronics and particularly to microprocessors.

As unemployment has risen the average duration of unemployment has lengthened. By 1981 almost half of Britain's jobless were long-term unemployed. A repercussion of rising unemployment has been the enormous increase in transfer payments in the form of unemployment and social security benefits referred to in Chapter 3. In addition, various job-creation and work-sharing schemes have been developed. At the same time government revenues have been diminished by the loss of taxation and social security contributions. Thus the ratio of social services expenditure as a percentage of GDP has continued to rise and increasing strains have been placed on the public finance system, so much so that in some quarters it has been argued that the dependent sector is in danger of overwhelming the productive sector.

In the context of prolonged and mass unemployment some writers have noted the emergence of a multi-sectoral economy in which new technology, including information technologies and the microprocessor, is leading to more automated capital intensive mass production and may also lead to more decentralized living and working as the local small business sector and the informal, often unpaid, household and neighbourhood sector are revived*.

The revival of the household sector is anticipated because microprocessors, microcomputers, and video terminals make it possible for much work currently performed in factories and offices to be done at home.

Other predicted changes in employment include:

- an expansion of part-time employment which already accounts for almost one in ten of the EEC's workforce, 90 per cent of these women, and the extension to these workers of the same legal and other rights enjoyed by full-time workers;
- work sharing in the form of shorter working weeks, earlier retirement, longer holidays, together with increased opportunities for part-time employment will help to share out the available work and enable people to choose more flexible working patterns;
- as attitudes to work continue to change, more people may seek flexibility, meaning, and personal development from their work, which will increasingly be viewed as a socially productive, personally fulfilling activity that meets deep and important needs rather than merely as a means to income;
- legal limits on the amount of overtime work. This already happens in other European countries. In West Germany, for instance, the legal limit is 80 hours per year; in Belgium 65 hours;
- possible government support for every collective agreement reached for changes in working hours that are coupled with the creation of more jobs. Lord Young, for example, has proposed a subsidy of £60 per week for each new job created, the amount tailing off in later years.

16.7 The Growing Demand for Employee Participation in Decision-Making

Despite the current economic recession demands for and progress towards

* Latham-Koenig, A. L., 'Changing Values in Post-Industrial Society and Implications for Management', *European Management Journal*, vol. 2, no. 1, Summer 1983

greater employee participation in corporate decision making are undiminished. In 1983, for example, Schuller* reported that

> At enterprise level patterns of decision making are changing, often in ways which significantly affect the extent to which employees directly and indirectly influence decisions.

Almost certainly this trend will continue into the future. Comprehensive research by Achleitner and others** into the challenges facing European business, for example, concludes that

> employees and new legislation will continue to demand increasing disclosure of information outside management. Demands for participation in decision making processes particularly as they affect employment will also continue

An important business management implication of the growing demand for more genuine participation in decision-making is that

> it will become increasingly difficult to get things done by appeal to hierarchical superiority and tradition ... many people will want to have a say in decisions and to feel that their opinions are taken seriously***.

We begin our brief analysis of employee participation with the important historical point that in many sectors of employment trade unions have already generated a substantial measure of employee involvement in decisions through the extension and widening scope of collective bargaining. Over a long period this has transformed virtually total management autonomy in organizational decision-making into a situation in which more and more decisions are jointly made by managements and employees through their union representatives.

Progress has, however, been uneven. Few organizations would claim to have gone as far as the Ford Motor Company whose Industrial Relations Director Paul Roots recently reported**** that

> We've greatly extended the areas over which we bargain with the unions ... union involvement has grown tremendously through collective bargaining machinery; in 1950 we just used to talk about wages, vacations and hours with the unions. Now we talk about things like investment, products, product strategy, marketing ... well almost anything you can think of.

---

* Schuller, T., 'Industrial Democracy and Participation', *Topics*, no. 9, March 1983

** Achleitner, P. *et. al.*, 'The Firm: Meeting the Legitimacy Challenge', *European Management Journal*, vol. 2, no. 1, Summer 1983

*** Latham-Koenig, A. L., 'Changing Values in Post-Industrial Society and Implications for Management', *European Management Journal*, vol. 2, no. 1, Summer 1983

**** M. Marchington in conversation with Paul Roots in 'Opinion Industrial Relations – Involvement and Intervention', *Management Digest*, 21 March 1983

By the late 1970s the experience of participation in several European countries had shifted the focus of debate to other forms of industrial democracy and, in particular, to worker directors.

16.8 Worker Directors

By this time workers on the board had already appeared in most West European countries. The two key features of the German 'co-determination' system dating back to the early 1950s are worker directors and works councils. Co-determination is based on a two-tier board structure. Workers are represented on a *supervisory board* which then elects a *management board*. Though the management board makes policy, its decisions on certain specified issues must be approved by the supervisory board. In coal and steel enterprises there is *parity* representation of workers and management on the 11-person supervisory board, i.e. five employee representatives, five shareholder representatives, and a jointly agreed 'independent' chairman.

In all other German companies employing over 500 workers the system is one of *minority* representation, with one-third of the supervisory board elected by a ballot of *all* employees. Following sustained trade union pressure, a second Co-determination Act was passed in 1976 extending equality of representation to all companies employing more than 2,000 workers.

In all establishments with five or more employees, an exclusively employee body called a *works council* must be set up. Its function is to represent the workforce in consultations and negotiations with plant management. Councillors serve for three years and are elected by secret ballot of the whole workforce.

The works council has the right to joint decision-making (co-determination) on hours, pay, holiday arrangements, health and safety rules, fixing piecework and bonus pay, and several other matters. On these questions, the employer must secure the approval of the council before acting. Failing agreement, the matter goes to arbitration. The 1952 Works Constitution Act makes it unlawful for councillors to initiate strikes.

There is conflicting evidence as to the success of the co-determination system. On the one hand, one can point to three or four decades of relative industrial peace in German industry. This record, however, is undoubtedly due to many factors, only one of which may be the co-determination system. On the other, however, research* carried out for the Bullock Committee in 1976 concluded that in the German case: first, worker

---

* Batsone, E. and Davies, P. L., *Industrial Democracy: European Experience* (two reports) HMSO, 1976, pp. 21 and 35

directors have generally had little effect on anything; and, second, consequently they have certainly had no catastrophic effect on anything or anybody.

The same research indicated that in practice German supervisory boards acted merely as advisers to management boards and as such had very limited influence over policy-making.

16.9 European Community Initiatives

Although the Bullock proposals for the election of worker directors in companies with more than 2,000 employees have not resulted in legislation, a number of legislative proposals for enhancing employee participation emanating from the European Community (EC) may have more effect.

In July 1983 the EC Commission issued a revised version of a draft Directive on Procedures for Informing and Consulting Employees – the so-called 'Vredeling' Directive first published in 1980.* If implemented, the Directive would require organizations employing 1,000 or more workers within the EC to disclose annually substantial general information on the group as a whole and specific information on their own subsidiary or establishment. Employee representatives would also gain the right to be informed before decisions are taken which are liable to have 'serious consequences' for employees' interests, and to be consulted thirty days before these decisions are implemented.

In August 1983 the Commission issued a revised text of the draft Fifth Directive on Company Law Harmonization first issued in 1972, proposing board representation for employees of companies with 500 employees or more on a German-style supervisory board within a two-tier structure. The revised version would require employee participation provisions in public limited companies (PLCs) which alone or with subsidiaries employed 1,000 or more, unless a majority of a PLC's employees opposed it.

The revised Fifth Directive would give PLCs a choice from three proposed methods of employee participation:

• worker directors elected onto a supervisory board of a PLC with a two-tier structure, or elected as non-executive directors to a single board;
• a works council;
• a system of participation established by collective agreement.

Each system is intended to have equivalent effect. Employee representatives, who should be elected by proportional representation in a secret ballot of all employees, whether worker directors or not, would have the

---

* DE and DTI *Press Notice*, 9 November 1983

rights to receive a quarterly report on company affairs, the draft annual report and accounts, and to request reports and undertake investigations where necessary.

In addition, representatives under the works council or collective agreement options would have to be consulted on major decisions such as closure or relocation.

At the time of writing both the revised 'Vredeling' and Fifth Directives are being considered by a working group of officials. Early resolution of the complex issues involved is not expected. The British Government, reflecting the view of most of British industry, is strongly opposed to the EC proposals, arguing that the precise form of employee participation is best left to employers and employees who are in the best position to judge what suits their particular circumstances.

STUDENT ASSIGNMENT 16.2

Workers on the Board?

I was never much impressed by the worker director idea and I never saw Bullock as inevitable. I've always thought that there was a fair bit of sense in the argument that the role of the union is to promote the interests of their members not the shareholders. It would be different obviously if there was a change in company law which equalised employee and shareholder interests, a worker director would have a different role. But there are practical problems as well; being on the board is almost certainly going to cut him off from the confidences of the shopfloor.

(Paul Roots, Industrial Relations Director, Ford Motor Company, 1983)

1. Identify and analyse the important issues relating to the introduction of worker directors contained in this quotation. Present your conclusions as a short oral report.
2. In your opinion *should* company law be altered in order to equalize employee and shareholder interests? What would be the implications of such a change in company law? Present your views as a short oral report.

16.10 Workers' Co-operatives

The ultimate form of employee participation is the situation in which workers themselves own and manage the enterprise. Indeed it has been argued by some that there can be no true employee participation without the rewards and responsibilities that go with ownership.

The most flourishing worker co-operatives in the West are those in the Mondragon area of Spain's Basque province*. The first of these was founded in 1956 with a labour force of twenty-three; by 1981 there were eighty-two Mondragon co-operatives employing 17,000 workers, producing mainly consumer goods and with a joint annual turnover approaching £400 million. By the same year when unemployment approached 10 per cent in the Basque country, the co-operatives had declared no redundancies, had suffered only one strike, and only one business failure.

The Mondragon co-operatives have been a spectacular success story, but perhaps one which cannot easily be emulated elsewhere. The Basque people's long tradition of entrepreneurship, their mountainous environment, and their separate language have combined to give them a strong sense of community and social cohesion which have been important preconditions for success.

16.11 The Social Responsibility of Private Enterprise

Throughout this book attention has been drawn to the inevitable interactions between business enterprises and the wider society and indeed global community within which they operate. There is no doubt that the importance of the limited company has been heightened in recent years by a new perception of the social role which companies may accept and the social responsibilities they should assume in societies increasingly concerned with accelerating social wellbeing. Social responsibility is difficult to define and measure. We take it here to mean 'the extent to which individual firms voluntarily serve social needs other than those of the firm's owners and managers even if this conflicts with the maximisation of profits'.**

In a recent major research project involving both academics from the European Institute for Advanced Studies in Management (EIASM) and the European Foundation for Management Development (EFMD), and managers from a group of leading European companies, the attempt was made to define the challenges facing European companies and the ways in which they were adapting to meet these challenges.*** An analysis of the

---

* Much of the account given here draws on a discussion between Mark Goyder, a personnel manager with GEC-Elliot Automation Ltd. and Mondragon's Personnel Director, Senor Martinez de Arroyo, reported in *Personnel Management*, March 1979
** Morgan, Eleanor 'Social Responsibility and Private Enterprises in the UK', *National Westminster Bank Quarterly Review*
*** Achleitner, P., *et. al.* 'The Firm: Meeting the Legitimacy Challenge', *European Management Journal*, vol. 2, no. 1, Summer 1983

present role of large European firms indicated clearly that the role and behaviour of firms differs significantly. The different roles could be classified according to the relative emphasis given to economic perform-ance (profitability and growth) and societal performance (social and political responsiveness). At one end of the spectrum are the 'dedicated profit seekers' who place almost exclusive emphasis on profits and who see societal demands as an unwarranted interference with the free enterprise system. At the opposite end are the 'social servant' firms, typically not profit seekers and often subsidized by society. Between the two are the 'societally responsible profit seekers' who whilst placing prime importance on profits, also assume some social responsibility and interact with government and public interest groups.

The second stage of the research forecasted which of the three roles would become most prevalent given future prospects and their likely impacts on business behaviour. Among the future prospects identified by the researchers were increasingly severe competition from newly-industrialized countries; low economic growth rates; increasing govern-ment involvement in the business system; a continuously evolving rela-tionship between the firm and its 'constituencies' including raw materials suppliers, communications media, consumer and environmental groups, local government as well as traditional stakeholders such as managers, unions, banks, government, etc; continued demand for increased em-ployee participation and information disclosure; the co-existence of tradi-tional and 'post-materialistic' values, the latter emphasizing quality of life, human rights, the common good, flexibility and variety in personal life, and greater personal freedom; and continuing high rates of unemployment and pressures to trade off economic performance against the provision of jobs.

The net impact of these trends, the researchers conclude, is likely to diminish the number of dedicated profit seekers, whilst increasing the number of firms in the socially responsive profit seeker and social servant categories. Society will not tolerate profit maximization at any cost and consequently the role of the dedicated profit seekers will become in-creasingly unacceptable.

Index